Márta Ujvári
The Trope Bundle Theory of Substance
Change, Individuation and Individual Essence

Márta Ujvári

The Trope Bundle Theory of Substance

Change, Individuation and Individual Essence

ontos
verlag

Frankfurt I Paris I Lancaster I New Brunswick

Bibliographic information published by Deutsche Nationalbibliothek
The Deutsche Nationalbibliothek lists this publication in the Deutsche Nationalbibliographie;
detailed bibliographic data is available in the Internet at http://dnb.ddb.de

North and South America by
Transaction Books
Rutgers University
Piscataway, NJ 08854-8042
trans@transactionpub.com

United Kingdom, Eire, Iceland, Turkey, Malta, Portugal by
Gazelle Books Services Limited
White Cross Mills
Hightown
LANCASTER, LA1 4XS
sales@gazellebooks.co.uk

Livraison pour la France et la Belgique:
Librairie Philosophique J.Vrin
6, place de la Sorbonne; F-75005 PARIS
Tel. +33 (0)1 43 54 03 47; Fax +33 (0)1 43 54 48 18
www.vrin.fr

©2013 ontos verlag
P.O. Box 15 41, D-63133 Heusenstamm
www.ontosverlag.com

ISBN 978-3-86838-180-1

2013

No part of this book may be reproduced, stored in retrieval systems or transmitted
in any form or by any means, electronic, mechanical, photocopying, microfilming, recording or otherwise
without written permission from the Publisher, with the exception of any material supplied specifically for the
purpose of being entered and executed on a computer system, for exclusive use of the purchaser of the work

Printed on acid-free paper
FSC-certified (Forest Stewardship Council)
This hardcover binding meets the International Library standard

Printed in Germany
by CPI buch bücher gmbh

Preface

This book has arisen from my research activity and teaching, over the last decade, in graduate and PhD courses on metaphysics in Hungary and some graduate courses in the UK. My main goal with this book is to develop a coherent account of the trope-bundle theory of individual substances (**BT**), their individuation and identity through time, and their individual essences that fares well on a cost-benefit analysis. The metaphysical account of substances is a perennial task of philosophy that has been brought into focus by works in the analytical style in recent years.

Students of metaphysics in the current Anglo-American analytical brand may find this book helpful to tackle some of the traditional and recent metaphysical problems typically discussed at metaphysics courses. Colleagues might appreciate the novelties of the book: its purported contribution to some of the unsettled issues of the topic.

Substantial part of the present writing is a renewed and corrected version of my book published in Hungarian (2009) with *L'Harmattan Publishing House*. A major part of the 6th chapter overlaps with my paper in *Metaphysica* (2004). The 7th chapter contains much of my paper in *Synthese* (2011), and contains the full text of my paper in *Metaphysica* (2012).

I express my *acknowledgment* to my colleagues. An earlier version of this book have been read and discussed by Howard Robinson from the *University of Liverpool* and David Weberman from the *Department of Philosophy of the Central European University*. I owe a special debt of gratitude to them for their useful comments and suggestions. I am also grateful for valuable comments and criticisms of an earlier draft of part of the 6th chapter to Robert Kirk, Stephen Barker and Robert Black from the *Department of Philosophy of Nottingham University*. The outline of the connection of trope **BT** and change developed more fully here took the form of a conference talk at the *Fifth ECAP,* in 2005 where it has been commented by Peter Simons, *Department of Philosophy of the University of Leeds.* I owe a debt to Peter Ohrstrom from *Aalborg University*, Denmark, who encouraged me in writing the part of the book that explores the Priorian theme of temporalized modality. I am indebted to Kornél Steiger from *Eötvös Loránd University of Budapest, Department of Ancient Philosophy* for his valuable comments and criticism with regard to my reading of Aristotelian essentialism. Also, I say thanks to colleagues from the *Philosophy Department of Zagreb University*, in the first instance to Tomislav Janovic, Pavel Gregorits and Dusan Dosudic who commented an earlier draft of the last chapter. I express my gratitude to Zoltán Szántó from the *Social Studies* of my home university, the *Corvinus University of Budapest*, who strongly supported my efforts in the analytical philosophy. I am grateful to my former PhD student in analytic metaphysics, Tibor Bárány who edited an earlier version of the book in Hungarian and polished its style.

Budapest, September, 2012

Márta Ujvári

Content

Preface 2

Content 4

Introduction 7

I. The Identity of Substances: Bare Substrata or Qualitative Bundles? 29

II. The Role of Tropes in Ontology: Accidents, Events, Particularism 59

III. The Individuation of Tropes and Substances in BT. The Main Criticisms of the Trope Theory 87

V. Two-tier Bundle Theories of Substance. Objections to BT 127

V. The Bundling Relation. Simons' Two-tier Bundle Theory of Substance 155

VI. Change, Temporal Parts and BT. Cambridge Change 183

VII. Individual Essences 217

Introduction

The goal of this book is to support a version of the trope-bundle view of individual substances. This preferred version is shown to match with a coherent account of change, individuation and individual essences. In particular, it is argued that qualitative individuation and qualitative individual essences can be defended on the basis of a trope account.

The main motivation for the qualitative approach to substances identifying them for the purpose of analysis with bundles of qualitative features is the aim to account for change and also, to ensure the possibility of contingent predication. That is, the individual substances are not conceived within a superessentialist scheme implying that all their qualitative features are essential to them. To the contrary, I argue that we need a two-tier modal trope **BT** that admits changes also in the determinates of the essential determinables constituting the hard core of the substance on top of permissible changes in the accidental tropes of the outer fringe. I argue that admitting change in the determinates of essential determinables does not violate the basic essentialist insights. Also, the momentary nature of tropes is explored and the temporal parts of occurrents vital to continuants are seen as the vehicles of change. Equipped with these resources, I hope to avoid set-theoretical essentialism threatening all the qualitative approaches to substances. As a result, room is made for contingent predication.

The main background assumptions of the book are the following. The principle of bearer-uniqueness with the non-transferability of tropes is assumed. Tropes are claimed to be individuated via the bearer substance. It is also claimed that essentialist commitments, more specifically, commitment to sortal essentialism and individual essentialism, cannot be dispensed with in a qualitative approach with explanatory purposes.

The adoption of a trope **BT** together with the individuation of tropes via the bearer substance might create the feeling of circularity: tropes and substances seem mutually to individuate each other. The novel solution to the problem developed here is this: it is shown that the individuation of concrete individual substances is independent, in crucial respects, from the fact that they are construed as bundles of tropes. For, concrete individual substances are the bearers of qualitative manifolds *qua* qualitative manifolds, while each constituting abstract trope encompasses only one qualitative feature. Bearing a manifold of qualitative features is one criterion of concreteness implying also independence. Thus, the concrete individual substances have the emergent property of independence even if they are construed as bundles of tropes. Further, the occupancy of a unique spatial-temporal position is also part and parcel of the individuation of concrete substances. But the occupancy of a spatial-temporal position serves only as a particularizer and not as an individuator for the abstract tropes: since the tropes, being abstract entities, can be co-located. So the individuation of tropes depends on factors other than the mere fact of their spatial-temporal position. Thus circularity proves to be only apparent.

The main problem of the qualitative approach lies in its essentialist commitment. That is, if substances are identified qualitatively and it comes to change and identity through time we have to face the counterintuitive consequences of our own essentialist commitments. I think that set theoretical essentialism can be evaded by the adoption of a modal two-tier **BT**. Sortal essentialism is a vulnerable position though, since Cambridge changes pose a challenge to it. I argue that commitment to sortal essentialism should not be abandoned since we have to identify substances *qua* tokens of essential sortals despite complications with Cambridge changes. The individual essences, within the overall sortal constraints, should not be repudiated either: they have a crucial role in the explanations about the individuals in counterfactual situations. I shall argue that the scheme of the explanatory resources would be deficient and gappy without the postulation of individual essences.

Since the notion of individual substances is heavily loaded, prompting various reactions, I spell out briefly my presuppositions. I take it that notion of substances as concrete particulars or continuants carves out reality for the understanding in an important respect that accommodates also our pre-theoretical intuitions. Rather than entertaining a mere flux of experience that cannot be revisited again, with this notion of substance we have a safe point of orientation for articulating experience, hopefully at the joints of reality. In this way the notion of individual substance can be seen as a prerequisite of a *significance condition* presupposed by the metaphysical analysis. Not even our ordinary claims about familiar items in the world could be empirically significant if the experiences backing these claims would not be appropriately structured. And substances are the important means of this structuring. The significance condition can also be referred to as an intelligibility condition.

This way of introducing the notion of substance may sound pretty much Kantian, although the notion of substance as a concrete particular was expounded by Aristotle.[1]

Since the present essay is not specifically historical, all that I have to indicate here briefly is that the notion of substance as developed in the *Categories* is the nearest to the present discussion. It is the notion of the so-called primary substance, like *this* man, *this* horse, etc., which is adopted here. These substances are the ultimate subjects of their properties and their designations occur always in the subject position and never in the predicative position. However, when such designations occur in the predicative position, like, for example, in the proposition "John *is a man*", they are treated by Aristotle as substances of another kind: the so-called secondary substances. In modern logic, the subject

---

[1] See Aristotle, *Categories*, in McKeon (1941); Aristotle, *Metaphysics Z*, in McKeon (1941).

position and the predicative position are relative to each other: what the term in the subject position denotes is a case of what the term in the predicative position denotes. This difference in the logical roles is turned by Aristotle into an ontological difference. Fortunately, primary substances can be legitimized on other grounds as well: I have just shown their role with the Kantian conditions of experience.

The main feature of the primary substances so conceived is that they retain their numerical identity through their career, although they can acquire, over time, incompatible properties. Obviously, the incompatible properties are not had by a particular substance at the same time: for example, Socrates is not hairy and bald at the same time but only in succession. This feature of the substance already brings with it a vital task for the analysis: it requires an account of its changing properties in a way that can also secure its identity through change. Otherwise an intelligibility condition would be violated: we would not know *what* precisely *is* the thing in its very being to which incompatible properties are ascribed through time. Change can be ascribed only against a relatively stable background that serves as the background *of* change; thus, a correct account must canvass how permanence is satisfied in the very notion of the substance. This *permanence* requirement is, again, straightforwardly Kantian in its spirit that I am ready to admit.

So, the *significance condition* supplied by the notion of individual substances can be supplemented by the *permanence condition*, supplied also by this notion. The permanence condition tells us that we can re-identify objects through time in virtue of a background of stable features against which change can meaningfully be described. These conditions are set forth for any intelligible talk about reality as we can comprehend it. The *significance condition* is ubiquitous; almost every metaphysics with some empirical leaning incorporates it. The *permanence condition* is typically associated with Kant's metaphysics of experience and also, it is emphasized in the empiricist reading of Kant.[2] As is known, Strawson in his *The Bounds of Sense* ascribes a special role to the external spatial objects as the vehicles of the *objectivity* of the judgements of experience. The objectivity of the judgements of outer experience which can help to confer an objective character on the judgements of the inner experience as well (see the argument of Kant's *Refutation of Idealism*) relies heavily on the sort of permanence that can be yielded only by the external spatial objects but never by the objects of the inner experience. In this sense part of the objectivity of our judgements of experience is due to the permanence, and hence to the possibility of revisiting, of external spatial objects. The standard Strawsonian interpretation is followed in this respect by some newer Kant scholarship as well.[3]

So it seems that the Aristotelian notion of primary substance can be legitimized through the Kantian role ascribed to external spatial objects. In fact, these objects can be subsumed under the Aristotelian criteria of primary substances, although Aristotle's chief examples of such substances are living organisms that exhibit particularly tight organic unity in virtue of being instantiations of biological kinds. However, there is no principled objection to extending this notion to other continuants as well: say, to individual exemplifications of non-biological kinds, artifacts, for example. An artifact, such as a chair, or a car, etc., exemplifies a kind. It enjoys a functional unity and can be the subject of predication. It may change some of its properties over time without ceasing to be what it is. Also, the semantic properties of artifact-terms permit dividing their reference without vagueness. Current metaphysics has coined the term *continuant* for Aristotelian primary substances taken in this extended sense, comprising also artifacts, other inanimate objects, etc., in order to contrast them with *occurrents*; i.e. events or processes.

---

[2] About the transcendentalist and the empiricist aspects of Kant's metaphysics of experience see Ujvári, M. (1989)

[3] See, for example, Paul Abela's recent book on Kant's empirical realism. (Abela: 2002)

Occurrents range from momentary episodes to extended entities. For example, a compound event like a theatre performance can be traced through the acts making it up. The main difference between continuants and occurrents acknowledged by dualist ontologies is that continuants have no temporal parts, only spatial parts, while events have temporal parts. Events are typically described as changes in the qualitative features of substances: for example, John's getting fat can make a lengthy event. Now a further difference between occurrents and events important from my perspective is that events enjoy permanence only derivatively, through the substances they are parasitic on: we can track the process of John's becoming fat in virtue of John's being a re-identifiable entity.

Here I shall discuss substances or continuants as identifiable mainly with the Aristotelian *criteria* of primary substances *and* the Kantian *legitimization* sketched above. This way of combining the Aristotelian criteria and Kantian legitimization about substances is not quite typical in the literature, though it can be shown to cohere with current approaches. David Wiggins, for example, follows Aristotle and Strawson in taking every concrete particular as a "this - such", i.e. an entity whose individuation requires a sortal concept *plus* a deictic component. He finds consonance between the Aristotelian and the Kantian approaches in the following respect. The former seeks the common natures or kinds of the individual substances captured by 'sortal predicates' in order to answer the 'what is it?' question; while the parallel of this strive in the Kantian philosophy is taking 'things falling under concepts' where 'concept' 'belongs on the level of sense' as Wiggins puts it. And to distinguish the organization of the objects of experience by concepts 'from the referential use' of concepts, Wiggins 'prefers the word "conception" to cover the Kantian use'.[4] So the job of the sortal element in the organization of things is a shared feature; though one has to realize that the Aristotelian mode is emphasis of the ontological aspect while the

---

[4] See Wiggins, D. (1980), (2001), pp.8-10. Reference is made to the 2nd edition.

Kantian mode is emphasis on producing metaphysics tailored to epistemic requirements.

There is also a further feature of substances which is, perhaps, the most familiar one, though not a feature that is ascribed to the external spatial objects in the Kantian approach. It is the putative independence, in an ontological sense, of substances that is their most salient feature. However, this feature can be linked to the permanence condition: the sort of *permanence* exhibited by continuants that is part and parcel of Kantian metaphysics is closely connected to the *independence* of continuants from entities of other kinds. They are independent in the sense that claims about their existence are intelligible without implying claim about the existence of other entities. It is partly in virtue of enjoying independent existence that substances are capable of exhibiting the sort of permanence they actually do; while momentary, fleeting entities, like smiles or gestures or any other accidents are typically dependent on some bearer substratum. Thus it is the permanent existence of a bearer substratum over a certain stretch of time that yields the underlying support for the existence of the fleeting entities. And individual substances or continuants can play the role of some such underlying substratum.[5] The independence of substances or continuants is ontological rather than conceptual: it means that they are capable of sustained existence without being parasitic, in their very being, on some other sort of entity. Also, it is the *independence* from other beings enjoyed by substances but not by events and accidents that marks the previous out as privileged entities on the ontological palette.

---

[5] A note of caution must be made here: when I am talking about substances providing a bearer substratum for the fleeting entities I am not implying the so-called substratum view of the substance. In fact, in *Metaphysics Z,* one of the meanings of substance offered by Aristotle is that individual substances are substrata. Currently, the label "the substratum view" is reserved for the dubious doctrine of non-qualitative substratum. Later in the discussion I shall elaborate on the substratum view of substance.

'Continuant' is a recent term for those concrete individual substances which are both spatially and temporally extended; however, with persons as individuals the criterion of spatial extension is typically suppressed for familiar Cartesian reasons. Without risking a verdict on personhood, I shall take it here that human persons have bodies, not only as a plain matter of fact, but also *qua* persons.

So far I have located independence and permanence mainly in the *spatial* character of continuants. These aspects are considered to be important for the very possibility of the objective judgements of experience in Kantian metaphysics. Having started with Kantian permanence conceptually linked up with Aristotelian independence, we can now turn to the familiar characterization of substances in terms of the *independence criterion*: among the things we can distinguish "...those which can be without other things while the others cannot be without them".[6] The independence criterion is picked up again by Descartes whose formulation is well known to students of metaphysics: "by substance we can understand nothing other than a thing which exists in such a way as to depend on no other things for its existence".[7]

The independence criterion of substances is endorsed here as well since it helps to distinguish substances from other sorts of entities like events and accidents. Still, this criterion might seem to conflict, at first sight, with the goal of the present essay. Since my goal is *to support a version of the bundle-of-tropes view of substances*, in this context the independence criterion might not be so easily satisfied. For, any bundle-view of substances construes substances as being made up, so to speak, from items of another sort, and so substances are dependent, even in their identification, on their qualitative components. There arises the worry that such construal conflicts with independence. We can evade this difficulty by observing that independence, as I have said, is

---

[6] Aristotle, *Metaphysics* Δ 11, 1019a

[7] Descartes, *Principles of Philosophy*, book I. 51.

ontological rather than *conceptual*; thus the conceptual analysis of substances in terms of other entities does not tell against their ontological independence. The further advantage of this position is that we do not have to be committed to a reductive approach to substances seeing them as derivative entities. An ontological reduction that is not preferred here would eliminate substances as entities of their own right in favour of bunches of qualitative features. A universalist, like Russell, would claim that all that exist are universals; what we take to be particulars are just bunches of qualitative features. This stance is clearly unacceptable since what I am up to is to justify a particularist position. What I offer is a conceptual analysis that is reductive, at best, in an explanatory sense: we need to approach the substance-particulars in terms of their qualitative features because only this approach satisfies the condition of significance, and, moreover, it accommodates change. For example, we have to apply analysis in qualitative terms if we want to explain why certain changes like breathing-in some poisonous gas is lethal to a living substance in the literal sense; or, why the destruction of a substantial form is lethal, in the modal sense, to an object *qua* a statue unlike *qua* a piece of clay, while, for example, the fading of the color of a piece of cloth leaves the identity of the cloth through time unaffected, etc. Differences in the impact of these changes would remain mysterious and unexplainable if, instead of the recommended approach, the non-qualitative bare substratum view of the substances were adopted. Later I shall defend my approach against this alternative. In sum, the conceptual or explanatory reduction in qualitative terms is metaphysically benign; we would face a conflict only if we strove at an ontological reduction as well.

The ontological reduction that I ignore here might square with a one-category ontology; for example, the one that uses tropes as building blocks for all sorts of entities. Now a few preliminary remarks have to be made before the full account of a trope theory. "Trope" as a technical term in current metaphysics refers to *property particulars*. The idea is that properties are particulars, just like substances or concrete events. For example, the particular shape of Socrates' nose is a trope not had by anybody else. The red shade of a given flower is a red-particular, or, a trope. The metaphysical meaning of "trope" has nothing to do with its etymology in rhetoric as a figure of speech. Santayana, the American philosopher is reported to have used it first in modern times for "the essence of an occurrence" or event. D.C. Williams, the father of trope theory as a particularist ontological theory has decided to convert the application of the term to denote the "occurrence of an essence", i.e. an abstract particular. It has to be made clear right at the start, that a trope is not equivalent to a particularized property or an exemplified universal. That is, the point is *not* that the particular shape of a concrete entity exemplifies or instantiates Shape-as-such; or, that a red shade instantiates Red-as-such. Such a reading would presuppose a common nature, a "one over many" which is the role of universals. But tropes are not tailored to common natures; these latter are explained by the tropists as sets of exactly resembling tropes. So, a trope is not a particularized property; it is a property particular.

To make clear, the recommendation of the trope-bundle view of substances does not imply the acceptance of the trope theory tout court as a one-category ontology. For example, we are not bound to accept the treatment of *relations* as tropes; similarly, we are not compelled to buy into an overall monistic trope ontology in order to support the application of tropes to the proper understanding of individual substances. Here I part company with Campbell who is the advocate of a one-category ontology and join rather with Bacon who emphasizes the non-reducibility of certain relations to tropes.[8]

The conceptual analysis has to account for the entities in terms of which substances are explicated. Sometimes these are misleadingly called reducing entities; but I have already made clear that they are reducing only in the explanatory sense and not in the ontological sense. Now these qualitative entities can be either universals or tropes. If the entities applied for explanatory reduction are universals, the account is committed to the so-called strong principle of the Identity of

---

[8] Campbell, K. (1990) ch.1., Bacon, J. (1995), ch.5.

Indiscernibles (Leibniz' principle: **PII**), which says that qualitative indiscernibility goes with numerical identity. So, the universalist's way is this: if substances can be understood only as collections of universals, those substances that share all the same universals would be indiscernible with respect to these qualitative features and hence, they would count as identical according to strong **PII**. But many scholars agree that the principle is clearly false. Just think of the qualitatively indistinguishable, still numerically distinct items of mass production coming off from the production lines. Now by simple modus tollens reasoning: the universalist bundle theory of substances (**BT**) implies strong **PII** which is false; hence (**BT**) itself is false as well. (What the weak version of **PII** offers us will be discussed later.)

The counter intuitive consequences of being committed to strong **PII** in the universalist approach serves to legitimize, at least partially, the alternative trope account. The trope account, as we shall see, does not suffer from many of those counter intuitive consequences that plague the universalist approach. A chief attraction of the tropist **BT** in comparison with the universalist **BT** has been spelled out recently by Howard Robinson: "if properties are conceived of as individuals - otherwise known as tropes...- then there cannot be a problem about the distinctness of exactly similar bundles, for the difference is built into the identity of the elements of the bundle, as it is not if the bundle is made of universals".[9]

In the standard reading tropes are property particulars, as I have already said. They cut across the orthodox division of abstract universals and concrete particulars: although they are qualitative features, they are not repeatable entities shared and sharable by many things. A trope is a quality instance which is intimately tied up in its very existence with the thing which it belongs to. There are some scholars though, Armstrong among others, who think of tropes as transferable entities.[10] But in my

---

[9] See Robinson, H. (2004), 18.

[10] Armstrong 1989b 117ff.

view the *supposition of bearer-uniqueness* accommodates better our intuition. So, a trope can be identified as a property particular that belongs to a concrete particular. For example, the trope of Socrates's being snub-nosed is a feature that characterizes exclusively Socrates; no one else is snub-nosed exactly in the way he is. Or, the old-looking grayness of the Houses of Parliament in London is, again, a shade of colour that no other building has. Now if tropes are so much intimately connected to the things they characterize and make up, then, obviously, they are dependent entities: they can only exist where and when their bearer does. What concerns us here as an ontological problem is that tropes are dependent entities. The snub-nosed feature of Socrates cannot exist apart from Socrates; the grayness of the Houses of Parliament cannot exist apart from the building of the Houses of Parliament, etc.

If this is the case with tropes, *and*, moreover, we acknowledge the independence of substances, how can we start out to support the bundle-of-tropes account of substances? Can we coherently claim that tropes as typically dependent entities make up substances as independent entities? Can the tropes be claimed to do their business in some non-circular way, particularly in view of the fact that the constituting tropes can be identified only by reference to the substance that they are supposed to make up? Apart from the threat of circularity, there is the following vexing question: how can we give an account of independent entities in terms of dependent entities? Can we, perhaps, argue for the *emergent* property of independence?

On the trope account the independence problem cannot be dissolved simply by taking recourse to the difference between the ontological and the epistemological senses of dependence. That is, it will not suffice to say that while tropes are ontologically dependent on the bearer substance, just as all instantiated qualities are dependent on the subject and the circumstances of instantiation, substances are dependent on the tropes from the perspective of the conceptual analysis. The epistemological dependence consists in that a thing is, for us, what it strikes us with in various forms of cognition, presumably in perception in the first instance. Thus we tend to identify things with their salient perceivable/cognizable features. At this point, however, an account is required of how an independent entity can be understood in terms of dependent entities. What makes us classify a particular collection of dependent entities as an independent whole? In this question the epistemological perspective merges with the ontological perspective. Hopefully, satisfactory answers will be found here to these questions. Ironically, this particular problem of the analysis does not threaten the universalist approach: universals are independent entities, at least in their Platonic reading, therefore the bundle-of-universals view of substances does not have to provide for the putative emergent property of independence. The universalist approach, as I have briefly indicated, has its major problem with the Leibniz principle. In the general assessment it will be argued that, despite all the difficulties, the trope account has its overwhelming merits and turns out to be the best available candidate compared to its rivals.

Independence was associated here with permanence, the sort of feature that substances or continuants have while events, accidents, etc., have, at best, only in a derivative sense, in virtue of being parasitic on substances. Accidents, like smiles and headaches, are temporary modifications of the substances in which they inhere. Accidents are dependent on the substances and they rarely last as long as the substances themselves. Sometimes accidents are said to be ambiguous between being quality instances *and* occurrents since quite often they come about as the result of an occurrent: say, the event of getting a headache, or the action of smiling.[11] When I claim that events have permanence only derivatively, in virtue of the permanence of the substance(s) involved, I do not thereby deny that they can have a long duration. For example, if the event of the death of Emperor Franz Josef becomes more and more distant from us receding into the past, an indefinitely long event can be generated by ascribing, to this event, the

---

[11] On these issues see Simons, P. (1987., 2000), 8.5. 'Some Related Concepts: Substance, Accident, Disturbance'

property of the temporal distance between its occurrence and the time of the actual speaker. Quite many people deny though that there are such temporal properties of events. However, the main point about permanence had by substances but only indirectly by events and their kin is *not* about duration; rather, what matters is that events can be identified and re-identified only by reference to substances involved in the property-changes typically making up events. Substances as the vehicles of the permanence condition for the grasp and proper articulation of experience yield the very background against which events and their kin are conceived to take place. All change can be meaningfully ascribed only against a relatively stable background; even if the substances themselves change through time in certain respects, they remain the fixed points for our grasp to latch onto. So, permanence is not to be conflated with invariance through time; rather, it is being identifiable through time.

I have mentioned events here to illustrate the contrast, in a vital respect, between substances and other sorts of ontological items. Let us see how events are considered today in the dominant view so that we can appreciate the full significance of this contrast. According to the received view events are tropes. They occupy a certain spatio-temporal region as many particulars do. But as opposed to continuant-particulars, several events can co-occupy a given region at a time since events are identified partly by reference to those qualitative features in respect of which a change occurs to some continuant. This explains the abstract feature of events. In familiar terms, events are ordered triples of things, properties and times. So, the abstract qualitative aspect and the particularity make events qualify as tropes. Especially the analysis of event causation relies in its ontological backup on the view that events are tropes. Recently Ehring has defended "the thesis that property instances, *qua* causal relata, are tropes, not exemplifications of universals".[12] The main reason for adopting this position is that events as

---

[12] Ehring, D. (1999), 19.

causal agents are always particulars and always qualitative. For example, it is the *given heat of the stove* as a property particular that causes the burning of my skin in a given situation and not heat in general.

Even apart from the causal role, there is a perfectly legitimate sense in which events can be claimed to be tropes: they can be seen as changes of the property instances of individual substances. This aspect is captured in Bennett's explanation: "If a sparrow's fall is a particular instance of the property *falling,* that would explain why the fall is so intimately linked with the sparrow yet not identical with it, how the fall is related to the universal property *falling*, why there cannot be a fall unless some thing falls, and so on. Everything that we know for sure about events flows from their being tropes".[13]

Now consider whether this standard reading of events as tropes is compatible with my goal of supporting the trope analysis of substances. More specifically, if we are out for construing substances as bundles of tropes *and* we accept, at the same time, the received view of taking events as tropes, are we still in the position of meeting criteria of *substancehood* that I have avowed of being committed to? How can we discriminate, within the overall trope-analyis, between substances and events once both are construed by tropes? Recall that yielding the permanence condition for experience, backed by independence, were found crucial for substancehood, constituting also the main division line between substances and events. We need the permanence or re-identifiability of substances to the possibility of objective judgements of experience. However, if we also buy into the trope analysis of events, while trying to maintain, at the same time, the crucial metaphysical distinction between substances and other sorts of entities, do we not thereby run into a plain conflict? If, in the overarching analysis, both substances and events are tropes, either simple or compound ones, what selects the previous out as the vehicle of permanence so vital for any

---

[13] See Bennett, J. (1999), 319. How tropes are related to universals and what role they play in predication will be discussed later. See chapter III.

metaphysics of experience? Is it not the case that by endorsing the trope analysis of events I thereby obliterate, at the level of the ontological account, the metaphysically vital distinction between substances and events?

It seems that the desideratum of metaphysics is to maintain the distinction between substances and events; or, in recent terminology, between continuants and occurrents. This might be obviated though by the desideratum of an occamised ontology. I shall show, the conflict can be resolved. Moreover, it can be resolved in a way that no recourse has to be made to the dubious claim that tropes are ambiguous between being tropes of substances *and* event tropes. Some authors though tend to speak about *continuant* tropes and *occurrent* tropes respectively in order to cover the difference. This verbal distinction, however, is not an explanation of how tropes can contribute to ontologically different items. We should not be reluctant to consider together the two areas by pretending that these are simply two different applications of the trope analysis. I will not follow here the cheap way of evading the difficulty by taking these as separate issues. To ensure the coherence of my account and to maintain my claims all I need is to examine the features of tropes and spell out the consequences of these features for both substances and events. Paradoxical it may sound at first hearing though, it is precisely the trope account of both categories that secures the vital metaphysical distinction between substances and events, as I shall show.[14]

---

[14] To anticipate the main line of my reasoning: the metaphysically vital distinction between substances and events can be secured precisely on the trope account, provided that tropes are taken as abstract entities (*pace* Simons who takes them concrete). The abstractness of tropes secures our desideratum in the following way: if, per impossibile, tropes were concrete, while events were identified as tropes, this would have the consequence that there would be only *concrete events*. Now concrete events as four dimensional entities make the notion of continuants or substances superfluous. That is, they make superfluous the idea of continuant things that are only spatially extended while preserving their identity through time. Four dimensional entities are both spatially and temporally extended and thereby the

Event-ontologies enjoy a reputation today. It is quite symptomatic of scientifically minded scholars that they tend to replace all talk about continuants by talk about occurrents. Substances are claimed to be dissolvable into their temporal phases and it is said that there is nothing more to the substance than the sequence of these temporal phases or parts. In short, event-ontologies are recommended in place of the usual dualistic substance/event division. Such position is sometimes claimed to be grounded in modern science; sometimes it is motivated by purely metaphysical considerations. The former can be illustrated by what Quine and Mark Heller say on the topic; the best exposition of the latter is David Lewis' view of things as being made up of their temporal parts.

Mark Heller, for example, proposes that "a physical object is not an enduring spatial hunk of matter, but is, rather, a spatio-temporal hunk of matter. Instead of thinking of matter as filling up regions of space, we should think of matter as filling up regions of space-time. A physical object is the material content of a region of space-time. Just as such an object has spatial extent, it also has temporal extent - it extends along four dimensions, not just three". [15] This four-dimensionalist view deprives objects of their distinctive ontological features and enhances the ontological significance of events. The same position is advocated by Quine who starts out with an interpretation of events that could also serve the goal of the four-dimensional view of objects.[16] As Bennett points out, "Quine uses his ideas about events ... as a basis for explaining what physical objects are."[17]

---

motivation for the distinction between substances and events would be partly lost. So we need the abstractness of tropes and the abstract feature of events in order to avoid the undesirable consequence just described.

[15] Heller, M. (1984), 324-5.

[16] See Quine, W.V. (1960), 171.

[17] Bennett, J. (1988), 104.

Now the question whether modern science explicitly implies, or, is only consistent with, event-ontology is not going to be settled in this book. Within the frameworks of metaphysics, however, a purely monistic event-ontology does not seem to be attractive: as long as the set of individual substances comprises also human creatures, the complete reduction of substances to events is simply inconceivable. For humans exhibit a special integrity amidst their changes that cannot be provided for in an event-ontology. Therefore a purely event-ontology will not be considered here as an attractive option. As to the scientifically motivated claims of such ontology, these claims are partly metaphysically irrelevant partly they are outside the reach of a comfortable decision.

The event-ontology is behind the doctrine of temporal parts that goes in tandem with the rejection of the traditional Aristotelian account of substances. According to the latter substances are *wholly present* in the successive phases of their existence, while exhibiting different properties in these phases. Thus we can flesh out the intuitively appealing claim that the *same* thing can be the bearer of different properties at different times. It is all too familiar that David Lewis has suggested, as an alternative, the temporal-parts understanding of substances persisting through change.[18] Lewis has coined his own terms for these two rival accounts: the traditional one is the so-called *endurance* theory of persistence; the temporal-parts doctrine is the so-called *perdurance* theory of persistence. Although the latter has a clear affinity to the event ontology because it takes the temporal parts as four-dimensional entities, the issue of endurantism *versus* perdurantism need not be seen as motivated by science. For, as we shall see, there are independent metaphysical considerations for the dilemma of endurantism vs perdurantism. I shall discuss the independent metaphysical aspects when I come to the identity and persistence of substances through time.

---

[18] See Lewis, D. (1983), 76-7.

See also: Lewis (1986), 202.

By now it has become clear that the purported defense of the trope-bundle view of substances or continuants splits into several sub-tasks. First of all, the bundle construal of substances has to be described and supported against the historically developed alternative, the so-called pure substratum theory of substances rooted in *Metaphysics Z*. I shall show that substances - rather than being taken as unanalysable primitives - should be conceived in terms of some qualitative features. The *first* chapter exposes the bundle-of-universals view of substances, and, as a contrast, it presents the bare substratum view. Criticisms of both theories is presented with special emphasis on the *modal* objections: bundle theories prove to be *ultraessentialist* while bare substratum theories prove to be *antiessentialist*. The inadequacies of the universalist bundle construal already points towards the need to consider a particularist version of the bundle view in terms of tropes.

The advantage of tropes over universals adjusted specifically to a substance theory is pointed out next. The *second* chapter is devoted to the ontological role of tropes: they are delineated from accidents whose kin, the events qualify as tropes, too, in full consonance with the trope-bundle view of substances. Davidson's notion of events as concrete particulars is discussed from a critical perspective. The coherent trope-theoretic reading of both substances and events requires the abstractness of tropes, as it is argued. Particularism that motivates the trope-theory will be distinguished from nominalism: I claim that it is wrong to understand the trope-theory as a kind of nominalism.

If tropes are particulars they must be individuated in some way. In the *third* chapter the various suggestions for the individuation of tropes is considered. The view I defend is that tropes can be individuated *via* their bearer-substance. Thus the whole problem of the individuation of tropes ultimately goes back to the problem of individuation of substances. Historically, there is the simple bundle view according to which the substance is "nothing but" the bundle of tropes; but this position is seen here as inadequate. For, in this case, one has to face the discomforting consequence that tropes and substances mutually individuate each other. This circularity charge will be evaded by explaining how and why a more sophisticated bundle theory is able to provide for the individuation of concrete substances so that the individuation of abstract tropes will remain dependent on the individuation of these concrete substances.

In this chapter much of Campbell's one-category trope ontology will be discussed and also, Bacon's polemic against the elimination of certain genuine universals in favour of tropes. Ultimately, Bacon's approach is assented.

More sophisticated bundle theories apply two tiers instead of identifying the individual directly with a cluster of qualitative features. Hopefully, this is a way to make **BT** (=bundle theory) more defensible against the standard charges. Accordingly, the *fourth* chapter discusses some bundle accounts of substances, notably those suggested by Castaneda, Casullo and van Cleve. Castaneda's "bundle-bundle view" and its perdurantist version developed by Casullo will be surveyed. The latter presupposes the temporal part doctrine of substances. Another two-tier account of substances exposed briefly by van Cleve presupposes a tight core to the substance going proxy for the substratum equipped with a looser outer fringe. The two tiers have different modal status: the core is constituted by essential tropes the outer fringe is constituted by accidental tropes. Cleve's insight is motivated mainly by the effort to avoid the standard objections that can be developed against the simple bundle theory in its universalist version. These objections will be discussed in Cleve's formulation and also, Casullo's defense of **BT** along perdurantist lines will be discussed. My reservations with perdurantism will be spelled out. All the bundle theories discussed in this chapter are *not* tropist.

The full elaboration of the Cleve-style two-tier account of substances can be found with Simons' trope **BT**. The special importance of Simons's version lies in his approach to the gluing relation going back to the Husserlian notion of *foundation*. So the topic of the *fifth* chapter is Simons's two-tier theory and his amendment on the bundling relation to make it efficient in explaining the *integral unity* of substances. Apart from achieving unity, this account is supposed to provide for change and identity through time. It will be pointed out, however, that these desiderata cannot be satisfied within the original frameworks of this theory: since the core of the substance is conceived as being made up of essential tropes in rigid (*de individuo*) mutual dependence, this conception does not provide for the possibility that the substances can change the *determinates* of their essential *determinable* tropes. Thus, rather than explaining change, this account proves to be too rigid in a counterintuitive way.

Further, radical essential change threatens the subsistence of accidental tropes on Simons's account, for these tropes would be left without a bearer with the destruction of the essential nucleus. This critical observation due to Denkel fits into the overall critical assessment of Simons's view. Moreover, one has to consider the possibility that the essential tropes of the substances can be affected by Cambridge events. Such events are typically represented as external relational changes from the perspective of the substance; still, some such events can lead to drastic change in the sortal status of continuants and their proper parts, as we shall see in the *sixth* chapter. Therefore the *sixth* chapter is devoted to the problem of change in the trope-bundle view of substances. The significance of this perspective is that the trope-view comes to be assessed against the requirement of accounting for change.

Ehring and Simons, for example, consider the coupling of trope **BT** with a perdurantist theory of identity through time. Here I will spell out my position with respect to these current doctrines and I make clear how change and persistence can be understood in tropist terms. Also, I examine how Cambridge changes affect certain sortal essentialist claims. The finding is that these trifle changes can bring about the destruction of the undetached proper parts of individual substances *qua* their proper parts. The general lesson is that Cambridge changes are far less trifle than they are typically thought to be: in a sense they are substantial and not bogus changes.

The last, *seventh* chapter tries to restate the good reputation of individual essences by showing their proper place within essentialism.

Two arguments are offered here for postulating individual essences of substances on top of their sortal essences. One is the explanatory gap argument, according to which many of our explanations concerning individuals would be gappy without exploring their individual essences as parts of the explanans. The other draws on the analogy with the individual essences of events presupposed in single causal explanations. These arguments are meant to support qualitative individual essences serving explanatory goals as opposed to hybrid impure relational essences accounting for origin and numerical identity. It is also highlighted why origin properties as components in the impure relational essences of individuals do not yield geniune *de re* constructions; and, as a consequence, why they cannot make individual essences. The distinction between the two types of individual essences is traced back to the ambiguity of the very notion of individuation.

I. The Identity of Substances: Bare Substrata or Qualitative Bundles?

Bare Substrata

There arises the dilemma of taking substances or continuants *either* as primitive, basic building blocks of ontology admitting no further reductive analysis *or* taking them as essentially structured by qualitative components. This dilemma owes itself to the inherent conflict of two different pulls in metaphysics: one is the empiricist pull that focuses on the perceivable, salient features of the continuants as the objects of experience and, accordingly, starts out to account for these continuants in terms of their perceivable, salient features. In this view the continuants are what the perceived qualities reveal to us. This leads to the bundle theories of substances. Among the classical British empiricists Berkeley and Hume may be credited with this view while Locke is the exception. As for modern empiricists, Russell advocates most clearly the bundle theory.[19]

The other pull in metaphysics is the desideratum of finding vehicles of *unity* that could stand firmly against the threat of constant flux in experience. Any coherent account of experience must provide for the possibility of the re-identification of the continuants that are so-called precisely because a stable unity and identity are presupposed with them. The underlying idea is that no trifle change can affect the identity of these continuants since their identity boils down to some deeper unity protecting them from falling apart into qualitative moments. Since no qualitative aspect arising in experience can just wander around without

---

[19] see Russell (1940)

belonging to something that already enjoys unity, there arises the need to pinpoint the locus of this unity.

But the main motivation for a primitive notion of unity derives from the insight that the explanation of any unity has a touch of circularity since the explanandum is already presupposed in one way or another. Therefore, those who put priority on unity suggest that substances are primitive wholes whose unity needs no special account. It is just part of the nature of the substances that they enjoy unity. A closely related point would be to observe that individual substances typically have sharp boundaries: no deliberation is needed to decide, for example, what the boundaries of a chair are and where the table "starts". In other words, we do not have to pick out, by deliberation, medium-size dry goods out of the chaos of qualitative features wandering around. All these considerations might pave the way to the so-called bare substratum theory representing the second horn of the dilemma. It is espoused, for example by Locke and it reaches back to *Metaphysics Z*. There Aristotle exposes it as one of the possible meanings of substance without fully endorsing it as an authentic guide to that notion.

The chief attraction of the bare substratum theory, as I have just said, is that the unity of the continuants and their distinct existence from their kin are primitive, built-in features not supervening on any of their other features. This theory, while not denying that continuants have ordinary properties discernible in experience, maintains that continuants have a propertiless component, their bare substratum, over and above the ordinary properties. Thus the bare substratum theory (with Gustav Bergmann as its main proponent) is actually a two-component theory: any substance or continuant is analyzable into its bare substratum *and* its properties and internal relations. So the substances are *not* unstructured concrete wholes or "blobs", as Armstrong prefers to call them, but they are, on the face of it, structured entities. Still, the two components do not equally lend themselves to recognition: while the properties and the relations are discernible, the bare substratum is an ontological posit not available to experience. It is postulated rather than detected. The bare substratum theory supresses the structure in favor of a primitive unity.

The basic tenet of the bare substratum theory is that the identity of the substances involves only these bare substrata as bare, propertiless particulars. In short, the identity of the substances is separable and is actually separate from their properties. Strange as it sounds though, the chief function of this claim is to circumvent the major problem of the rival bundle view. The latter makes the identity of the substances supervenient on their qualitative features objectionable on several grounds. The main objection is that the bundle view cannot account for the numerical diversity of substances sharing all their qualitative features, more precisely, their pure properties. The role of accounting for numerical diversity where no difference in terms of properties is detectable is performed by bare substrata. Say, numerically different cars of the same trade-mark, colour, etc. coming off from the production line are identical in all their pure properties; still, they owe their distinctness to the distinctness of their bare substrata. This is a difficult notion though, since it is unclear how bare entities can perform this putative role.

Sometimes we still buy into unintuitive accounts provided the payoff seems promising. There is the temptation to think that this is the case with the positing of bare substrata: maybe, it gives us what we need without producing more problems than what it solves. Many critics find though, that it is not really worth positing bare substrata. However, before displaying the shortcomings of this view let us see what the bare substrata are supposed to accomplish for the analysis.

Bare substrata are often appealed to as things with the duty of accounting for the numerical diversity of qualitatively indiscernible substances. So they are a kind of *individuator*. The inclusion of such non-qualitative components into the structure of substances is a way of fulfilling the requirement of the principle of Constituent Identity. The principle tells us that things with the same constituents are numerically identical. For example, if Hamlet and the tragic prince of Denmark share blood and flesh, etc. they are numerically identical. Or, to take a somewhat controversial example, if a lump of clay and a statue are made up of exactly the same clay-molecules, again, they count as numerically identical. Now things with the same qualitative features but with different substrata incorporated also as constituents, would count as numerically different satisfying thus our commonsensical intuition.

Numerical identity may be displayed together with non-identity under a sortal. The statue and the lump of clay do not fall under the same sortal or Form in the Aristotelian sense: one being, as a statue, a work of art, the other being the token of a mass-type. Thus, while numerical identity obtains, identity under sortals becomes relativized to these sortals. Those who find repugnant the idea of relativized identity propagated, for example, by Peter Geach, put emphasis on numerical identity as the only conceivable way of talking about the identity of concrete, empirical things.[20] However, the notion of numerical identity is retained in any case, whether we are prepared to countenance other notions of identity or not.

So numerical identity needs to be explained; and the claim is that each token of a substance-type is a separate token or individual in virtue of having a bare substratum of its own. These bare substrata must be bare, i.e. propertiless; otherwise they would be just additional qualitative features of the substances and the bare substratum view would collapse into a kind of bundle view explaining numerical diversity with the help of qualitative diversity.

One might say that numerical diversity could equally be explained by reference to the unique spatio(temporal) position that each concrete individual occupies. This suggestion would spare recourse to bare substrata as individuators. Soon I will come to the problem of ascribing individuating role to spatio(temporal) properties in the bundle theory.

Turning back to substrata for the moment, the question arises whether these putative individuators can really be propertiless items. Quite many

---

[20] It has to be noted here that the identity conditions of abstract entities are a separate issue. These should not be conflated with the identity conditions of concrete, empirical things.

scholars find this idea perplexing. For example, Denkel has argued that "the bare substratum as individuator is a logically inadequate notion".[21] The main point, to anticipate, is that bare substrata cannot yield identity conditions just because they are propertiless. To see this just consider two substances *a* and *b* sharing the same bare substratum; would that be sufficient to render *a* and *b* identical, as Denkel invites us to consider? Obviously not since "this condition can hold regardless of the fulfillment of the rival condition that *a* and *b* should share exactly the same properties." We can concede that this scenario is logically possible: i.e. that two or more individual substances have different properties while sharing the same bare substratum. Therefore the latter cannot fulfill the role of individuator.

In order to see this more clearly, let us refine the example just considered. Let us take it now that the bare substratum *and* also, all the determinable properties, are shared by substances *a* and *b*; however, the shared determinables are exhibited under different unshared determinates. Roughly speaking, determinable properties stand to determinate properties like genus stands to species: for example, being coloured is a determinable property, while being red is a determinate one; having weight is a determinable property, while being 50 kg is a determinate one, etc. It is worth noting that one and the same property can be both a determinable and a determinate but in different contexts. For example, being red is a determinate with respect to being coloured, while it is a determinable with respect to shades of red, say, maroon. Now to apply these considerations to our imagined case, let us take that *a* and *b* are substances with the same bare substratum and the same determinable properties, e.g. being plastic toys of a cubic shape both coloured and having size, etc. These would render them identical on the substratum view; but say, one is red, the other is blue, one is two inches big, the other is three inches big, etc. We can see that the bare substratum equipped with the same determinables exhibited under

---

[21] See Denkel, A. (2000)

different determinates cannot play the role of guaranteeing the identity of the substances. The implication is that "on the substratum hypothesis there may be objects with contradictory properties: an intolerably absurd consequence".[22]

One way to avoid this absurd consequence would be to say that difference of properties, more precisely, difference at the level of determinates, implies difference in the individuating bare substratum. So, the bare substratum of the red plastic cubic toy of two inches big is necessarily different from the substratum of the blue plastic cubic toy of three inches big. Unfortunately this escape route out of the absurdity is not available. We can not say that the different bunches of properties had by *a* and *b* respectively commits us to posit different bare substrata to *a* and *b* since propertiless substrata do not stand in the logical relations of either entailment or exclusion to the bunches of properties. We cannot say that one bunch or bundle of properties entails a given bare substratum while it excludes some other since the bare substratum has no property in virtue of which the entailment/exclusion would hold. Therefore Denkel's scenario about two substances *a* and *b* sharing the same bare substratum is not so much weird as it might seem at first sight. We can even swap the bare substrata of substances of the same kind; indeed, we can even swap bare substrata of substances of *different* kinds, without ever being in the position to discern the difference. So we have found a further argument to back the earlier point about the "intolerably absurd consequence" of the bare substratum theory.

Before abandoning, however, this theory across the board, the other role of bare substrata should be considered. The bare substratum theory is saved from a wholesale dismissal, provided it is not found so much vulnerable in its other role. The other role is this: bare substrata are said to be the *literal possessors of the properties* of the substances. In this role bare substrata are the ultimate subjects of predication. The key term is predication. It must be shown now why predication needs the positing

---

[22] *ibid.* 433 - 4.

of bare substrata. Here the argument proceeds by reductio. Suppose that substances could be taken as bunches of qualitative features; in this case they could not count as subjects for predication, or, metaphysically speaking, as the literal bearers of the properties. This point is easily demonstrable. Consider an ordinary, concrete, empirical object, say, a plastic cube toy and predicate of it one of its qualitative features. Suppose, we want to predicate of it its colour, or its size, etc. What would be the so-called ultimate subject of predication in this case? Obviously, it cannot be the object *qua* a bunch of its qualitative features because then predication would be redundant: one of the features constituting the object would be predicated of it, in which case the subject-concept would already include the predicate-concept. All predication would turn into *tautology* on this account, which is clearly absurd.

One way of coping with this problem would be to stipulate that it is not the whole bunch of properties making the thing that counts as the ultimate subject of predication. Rather, it is the bunch of properties *minus* the property that we want to ascribe to it in predication on the given occasion. So, if we want to say that the toy *is* plastic, we comprise into its subject-bunch all its features that normally count, *except* its being plastic; or, if we want to say that the toy *is* red, we comprise into its subject-bunch all its features that normally count, *except* its being red, etc. So far so good, the move is *ad hoc* but it seems to work; or, does it really? Compare two or more such "predications" all purporting to be about the *same* toy. The trouble is that we do not achieve *sameness* of the toy under such predications, since the subject-bunch keeps on varying according to the inevitable selection: i.e., which of the components has to be deleted from it in order to secure the non-tautologous character of the subject-predicate discourse. Therefore the substance, taken in terms of its properties, cannot be the literal bearer of its properties required to predication. Therefore a component has to be posited, besides the properties, as the literal bearer of properties that plays the role of the ultimate subject of predication; this is the bare substratum.

There arises now the question how this bare substratum as *the* subject of predication is identifiable; what makes one bare substratum different from another; what makes one, rather than the other, *the* subject *of* predication in one particular individual substance. These questions already presuppose a close connection between the first and the second roles of bare substrata: the vital point is that the second role cannot be performed without the first role being successfully performed. That is, bare substrata *as individuators* must be found impeccable first, before the second role of yielding the ultimate *subject of predication* could be considered. But we have already seen that the notion of bare substratum as individuator is absurd with unacceptable logical consequences. Most critics of the bare substratum theory point out the inadequacy of the theory of bare substrata as individuators without making it clear how the two roles hang together.

Therefore my suggestion is that there is no point in staying with the notion of bare substratum solely on the basis of the second function, i.e., its being the ultimate subject of predication, even though the deficiency of the rival view in this respect plays into the hands of the bare substratum theory. As I have already shown, bare substrata cannot be vindicated as the ultimate subjects of predication because the successful performance of this role hangs together with the successful performance of the individuating role; but substrata fail in this latter role.

Thus the individuating role proves to be critical. It is easy to see that bare substrata cannot perform the role of individuating the substances, since they themselves are in need of identity conditions. Substrata must also differ in their identity-properties, as Loux points out, echoing the criticism of Sellars.[23] As is known, there is a way of supplying identity-properties by making recourse to the dubious notion of *haecceistic* properties. If this solution is adopted, then we can claim, for example, that substratum Φ has the haeccesitic property of being identical with Φ ;

---

[23] See Loux, M. (1978) and Sellars, W. (1963a)

substratum Γ has the haecceistic property of being identical with Γ, etc. However, such identity properties meet serious objections. I follow the lead of those metaphysicians who refuse to countenance haecceistic properties because they do not find them to be *genuine* properties.[24] And any other candidates for the identity property of substrata would face the same fate by contravening the very notion of a "propertiless substratum".

The notion of the bare substratum cannot exclude, however, at least one second-order property, i.e. the property of "having no property essentially". But we are not better off either with this move. Since now it is perfectly legitimate to ask whether this property is had by the substratum contingently or essentially; the meaningfulness of this question shows that the property is a genuine one. Another second-order property of substrata would be the property of "being the literal bearer of properties". And bare substrata cannot avoid having decent first-order properties either, such as: "being essentially subjects for attributes", "being essentially diversifiers", etc.[25] The problem for bare substrata arises at this level: if substrata are "all essentially subjects for attributes, all essentially diversifiers..."etc., then, "while being numerically different from each other, they begin to look like qualitatively indiscernible entities". These qualitatively indiscernible entities are, then, in need of explanation of their numerical diversity by some further entity, say, a further "lower- level substratum", as Loux says.[26] But since the same point can be made for this lower-level as well, that is, further numerical diversifiers of qualitatively indiscernible entities have to be posited, regress ensues from each lower level substratum to further lower level substratum, etc.

---

[24] See Chisholm, R. (1981), chapter 1, especially pp. 7, 16. See also: Armstrong, D. M. (1980), p.93. Their objections are discussed at length by Losonsky, M. (1987b)

[25] See Loux, M. (1998), 117.

[26] *ibid.*

The discomforting consequences of the bare substratum theory already yield some arguments for espousing the rival bundle theory. Moreover, there is a main independent motivation for the latter: philosophers of empiricist vein have always found that concrete things can be conceived only in terms of their perceivable/cognizable features. The verificationist conviction is always lurking behind any defense of the bundle view. From Berkeley through Russell up to contemporary proponents of the view like Castaneda and Cleve, individual concrete substances are thought to have a certain structure specifiable with the help of their discernible properties. Since these empiricists deny that there is an underlying bearer of properties over and above the properties that actually make up the substance, they must give an account of substancehood different from, still completely analyzable into, qualitative features.[27]

Substances as bundles of universals

Here substances are taken as mere "bundles" or "collections" of sharable qualitative features and substancehood is explained with the help of "bundling" as the gluing relation. This relation is supposed to turn a mere aggregate into a more unitary whole. It is variously referred to by different authors: Russell, for example, calls it "compresence", D.C. Williams calls it "collocation". Castaneda's idiosyncratic term for the gluing relation is "consubstantiation". All these locutions express the claim that a substance is constituted by the spatio-temporal co-occurrence of certain instantiated properties. Now some bundle theories are realists: they take properties as platonic universals; i.e. as multiply exemplifiable entities implying that the very same universal can occur in different exemplifications. The redness that is exemplified by the rose is

---

[27] The only exceptions are minds or selves; even Berkeley refrains from giving a reductive account of these special substances in terms of their qualitative features. The substancehood of minds/selves reveals itself in a privileged unity; obviously, this is not to say that minds/selves make a supporting case for the bare substratum theory.

the same redness that is exemplified by the carpet or the post box. Thus a universal is a "*one over the many*"; and this gives a sharp contrast with particulars.

Universalism is not an indispensable feature though of the bundle theory of substances. Properties in the bundle can be conceived metaphysically in a particularist way as well: instead of insisting on the multiple occurrence of exactly the same universal feature, properties can be seen as being "adjusted" to the substances they characterize. So the redness of the rose is very similar, but not strictly identical to, the redness of the carpet; and both are very similar, but not strictly identical to, the redness of the post box. The particularist version of the bundle theory takes the form of the trope-bundle theory: this will be recommended here as the most plausible theory once all the pros and cons have been assessed. To anticipate, the most serious objection against the universalist bundle view does not arise, as we shall see, on the trope-bundle view.

So the bundle approach, in general, recommends itself as the implementation of an empiricist approach to the individual substances. It avoids the logically intolerable consequences of the bare substratum theory by making talk about substances intelligible according to verificationist requirements. Still, there are some significant objections against the universalist bundle theory that have crystallized in the long course of debates.

It is objected, *first,* that the constituents of substances are platonic universals rather than constituents of some other sort. Now universals as abstract entities are necessary beings. The necessary existence of universals as the constituents of concrete individual substances cannot, however, be inherited by the substances. The latter are contingent beings and the question is how the contingency of the concrete individual substances can be provided for, given that the constituents are necessary beings. Should we let ourselves be tempted by the idea of contingent bare substrata in order to resolve the difficulty? Do we have to fall back to the rival view? Fortunately, we do not have to, since the required contingency is said to be provided by the gluing relation of "compresence". This relation itself is contingent: it is contingent whether a certain universal is compresent with another universal in the substance-bundle. For example, "hairiness" in Socrates is contingently compresent with his "being snub-nosed". It can easily be seen that the contingency of the gluing relation stressed by many authors owes much to the contingency of the relation of exemplification or instantiation. While universals are necessary, it is purely a contingent matter whether they are exemplified or not, and, as a consequence, whether they are co-exemplified or not with other universals to make a given individual. Thus one needs to explore the distinction between universals themselves and their instantiations in order to explain the contingency of the gluing relation. In short, gluing can count as contingent only in virtue of property-instantiation being contingent. The familiar difference in this respect between the platonic and the Aristotelian tradition is that while the former admits independently existing, uninstantiated universals as well, the latter denies them. So, the argument for the contingency of gluing is also a watershed between the two traditions.

Perhaps, the only exceptions to contingent gluing are the instances of the so-called natural kind-universals. These latter determine, in Aristotelian fashion, the nature of the individuals falling under them. E.g. a rabbit could not but fall under the universal "rabbithood", otherwise it would not exist *qua* a rabbit. Apart from such kind universals, the other universals entering into the constitution of a substance are glued together contingently unless one is prepared to embrace excessive essentialism.

So the first objection, which is a modal one, falls. Unfortunately, there is another modal objection against the bundle view that cannot so easily be dismissed.[28] The second modal objection concerns precisely the

---

[28] I shall examine it more closely from the perspective of the two-tier trope bundle view put forward by Simons. There my concern will be to account for both the essential and the contingent properties of the substances.

ultraessentialism of the bundle theories; and, by parity, one has to remark the *antiessentialist* feature of the substratum theories not mentioned before.[29] First let us do the latter. The antiessentialism of the substratum theory consists in that no property whatever is necessitated by the propertiless substratum. Such substratum does not stand, either in the relation of entailment or exclusion, to properties. Although I have pointed this out before I have not labeled it as a modal problem. That is, I have not mentioned antiessentialism as a special weakness of the substratum theory since the problem it generates is just a modal variant of the more general problem that the notion of a thing without properties is incoherent. To recall, it is incoherent because it leaves the second order property of "having no property" unexplained. Obviously, the same applies to the second order property of "having no property essentially" characteristic of bare substratum.

The modal problem of the rival view, i.e. the ultraessentialism of the bundle theory is more perplexing for it affects the problem of substance-identity through time. Let us have a closer look at it. In the reductive approach of the bundle theory, substances are "nothing more", than bundles or clusters of properties. Therefore all the properties making up substances are essential or necessary to them in the following sense: "if the attribute did not enter into the constitution of the object, that object would not exist".[30]

When talking about these modal traits I occasionally use "essential" and "necessary" interchangeably. Although there is an important difference, its subtlety plays no role in the present discussion.[31] So, the

---

[29] About ultraessentialism and antiessentialism see Loux (1998) 101-115.

[30] See Loux (1998), 105.

[31] "Necessary" and "essential" are used almost interchangeable because essences are typically analysed as *de re* necessities in logic. Despite this prevailing treatment, I appreciate Kit Fine's insight that essence is, in some sense, stronger than logical modality. For example, there are necessary truths involving a thing such that these truths do not obtain in virtue of the thing's essence. See Kit Fine (1994)

main point is that the identity of the individual substances boils down to complete constituent identity and the constituents are, in the bundle-view, the properties. The substance is identified thus with the actual collection of its properties. As a consequence, a different collection of properties yields a different bundle and hence another individual substance. As it might be guessed, this notion of the substance makes substances extremely fragile: change in the actual collection of properties, however trifle it might be, would give a different individual substance. So the identity of the substances through time cannot be secured on this account; this is a chief vulnerable aspect of the bundle theory.

The overarching modal problem, to repeat, is that ultraessentialism plagues one, and antiessentialism plagues the other, member of the pair of the competing theories. This extremist distribution of the modal traits has a bearing even on a promising version of the bundle-of-tropes view, as we shall see. The antiessentialism of the substratum theories, however, is not without some advantage. As it has already been pointed out, substratum theories are antiessentialist in the following sense: all the properties ascribable to a substance are contingent to its substratum as the literal bearer of these properties since a propertiless substratum does not necessitate any property. The set of properties characterizing the individual substance does not entail, and is not entailed by, the bare substratum of the substance. In a dialectical spirit, this might be seen as an advantage of the substratum theory. For substratum theorists typically claim that substances with the same set of pure properties can be numerically distinct by virtue of involving distinct substrata. Now if entailment held, per impossibile, from the set of properties to the bare substratum, then, clearly, sameness of the set would imply sameness of the substratum. But this unwelcome consequence is successfully avoided by the antiessentialism of the substratum theory which rules out such entailments.

However, supposing entailment from the substratum to the set of associated properties would not be quite unreasonable. For, it would help to restrict the options: for example, "cat-substrata" would turn to be compatible only with "cat-like" associated properties and so these could join only to "cat-individuals"; rather than being compatible with "car-substrata" and joining thus to "car-individuals". In the lack of such entailment substrata are most often claimed to be individuated in a *haecceistic* manner: say, substratum Γ has the haecceistic property of being identical with Γ, etc. and the same holds for each substratum. This manouvre still does not secure the unique link of the substratum to the substance whose substratum it is. Since any recourse to genuine qualitative features is a forbidden move in this theory, substances are also said to be identifiable in a haecceistic manner: cat Tibbles has the unique, non-sharable property of "being identical with Tibbles", etc. The question, then, is how one can match the haecceistically individuated substratum with the haecceistically individuated substance? What belongs to what and why?

The upshot is this: the lack of entailment from the properties to the identity of the substances is an advantage of the substratum theory as I have suggested, since it does the job of providing for the possibility of qualitatively indiscernible, still numerically distinct substances. However, the tie of the individual substrata to the individual substances is inadequately accounted for on the bare substratum theory. For example, a swap of substrata between any two individual substances would be conceivable. Verificationists would also explore the fact that the swap would be undetectable. Moreover, all the criticisms that target the notion of a thing "having no property" can be repeated for the notion of a thing "having no property essentially". For, one might wonder whether the property of "having no property essentially" is contingently or essentially true of bare substrata? And modal questions of the same form can be asked about each second order property of the bare substrata.

Let us return to the modal problem of the ultraessentialism of the bundle theory and the other objections. Vulnerability to qualitative change has just been indicated and the *second* major charge against the theory is precisely this: it cannot provide for the identity of the individual substances through time. The obvious reason is that any change in the bundle of qualitative features, however trifle, results in change of the individual substance identified essentially in terms of the actual elements of the bundle. So the counter-intuitive result is that whenever there is a slightly different bundle, there is another individual.

Now identity through time, or, better, identity *despite* minor qualitative changes in time is a big issue. All the attempts to cope with it run into conflict with the logical feature of identity, namely, that identity involves property-indiscernibility. It is not at all trivial how we could satisfy the two desiderata: to get both logic working according to its principles and also, to provide for the pre-theoretical intuition that the identity of concrete substances is loose enough not undermined by minor changes. Admittedly, if the bundle theory fails this test, it still has to be treated with some charity since other theories are not much better either in this respect.

When talking about change, a distinction must be made between its two notions: one is change in certain qualitative respects, the other is the *radical* change of coming into being or perishing. Metaphysicians are usually keen on the distinction since the two notions of change carry different implications. Qualitative change, for example, is a problem for identity through time; while it is a problem for coming into being how to avoid the dubious claim of creation *ex nihilo*. Being aware of these implications, Kant has also used two different expressions, notably, *Wechsel* and *Veränderung*, to indicate the difference.

Further, perishing can be literal as passing from life to death with living beings. But it can also be perishing *qua* the particular exemplification of a *sortal* ceasing to be the exemplification of that sortal. In the latter case the presupposition is that the doctrine of sortal essentialism holds. For example, a clay statue can be destroyed, *qua* a statue, by being squeezed not satisfying any more the formal principle of a statue. So ceasing to exist *as* an individual substance *of a certain sort*, either animate or inanimate, qualifies as perishing in the latter sense.

There is also a third notion of change that has not been considered, until quite recently, to pose any challenge to the identity of substances through time. It is a "*Cambridge change*" named after the treatment of change by some Cambridge philosophers, notably Russell. Such change is typically described as mere relational change not affecting the intrinsic features of the substance. For example, Xanthippe's becoming a widow is due to Socrates's dying and not to any intrinsic qualitative change of Xanthippe as a human being. If identity involves sameness of intrinsic qualitative features, then, obviously, Xanthippe does not undergo any real change by becoming a widow. So the impression is that Cambridge changes are too trifling to generate any metaphysical problem for the identity of substances. But this impression is misleading and the traditional understanding of Cambridge changes is highly disputable. I shall come to it when discussing, in the sixth chapter, the consequences of sortal essentialism for the identity of individual substances.

Here I consider only genuine intrinsic qualitative change supplying a charge against the property-bundle view.

To admit, the notion of qualitative change is perplexing in itself, consisting in an object having a certain property at one time and having another property at a successive time. This flies in the face of the principle of identity sometimes referred to as Leibniz's Law: according to it, whatever is true of a given thing must be true of anything identical with that thing.[32] For example, the soup which is hot first is identical with the same portion of soup that has become colder a few minutes later. In other words, identity entails indiscernibility: the sameness of a portion of soup on the table precludes the soup's being discernible from itself. Otherwise the same soup would be both hot and cold; but no thing can have contradictory properties. The familiar reply is that it is not the same temporal segment of the soup that is *both* hot and cold but different temporal segments of the liquid possess different properties.

The term 'Leibniz's Law' is, in fact, misleading here since the term is reserved not for the *indiscernibility of the identicals* but for its converse

---

[32] See Lowe, E. J. (2002), 41.

that seems to hold equally; i.e., it is reserved for the *identity of indiscernibles*. I shall stay with this latter usage and will rather refer to identity's implying indiscernibility as a logical feature of identity. This logical feature holds even if the converse, Leibniz's Law is not accepted. This distinction between the two directions of the entailment has an important bearing on the present discussion. For those who question "Leibniz's Law", meaning the Identity of Indiscernibles, formulate a further charge against the bundle theory which is clearly distinct from the charge that substance-identity through time does not meet the logical requirement of identity's involving complete indiscernibility. The further charge, to remind, is that there are numerically distinct while qualitatively indiscernible things, *pace* the Leibniz Law.

Let us return for a moment to the idea of the temporalized solution to identity through time. It must be noted here that this solution produces even more complications for the bundle construal of substances than the traditional Aristotelian view according to which individual substances are "wholly present" in each phase of their existence. For, instead of having just one bundle going proxy for the substance, a whole temporal sequence of bundles has to be postulated in order to account for identity through time. In fact, this leads to the *bundle-bundle* view, considered later.

Now the moral I want to draw from considering the *second* charge is this: the indiscernibility of identicals is violated in qualitative change, whatever construal of substances is adopted. So this problem is *not* specific to the bundle view. What is specific to it is the excessive fragility of the substance individuated in terms of its properties. The bundle view invites a very static approach to identity. This could be overcome, perhaps, by some *essentialist* manouvre. Such manouvre would amount to claiming that the identity of the substances hinges on a proper subset of the properties containing only the essential ones, while the changing contingent properties do not affect their identity. That is, some modal two-tier version of the bundle view seems appropriate. As we shall see, this is the solution adopted by some current two-tier tropist bundle theories.

The charges discussed so far might urge one to abandon substance-identity being pinned down to mere *constituent-identity*. For the feeling is that there is a perfectly legitimate notion of substance-identity over and above constituent identity. Let alone the dubious claim that the constituents of concrete particulars are, literally, abstract qualitative features. Now if one does not want to retreat to the bare substratum view, one might concede the Aristotelian view according to which individual substances are the numerically distinct instantiations of their kinds. For example, an individual horse is the numerically distinct instantiation of the kind "horse"; an individual man is the numerically distinct instantiation of the kind "man", etc. Accordingly, such kinds are determined by substance-universals as opposed to other universals not constituting the essence of a kind. The Aristotelian view is saturated by an organic conception of these kinds; the typical examples from the *Categories* are tokens of living types. But, as I have said, the same conception can be extended, with minor modifications, to non-organic kinds as well, say, artifact-kinds.

Now this Aristotelian reading of substance-identity distinct from mere constituent identity is not a modification of the bundle view any more; rather, it is the replacement of a reductionist account by a basically non-reductionist account. The difference between a reductionist and a non-reductionist account is this: on the Aristotelian view substances are no longer constituted by all the properties they have; it is only their substance kind that determines their identity qua tokens of the kind.

The revival of the Aristotelian approach to substance-identity is not rare among contemporary metaphysicians: just to mention a few, Loux, Lowe and Wiggins are the most prominent representatives of this approach nowadays. The revival of this approach is in tandem with the revival of Aristotelian *sortal essentialism.* This doctrine, briefly, says that individual substances persist *qua* instantiations of their kinds or sorts as long as they satisfy the sortal principle. For example, a man is a man as long as he properly falls under the criteria of manhood (though not necessarily the *same* man). Someone with a functioning human body but with a loss of consciousness and memory, counts as a man "in name alone", to borrow Locke's phrase. Within the Aristotelian approach I shall focus only on the implications of sortal essentialism.

In sum, the second charge against the bundle theory needs some caution since there does not exist an adequate final solution to the problem of the identity of concrete substances through time. Though there are various attempts to meet the problem but each attempt pays a price for the solution offered. What is specific, however, to the property-bundle view is its excessive fragility. This can be mitigated, as far as I see, only by a *modal* two-tier version of the bundle view. More space will be devoted to this later.

The *third* charge against the bundle view is *semantic*, saying that it makes all predication tautology. To remind, according to the bundle view the whole set of properties goes proxy for the substance as the subject of predication. In this case, say, a colored plastic cubic toy as the set of all these salient and other non-salient chemical, etc. properties *is* the subject. Thus, in predication, one of the properties from this constituting set is picked out and predicated of the set which already contains the predicated property as well. The toy as the set of the properties of being cubic, red, light, plastic, etc. *is* red, *is* cubic, etc. Thus all subject-predicate discourse turns out to be *tautologous*.

Now this is an undesirable consequence, and not for the only reason of depriving predication of its informative character. Tautology statements are necessary and so leave no room for *contingent* predication. That is, they leave no room for a subject's having some of its properties contingently. It is intuitively clear though, that the plastic toy, while it is probably essentially plastic, is only contingently red for it might have other color as well without ceasing to be what it is, a plastic cubic toy. The ability to provide for contingent predication is an urgent requirement for any metaphysical construal of the concrete individual substances since these are contingent beings that cannot have all their properties essentially. A toy, or a dog, etc., only contingently exists: the very same world might contain other inhabitants. Or, to put it differently, in some worlds the given toy, the dog, etc., do not exist. Since contingent beings cannot have all their properties essentially or necessarily, contingent predication must be secured somehow. Otherwise the universalist bundle theory would be committed to an ontology comprising only necessary entities.

The metaphysical requirements for contingent existence and contingent predication go in tandem with the semantic requirement for significant, informative predication. Contingent predication and informative predication merge in the stipulation that the bundle individuating the subject is not to be taken as exhaustive. That is, the bundle should not comprise all the properties of the subject but only those that suffice for individuation[33].

Apart from avoiding ultraessentialism this stipulation also helps to avoid tautologous prediction. For now, when 'being plastic' is predicated of the toy, this property is left out from the identifying bundle. But the individuating bundle is not any *arbitrary* subset of the whole set of properties sufficing for successful unique reference to the given thing. A decision has to be made on the metaphysical level about the sortal and the individual essences of the things that the individuating bundle is supposed to comprise. The full significance of this requirement will become clear in the last chapter. I just indicate here a discomforting scenario: the toy is said to be the bundle of all its properties *except* for the one predicated of it in a given predication. This applies for each case of predication; the predicated property is always deleted from the bundle. This cheap manouvre spares tautologous predication though, but the price is high. No two predications about the toy are literally about the

---

[33] Obviously, the suggestion is not new. For example, Arnauld makes clear in his correspondence with Leibniz that he is prepared to countenance only the essential properties in the individual concept of persons and that these properties do not exhaust the complete qualitative characterizations of persons. Here Leibniz's theory is disputed according to which the individual concept is the *complete concept* approving thereby superessentialism. See: Arnauld to Leibniz, May 13, 1686. Quoted by: Rosenkranz, G. S. (1993), p. 42.

same individual. One is about the bundle of toy-features except for being plastic; another is about the bundle of toy-features except for being red, etc. This flies in the face of our intuition that the very same subject can enter into different predications. To secure individuation it becomes compelling to rely on essentialist considerations, both sortal and individual.

The semantic charge can, perhaps, be evaded by saying that the bundle view need not be committed to the Fregean semantic interpretation of proper names according to which these are disguised descriptions specifiable in terms of the associated properties. For example, the bundle theorist could be more "Millian", insisting on the accessibility of the referent without the invocation of the associated properties. This would amount to the loosening of the tie between the metaphysical and the semantic doctrines. However, there does not seem to be any other way of discarding the Fregean theory of proper names as disguised descriptions, than espousing, at the metaphysical level, some sort of a non-qualitative substratum view. In this case coherence would be achieved between metaphysics *and* semantics, since in both areas the qualitative aspect would be suppressed in favor of a primitive, underived unity. The moral is that we are not free in combining any metaphysical position with any semantic theory. As I see it, it is Simons' two-tier trope theory that can evade the semantic obstacle by positing a nucleus to the substance. This nucleus, although it consists of a bunch of essential properties, is able to function as a subject of predication in virtue of its integral unity.

The most familiar and, perhaps, the most devastating charge against the universalist bundle view is that it implies commitment to the "*strong*" version of the principle of the Identity of Indiscernibles (**PII**). Let us come to this *fourth* charge. The idea is this: the bundle view can specify the identity of substances only in terms of the constituting properties; hence two substances are the same iff they share all their constituting properties. This is precisely what **PII** says: it is impossible for numerically distinct concrete particulars to share all their properties. I have formulated now **PII** without qualification: i.e., whether it is "strong" or "weak". The basic idea is that property-identity implies numerical identity.

This idea is, however, repugnant to those who find the familiar counterexamples convincing. Say, a universe consisting of two spheres exactly alike in all qualitative and relational respects would not collapse into one sphere just because of the indiscernibility of these two objects. In our times Max Black started the debate about the identity of indiscernibles with his provocative essay.[34] Black points out that the numerically distinct two spheres make a case for being identical twins that are not discernible even with respect of their spatial arrangements, for, "there isn't any *being to the right* or *being to the left* in the two-sphere universe until an observer is introduced, that is to say until a real change is made."[35] In the absence of such spatial relation smuggled in by an observer, **PII** proves to be intuitively false. The version of the principle that seems to be so clearly false is, therefore, the one that focuses only on intrinsic properties. Provided that spatial relations are also incorporated, the identical twins can be shown to be discernible. Similarly, items of mass production can be shown to be qualitatively identical still distinct as to their spatial and temporal relational properties. So their numerical distinctness can be explained by these relational differences. If these spatio-temporal properties are also incorporated into the principle of **PII**, then it seems to be basically acceptable: it comes down to the familiar claim that no two numerical distinct concrete particulars can occupy the same spatio-temporal region, whether they share other properties or not.

Now let us call properties of spatio-temporal location *impure* in the following sense: the designations of these properties esentially contain reference to particulars. For example, "North of London", "1200 before Christ", etc. That is, they count as impure from the perspective of the

---

[34] See Black, M. (1952)

[35] Black (1952) 112. Reference is made to Loux, M. J. ed. (2001.)

ontological division of particulars and properties. In fact, they cross over this division by bringing in individual constants into the content of compound properties. Pure properties, by contrast, are those that are formulated without reference to particulars. For example, while "being a king" is a pure property, "being an Anjou king" is an impure one. Or, "being greater than Venus" is, again, impure; so it is not only the properties of spatio-temporal location that qualify as impure ones, though they are the salient cases. The distinction between pure and impure properties is formulated technically by Loux as follows: " a property P is impure just in case there is some relation, R, and some contingent concrete particular, s, such that necessarily, for any object, x, x has P if and only if x enters into R with s and that a property, P, is pure just in case it is not impure".[36] So, for example, "being an Anjou king" is an impure property, because for some individual x, in order to have it, x must stand in the relation of descendance to an Anjou as a contingent concrete particular. "Being a king", on the other hand, qualifies as a pure property because for someone to have this property it is not required to stand in relation to a contingent concrete particular.

Weak **PII** comprises both pure and impure properties, saying this: it is impossible for numerically distinct concrete particulars to share all their pure *and* impure properties.

The question arises: if weak **PII** is defensible, why cannot the bundle theorist help himself by relying on weak **PII** at the specification of the identity conditions of the concrete individual substances? In other words, if the bundle constituting an individual comprises both the pure and the impure properties, including, in the latter, properties of unique spatio-temporal location, then, clearly, no two numerically distinct individuals will be constituted by the same bundle. In this case no counterexamples can be devised to the principle; the bundle theory and weak PII will prove co-tenable.

---

[36] Loux, M. J. (1998) 128. footnote 19.

Unfortunately, this solution is not available, except on pain of circularity. For the bundle theorist starts out to account for particulars which he cannot do in terms of other particulars. If the reductive construal of an individual in terms of its properties already contains impure properties with built-in references to other particulars, then the bundle theory will not count as a genuinely reductive account of individuals. For individuals would already be presupposed on top of their properties.[37] So the only possibility for the bundle theorist is to espouse the *strong* version of **PII** and thus reduce individuals to sets of pure properties.

Strong **PII** says: it is impossible for numerically distinct concrete particulars to share all their pure properties.

Thus the main objection leveled against the universalist bundle-view is that it implies the *strong* **PII** whose falsity has already been demonstrated. It is not only the example of the two sphere universe that clearly shows this; numerous other counterexamples with identical twins can be devised. This line of criticism is stressed, among others, by Van Cleve.[38] He points out that the bundle theorist cannot admit impure properties in the bundle and so is forced to embrace the stronger principle: "the bundle theory cannot admit impure properties, and is committed to the consequence that no two individuals can have all the same *pure* properties."[39]

To avoid this consequence defensive strategies have been developed. They proceed by weakening the modal force of the bundle theory and its consequences with the help of some independent considerations. Casullo, for example, suggests that the bundle theory need not be developed in a necessitarian version; it can be formulated in terms of

---

[37] This criticism of the bundle theory can be found in Armstrong (1978) vol. I.

[38] Van Cleve (1985) p. 96.

[39] Van Cleve (1985), 122. Reference is made to Loux, M. J. ed. (2001).

contingency.[40] Accordingly, a concrete individual is only contingently identical to a set of co-occurring properties and not necessarily. This claim is central to what Casullo calls the "weak bundle theory" (**WBT**)

Quote: " (**WBT**) A (momentary physical) thing is *contingently* identical to a complex of mutually co-instantiated properties".

Its advantage, according to Casullo, is that "it is not committed to the *necessary* truth of **PII**." That is, (**WBT**) is not committed to the doctrine that it is *impossible* for numerically distinct individuals to have all their pure properties in common. Apparently, it is committed only to the weaker claim that numerically distinct individuals do not, *in fact*, have all pure properties in common".[41]

Clearly, (**WBT**) is technically "weak" in the sense of being formulated in terms of contingency and not in terms of necessity. But it is not "weak" in the sense of admitting *impure* properties to the identification of the individual substances. For, as we have just clarified a bit before, *all* reductive bundle accounts of substances in qualitative terms rule out recourse to impure properties that smuggle in individuals, and thus turn the account circular. In other words, the bundle theories, whether they are developed in the necessitarian version or in the factual, contingent version, are all committed to *strong* (**PII**) and this commitment is seen as the major defect of (**BT**). Thus Casullo's *weak* (**BT**) is also committed to *strong* (**PII**).

The position of (**WBT**) is not a safe harbor for the bundle theory since there are numerous counterexamples to *strong* (**PII**). Casullo is also aware of this "grave difficulty". In the face of this difficulty a second step is suggested. It consists in restricting the range of those things that do not, in fact, have all their pure properties in common with any other thing. The restriction involves those elements of the spatio-

---

[40] See Casullo, A. (1988)

[41] Casullo, *op.cit.*, 140-41.

temporal framework that serve as "landmarks" for the specification of the spatio-temporal position of the concrete individuals. Then Casullo claims that **(WBT)** is committed only to the *existence* of these entities satisfying the requirement of strong **(PII)**. As examples, think of the calendar system or the system of longitude and latitude. These landmarks have two distinctive features: "(1) all *other* things have their spatio-temporal location by virtue of standing in certain relations to the landmarks; (2) the landmarks do *not* have their spatio-temporal location by virtue of standing in certain relations to any *other* things".[42] So the landmarks are those things whose identification does not involve reference to other individuals; thus one need not make recourse to impure properties with landmarks, unlike with other things. Landmarks are characterized only by unshared pure properties. Moreover, they are numerically distinct in virtue of their pure properties, so they constitute the impeccable cases of **PII** with pure properties.

Casullo's strategy, however, is not impeccable. Although **(WBT)** is correctly formulated and the factual claim about such landmarks may be true as well. What is not convincingly true, however, is that **(WBT)** "is committed" to the factual claim about landmarks. Undeniably, it is consistent with it, but **(WBT)** is just the formulation of the general bundle-theoretical conditions of substance-identity in terms of contingency where no mention is made of *individual constants*, such as these landmarks. Therefore, it is questionable to claim that such general formulation "is committed" to an *existentially quantified* statement about landmarks, or whatever else. So, Casullo's suggestion is not much advancement over the necessitarian version of the bundle theory.

Apart from the Casullo-type suggestion to evade the chief charge against the universalist bundle theory, the more traditional line of defense put forward first by Russell focuses on **(PII)**.[43] It does not

---

[42] See Casullo, A. (1988), p. 142.

[43] Russell, B. (1948), 298-9.

recommend (**PII**) as a contingent truth; rather, it claims that the modally stronger (**PII**) is to be maintained. Accordingly, concrete objects are *necessarily* constituted by their properties, among them by properties determining the location of these objects in the visual field *qua* objects of perception. The claim is that these properties are *monadic* positional properties rather than relational spatial properties and, since different visual objects always differ with respect to these monadic properties of visual location, there do not exist counterexamples to strong (**PII**).

Various objections can be raised to Russell's solution. For example, it can be pointed out that these visual properties are of no help in finding uniquely individuating properties for numerically distinct concrete physical objects since the structure of physical space is different from the structure of perceptual space.[44] This retort may not be, however, quite convincing for a phenomenalist who always takes physical objects as the possibilities of perception. The weakness of Russell's suggestion lies, in my opinion, in that these visual monadic properties are also *impure* ones since they can be specified only by reference to the observer as an individual. But (**PII**) cannot make recourse to impure properties in yielding a reductive account of the concrete individuals since impure properties already have individuals as their built-in elements. Therefore Russell's suggestion does not successfully cope with the standard charge against (**BT**): i.e. its implying the strong version of (**PII**).

Let me note here that the various defenses of the universalist bundle theory use "*strong*" and "*weak*" (**PII**) ambiguously. In one of its use, the pair of qualification is *modal* and it refers to whether the object is necessarily or contingently identical with the bundle of its properties. As we have seen, Casullo applied this criterion; whereas the charge against the universalist bundle theory is formulated with the other criterion. The other criterion is non-modal *logical* and it refers, to repeat, to that whether the constituting properties are pure or impure. Both uses of

---

[44] See Casullo, p. 139.

strong/weak (**PII**) are legitimate but they should not be conflated since they carry different implications, as we have just seen.

I have started to assess the *pros* and *cons* of the universalist bundle view *and* the bare substratum view of concrete individual substances and have found the following. Given the absurd consequences of the bare substratum view, the approach with qualitative aspects seemed to be more promising, although it is still objectionable on various grounds. As we have just seen, commitment to strong (**PII**) (with pure properties) cannot be avoided and also, the semantic problem of trivializing the subject-predicate discourse by making all predication tautologous has also remained unsolved. These charges hold, even though the metaphysical doctrines can be loosened, to a certain extent, from the respective semantic doctrines.

The bundle view may be unsatisfactory in its *universalist* form; but, presumably, its *particularized* version is more promising. This is what I am going to argue for. The particularized form of the bundle theory takes *tropes* as the constituting elements of the bundle. Before elaborating on the current trope views, two main advantages of the bundle-of-tropes view can be anticipated. These are connected to the fact that some of the objections against the universalist bundle view do not arise on the bundle-of-tropes view. For example, the universalist bundle view has to face the threat of arbitrarily postulating particulars on the basis of any set of properties. Although it is intuitively clear that not *any* set of properties make a particular, the universalist approach cannot offer here any constraint. This threat does not arise on the trope-approach. Tropes are property-particulars pertaining already to concrete individuals. Mona Lisa's smile is not just a smile that could be had by anyone else; it is a smile that is intimately connected to Mona Lisa. In other words, this trope is individuated partly by Mona Lisa and this fact excludes the possibility of the ad hoc assignments of individuals to any collections of qualitative features.

The best support, however, for the trope-bundle view is that it avoids commitment to the strong version of (**PII**) (with pure properties). Since tropes are not sharable entities, we are not in the predicament of strong **(PII)**: Mona Lisa's smile is different from, although resembling Lollobrigida's smile and the same applies to all the different, although resembling, tropes making up Mona Lisa and Lollobrigida respectively. On the trope account, substances can have only exactly resembling tropes and having exactly resembling tropes does not imply the numerical identity of distinct substances.

The trap of strong **(PII)** can be avoided if tropes are taken as dependent entities that are intimately connected to their bearers. Appeal can be made here to the *principle of bearer-uniqueness*. This principle states that for all tropes a, b and all things x, y if a is a quality of x and b is a quality of y and x and y are nonidenticals, then a and b are nonidenticals as well.

The principle of bearer uniqueness guarantees that tropes are non-sharable, but it does not explain what makes a trope pertaining to one individual "exactly similar" to another trope pertaining to another individual. In other words, if the trope-theory denies that there are common natures and, moreover, bearer uniqueness secures the disjoint character of the sets or bundles making up the individuals, then there is no ground for the claim of exact similarity. But this is not a compelling reason to give up bearer uniqueness; rather, some other explanation must be sought for the existence of common natures outside the trope theory. My motivation for doing so will become clear in the next chapter. Some authors deny bearer-uniqueness and think of tropes as transferable entities. This is one of the complications of the trope-theory that will also be discussed in the next chapter.

II. The Role of Tropes in Ontology:
Accidents, Events, Particularism

As to its etymological origin, "trope" means a "figure of speech" or "turn of phrase". This has little to do with its current technical meaning in metaphysics, for a trope in the technical sense is a property-particular. The history of its current philosophical use can be traced back to George Santayana: he is reported to have given a metaphysical meaning to "trope". Later, in the 50's, D.C. Williams defined a trope as "a particular entity either abstract or consisting of one or more concrete entities in combination with an abstraction. Thus Napoleon and Napoleon's forelock are not tropes, but Napoleon's posture is a trope and so is the whole whose constituents are his forelock and his posture, and so is his residing on Elba".[45] Williams's definition leaves no doubt that a trope is not a concrete particular even though concrete entities can enter into tropes as composite parts. The explanation of why Napoleon's forelock does not qualify as a trope, though it is a particular and is part of Napoleon, while his posture does qualify as a trope, is this: tropes are always the abstract parts or components of the individuals, and never their concrete parts. So Napoleon's forelock, being his concrete part, cannot qualify as a trope.

The various criteria of abstractness and concreteness will be discussed soon. Here it suffices to say that concrete things typically are the bearers of qualitative manifolds; while these things specified from

---

[45] Williams, D.C. (1953), 6.

the perspective of one perceptual mode or one qualitative feature, abstracted from the rest of their qualitative features, yield abstract individuals. So, for example, a sugar cube is a concrete individual, while a tangible cube, a visual cube, etc. is an abstract individual. This interpretation of the abstract/concrete division is explanatory of Williams's definition of trope. Obviously, it does not rule out other criteria that permit abstract individuals, say, mathematical objects, to bear more properties.

The significance of Williams's early point about the abstract character of tropes, in the present context, is the following. Peter Simons has recently characterized tropes as *concrete entities* and now we have to consider this option. In this respect I part company with Simons and will urge that we return to the original conception. What is at stake here is to find a coherent ontological reading of substances together with their constituting tropes.

Now someone's posture or residing on Elba look pretty much like *accidents*; thus Williams's definition seems to be flirting with the idea of just renaming accidents under the coined term "trope". This suspicion can be supported by observing that Williams's definition of tropes splits in exactly the same way as the traditional approaches to accidents do. I shall elaborate on this soon. Accidents, traditionally conceived, are entities depending permanently on the ontological fundament, where the latter is most often an Aristotelian substance capable of independent existence. For example, "smiles", "thoughts", etc. are accidents *of* the smiling, thinking etc. individual substances. These accidents are ambiguous in that they are both property-instances *and* actions or events. For example, the "smile" and the "thought" accidents are both the instances of having a smile, entertaining a thought, *and* also they are the actions of smiling and thinking. As Simons observes, "many of the events involving particular continuants are accidents of them".[46]

---

[46] Simons, P. (1987, 200), 306.

The double feature of the accidents, i.e. that they are both property-particulars *and* events, is inherited by the *ontological scope of tropes* as they are currently conceived: tropes are not only the abstract constituents of the concrete substances but also events are claimed to be tropes. I shall comment on the metaphysical consequences of this double ontological role of tropes; clearly, their prevalence today extends far beyond Williams's initial conception that fits so well to accidents.

Now accidents involve both an *abstract* component which is the property instance and the *concrete* individual substance as the bearer or fundament of the instance. In Aristotelian terms, accidents have an abstract or formal component and a concrete or material component. Interestingly enough, it is Aristotle who deviates from Aristotelian doctrines in his conception of accidents, while Brentano picks up orthodox Aristotelianism in his approach. The point is that for Brentano an accident is the combination of a form with some underlying material: for example, a fist is the clenchedness of the hand and Brentano takes it that both the clenchedness *and* the hand as an improper material part of the fist make the accident. That is, Brentanist accidents have their substances as their parts. By contrast, for Aristotle the accident is the individual clenchedness "inhering" in the hand.[47] That is, the Aristotelian accident is purely the abstract component of the substance.

Now we can see that these two ways of conceiving accidents are mirrored in Williams's definition of tropes. Williams is, in fact, permissive about these two ways, for he incorporates both into his definition. To recall: a trope "is a particular entity either abstract or consisting of one or more concrete entities in combination with an abstraction". So, the clenchedness of the hand is a trope, but equally, the clenchedness *plus* the hand is a trope as well, perhaps a different one.

---

[47] See Simons on the difference between the Aristotelian and the Brentanist conception of accident. Simons (1987, 2000), ch. 8.:"Some Related Concepts: Substance, Accident, Disturbance".

It is not by chance that accidents serve as guides to tropes. Historically, the trope-theoretic view of events goes back to Locke's "modes" and Leibniz's "individual accidents".[48] The individual or particular aspect of the tropes is emphasized also today, but tropes need not be accidental. That is, tropes are not confined to the role of being the contingent abstract components of the substances. The trope-bundle view requires, for example, essential tropes that constitute the individual nature of the substances. By contrast, accidents like "smiles" or "thoughts" are always contingent entities. Moreover, accidents are ambiguous between being occurents and being short-lived continuants: they are partly thing-like and partly event-like. Thus one can take "smiles" or "thoughts" either as acts or as short-lived entities.

Here I focus on the virtues of taking tropes as constituents of individual substances. But the tropehood of events and accidents is also appreciated from the perspective of ontological parsimony and coherence and also, from the perspective of accounting for "identity through time". In fact, the latter phrase is a euphemism for identity amidst minor diachronic changes.

Tropes also score well as *truthmakers* for non-existential propositions about particulars. For example, if one wants to account for the truth of this piece of paper being white one has to make recourse only to the presence of the whiteness-trope that constitutes, together with other tropes, the piece of paper at a given time. The theory of truthmakers needs no states of affairs as additional entities to particulars and qualitative features; it suffices to make appeal only to tropes.[49] At least, this is what the proponents of the truthmaker theory claim, for example, Simons. In his version tropes correlate semantically with *predicates*: the

---

[48] Locke, J. (1975), Leibniz, G.W. (1981)

[49] See Simons, P. (2000) See also for the theory of truthmakers: Mulligan, K., Simons, P., Smith, B. (1984)

whiteness-trope is what the predicate "white" stands for; the smile-trope is what the predicate "smile" stands for, etc.

The suggested truthmaker theory for tropes is semantically *sparse*. While each trope is said to be semantically discernible, so, that it can be expressed with the help of a predicate, it does not generally hold that each predicate stands for a separate trope, or, that it stands for a trope at all. If this is the case, then, clearly, propositions with predicates lacking the ontological backing in the form of tropes would be without their own separate truthmakers. Only the "world" as such would be indirectly relevant to their truth. In other words, a weak or sparse truthmaker theory fits the ontological theory of tropes.

The semantic behavior of tropes still seems unsettled in the analysis: it is not tenable that while there might be predicates without the appropriate trope content, the tropes are semantically fully expressible. For the point is that the linguistic resources might not be sufficiently fine-tuned to express the semantic nuances between the resembling individual tropes. Perhaps, this is the reason behind Simons' concession that "tropes are ... elusive to linguistic analysis".[50] The semantic connection between tropes and predicates is also discussed by McDaniel.[51]

Another semantic approach to tropes is motivated by appeal to ontological abundance. Those who acknowledge the existence of both substances and attributes, not staying with a one-category ontology of tropes, are naturally inclined to see tropes as being composite in nature rather than primitive and unstructured. In this vein some authors claim that the tropes exhibit composite structures akin to propositions. For example, the trope of "Socrates-being-snub-nosed" involves an individual, a property, and the tie of exemplification between them.

---

[50] Simons (2000), 153.

[51] See Kris McDaniel (2001)

Recently, they have been called *propositional* tropes. This account of the tropes largely features the subject-predicate discourse of language. I find the notion of propositional tropes appealing since with it tropes can be *individuated* by reference to the bearer substances: individuation requiring the ordered triple consisting of the bearer, the trope and the bearing relation. All of these together look pretty much like a composite with a propositional structure.

The question still arises whether the ontological parsimony of the trope theory dispensing with states of affairs is not lost by the recognition of propositional tropes. For the point is that the propositional tropes can exist only if the corresponding states of affairs exist, too. It does not suffice for the existence of a propositional trope like, for example, "Socrates-being-snub-nosed" that there exist Socrates, snub-nosedness and the tie of exemplification.[52] The state of affairs that "Socrates is snub-nosed" must also obtain over and above the constituents in order for there be a truthmaker for the respective propositional trope.[53] An ontological implication of this worry will be spelled out in the end of this chapter.

The alternative to ascribing a composite structure to tropes is to accord them a primitive nature. Primitive tropes can be incorporated into a *moderate nominalistic* ontology or, in an equally *moderate realistic* ontology. For example, Stout, Williams and Simons place the tropes within the frame of a nominalistic bundle construal of both universals and individuals.[54] Thus individuals are construed as bundles

---

[52] It should be noted here that the "*is*" of exemplification can be understood either *atemporally*, meaning that "being Socrates" involves "being snub-nosed" or, it can be understood with a *time-index* meaning that the connective applies for the temporally determinate life-span of Socrates. The latter notion implies that the propositional tropes are contingent entities, while propositions are obviously not.

[53] About states of affairs being non-mereological composites see: Armstrong, D.M. (1978) vol. II.

[54] See Stout, G.F. (1971a), Williams, D.C. (1953), Simons, P. (1994), (2000).

of co-occurring tropes; and universals are construed as bundles of exactly resembling tropes. This approach is nominalistic because it recognizes only particulars; it is moderate because it provides for the qualitative features in a way that does not involve a full reduction of properties to individuals unlike the typical varieties of nominalism, i.e., class nominalism and resemblance nominalism. In the non-reductive treatment of properties, tropism departs from standard nominalism. Later in this chapter I shall say more on why I refrain from labelling the trope theory as a kind of nominalism. As I make clear there, it is more appropriate to take the trope theory as a systematic attempt for a *particularist* ontology rather than trying to squeeze it into the gap between traditional nominalism and traditional realism.

For this very reason I would not endorse trope theory as a kind of moderate realism either. Some authors take this option though, because they find that certain versions of the trope theory accept immanent universals, i.e. universals that exist only through their instances. For example, Mertz represents this approach.[55] In fact, tropes can be combined with the admission of either primitive universals or immanent universals; there remains still the difference between tropes as genuine abstract particulars *and* abstract universals either exemplified or non-exemplified. However, the basic tenets of trope theory need not be discarded, whether one feels the need for universals as ineliminable items in the ontology or not. In fact, I think that universals cannot be dispensed with because certain relations cannot be explained away in favor of tropes. This insight puts me closer to Bacon and separates me from Campbell.

Apart from being truthmakers in ontology, the epistemological role of tropes seems to be the best argument for positing them: we encounter first specific qualitative features when we get acquainted with things in experience. And we appeal to these features at the level of explanation, too. Therefore the trope-cluster theory of individuals is seen here as the

---

[55] Mertz, D. W. (1996)

best application of tropes. This theory, however, is not fully reductionist: it does not claim that individual substances are "nothing more" than collections of tropes. As will become clear later, there is a qualitative, still substratum-like tight bundle to the substance in virtue of which it does make sense to speak of independent substances *and* their dependent tropes, despite of the overall correctness of the official theory that substances are analyzed best as bundles of tropes. Also, I shall explain in the next chapter how the individuation of tropes can be conceived via the individuation of their bearer substances in a non-circular way.

The abstractness of tropes has been recently challenged. Let us see now how the abstractness of tropes can be restated and also, how this secures the metaphysical distinction between substances and events anticipated in the *Introduction*.

Tropes: abstract or concrete?

Tropes are concrete in the sense of being spatio-temporal occupants existing when and where the bearer-substance does. But they are abstract according to two criteria: first, they are dependent entities depending on the bearer substances and thus they are not concrete in the sense of being capable of independent existence associated traditionally with Aristotelian substances and the Cartesian definition of substances. Second, they are abstract in another sense as well, because what they are instances *of*, are properties featuring the substance only from one aspect. Thus they are not concrete in the sense of comprising all features of the substance.

Now ordinary particulars are both capable of independent existence and comprise all their features; so they are concrete particulars by these two criteria while tropes qualify as abstract particulars. But tropes are concrete if their spatio-temporal occupancy plays a decisive role in their categorisation; Peter Simons prefers to stay with the criterion of spatio-temporality and hence regards tropes as "dependent concrete particulars". His resolution of the question, however, is not quite felicitous since he also considers the different criteria according to which tropes would qualify as abstract particulars. And there is no fact of the matter to show why one criterion supporting the contrary view outweighs the others in the general assessment. Further, it does not seem to be quite legitimate to blend one criterion leading to one resolution with another criterion leading to another resolution: the dependency-criterion suggests that whatever is dependent *cannot be* concrete; the spatio-temporality criterion suggests that whatever is spatio-temporal *must be* concrete. In face of these facts, what sense can we make of the notion of a "dependent concrete particular" as suggested by Simons?

There is a further aspect of concreteness in the light of which the concreteness of tropes is hardly tenable. The point is that independent particulars typically exhibit a *manifold* of properties/ relations and their independence is closely connected to their ability to sustain such a manifold. Here I use "manifold" mostly in the Kantian sense that provides for qualitative diversity requiring synthesis in terms of the notion of an object. Dependent particulars, however, cannot sustain a manifold; rather, they pertain to other particulars which have this magic ontological ability. So it seems, at least with ordinary objects as particulars, that the independence criterion of concreteness and the other criterion of sustaining the manifold of properties support each other in the way just indicated. Therefore tropes, being dependent particulars, can only be abstract.

The trope view of events also lends support to the idea that tropes are abstract particulars. Here the argument can proceed by reductio: if tropes were concrete, while events were identified outright *as* tropes, this would have the consequence that there would only be *concrete events*. It cannot be assumed, however, that all events are concrete; for example, repeatable event types are clearly abstract.

Now a concrete event is something that comprises all features of the substances they involve, including the spatio-temporal qualifications of the latter. Admitting only concrete events would help to obliterate the vital metaphysical distinction between events or *occurrents and* concrete *continuants* (thing-like particulars). For on this view, equipped with concrete tropes as the building blocks, a concrete event would be indistinguishable from the substance(s) they involve: both would be four-dimensional entities. In short, they would be indistinguishable in a four-dimensionalist framework. Four-dimensionalism is supported, for example, by Quine; according to him events are only concrete. In his critical remarks about Quine, Bennett states that Quine "is interested in the events that he thinks can plausibly be identified with physical things, when these are viewed as four-dimensional, and he assumes that all such events are concrete".[56]

I want to retain, however, the distinction between substance-continuants *and* events for a metaphysical reason: this being commitment to substances as entities existing on their own right and doing their job for the significance condition and the permanence condition of the metaphysics of experience. Conceding the abstractness of tropes removes already an obstacle to this position. There is no principled objection to ontologically construing events, both types and tokens, with abstract tropes as components. The same applies to concrete continuants. The main point is that the concreteness of an entity, whether a substance or an event, is due *not* to the concreteness of its ontological building blocks in a simplified scheme; but it is a feature of the complexity resulting from the combination of the constituting tropes. Once this point is appreciated, concrete continuants can be seen to exhibit a complexity different from the complexity of the concrete events making up their temporal career. This approach allows us to see a given complexity of abstract components under the label 'substance',

---

[56] See Bennett (1988), 115-16.

while it allows us to see a different complexity of abstract items under the label 'event'.[57]

Given that tropes play a role with substances *and* also, that events are tropes, a series of questions suggests itself. For example, is there a good fit between the trope-bundle view of substances *and* the trope view of events? Or, is the bundle-*cum*-substratum view more appealing whenever we want to stress *unity*, in the notion of an object, of those features of which some, but not all, are affected by changes? A further question is whether tropes show the same features with respect to substances and events. For example, the Armstrongian view that tropes are *ways* seems to be less controversial when applied to events that have a natural propensity to take adverbs than when applied to substances inviting, basically, a nominal account.[58]

Although the trope account of events may seem to be intuitively correct, given the wide range of disputes in the literature about the status of events, next I briefly survey the main arguments in favour of events being particulars and the main arguments in favour of their being universals. My aim is to arrive at the trope account as a tenable alternative.[59] Within this part I also examine Davidson's construal of events as objects of verbs.

---

[57] The role of tropes with events and substances is discussed in Ujvári, M. (2000a)

[58] Armstrong (1978), 115.

[59] The tropehood of events is defended in Ujvári, M. (2000b)

Events as particulars, events as universals

Events seem to cut across the exclusive ontological characterisation of being either particulars or universals: in some respect they behave like particulars; in others, they behave like universals.

Particulars as individuals are represented logically by singular terms: names or definite descriptions. Some but not all events have separate names or identifying definite descriptions. However, what is not supplied by ordinary language can be supplied by a logical device. Davidson quantifies over event-objects that are not named in sentences. His main reason is that this is how one can account for adverb-dropping inferences. For example, if one wants to secure the inference from the sentence "Sebastian strolled through the streets of Bologna at 2 a.m." to the sentence "Sebastian strolled through the streets of Bologna", one has to construe the predicate with the same *arity* in both cases. The obvious reason is that if the first occurrence of "strolled" were construed as an irreducibly three-place predicate while its second occurrence were construed as dyadic, the inference would not go through. Therefore Davidson suggests that we "provide each verb of action or change with an event-place; we may say of such verbs that they take an *event-object*."[60] So, the proper form of the sentence that admits adverb dropping inference is this: "There is an event x such that Sebastian strolled x, x took place in the streets of Bologna, and x was going on at 2 a.m."[61] Now from this sequence of conjunctions any one of its conjuncts logically follows.

---

[60] Davidson, D. (1980), 167.

[61] See Davidson (1980) ibid. Following Davidson, Myles Brand also supports the particularist theories of events which have the advantage of ontological simplicity, as he says. Also, these theories assimilate, by naming and counting, the talk about events to talk about physical objects. See Brand (1975).

There remains a further problem not envisaged by Davidson: namely, that the verb may take, apart from the suggested event-object, a direct object as well, say, a concrete particular. For example, instead of strolling, Sebastian might drive a car through the streets of Bologna at 2 a.m. The verb 'drive' takes an event-object since on Davidson's construal verbs of action and change take event-objects even if there is no other kind of object to be taken by them. And, in virtue of being a transitive verb, 'drive' invites also a concrete particular *as* object which is not part of the event-object. So, we would have to say according to Davidson: "there is an event x such that Sebastian drove x, *and* Sebastian drove a car, and x took place in the streets of Bologna, and x was going on at 2 a.m." Now quite evidently, in "Sebastian drove x", x cannot stand for the ordinary substance-object, viz. the car, because it stands for the event of driving. So there are two things that Sebastian drove at the same time: he drove the concrete particular, the car, and he also drove the abstract particular, the event of driving.

What is wrong with Davidson's construal is not that the agent, while doing something, thereby does something else; *"by"*- *locutions* are perfectly acceptable. By driving the car Sebastian performs the act of driving. The action or event *consists in* driving and the car is its *object*. However, this would not serve Davidson's goal: he wants to assimilate events to ordinary substance-particulars. Therefore he supplies the verb with an event place; thus events, like substances, are taken by verbs *as* objects. With this construal one can quantify over event variables on *a par* with ordinary individual variables.

The disanalogy is still there. Events are not objects in the sense in which concrete particulars are: one can draw on the familiar distinction that while events have temporal parts substances have only spatial parts. In addition to this I further suggest that events and actions, *qua* objects of verbs, are different from ordinary substances *qua* objects of verbs. Events, actions are the *internal* objects of something's acting, taking place, etc. in a certain way. They are internal just in the sense in which waltzes are internal objects of the act of dancing; or, strolls are the internal objects of the act of strolling: they exist in so far as these actions do.

By contrast, ordinary substances are the objects of verbs in a different sense. They are not the kinds of things that become reified through the process of something's acting or taking place in a certain way. Therefore *what* they are *can not be read off directly from the meaning of the verb that takes them as objects.* If two object places are supplied in a sentence, one for Davidson's event and the other for the object of the transitive verb, they behave differently. For example, applying Davidson's construal we would have to say that "there is an event x such that Sebastian drove x, x took place in the streets of Bologna, x was going on at 2 a.m., etc. *and* there is a y such that Sebastian drove y". While we can immediately read off here the internal event-object x, i.e., that there happened a driving, and so can fill in one place, we do not have the faintest idea as to what particularly object y was, invited by "drove" in the second conjunct. Sebastian could drive, in an old-fashioned way, a coach instead of a car. Let alone the fact that what the quantified sentence stands for is highly counterintuitive: *Sebastian drove a drive* which took place in the streets of Bologna, etc. and *he drove a car* (or a coach, etc.).

In sum, what objects the transitive verbs actually take cannot simply be read off from the verb. Ordinary substance objects of transitive verbs are *external* to the action or change expressed by the verb; they have to be provided as extra items. But event-objects, being the internal and immediate objects of change, are yielded by, and are also computable from, the verb itself.

One might object that the argument rests on the conflation of the metaphysical notion of a *particular* with the grammatical notion of an *object* occupying the object-position in the grammatical structure. The feeling of discomfort evaporates once we realize that quantification is a test for the metaphysical status of being a particular. That is why Davidson supplies an event-place in a grammatical context where originally there has been none. So, the background metaphysical requirements are met by adjustments in the grammatical structure. Similarly, my attempt is also perfectly legitimate: i.e. to trace back, in the metaphysical background, what makes the newly created placeholder, the events, different from the more conventional placeholder, the typical substance-objects of transitive verbs.

My first conclusion is that the Davidsonian arguments purporting to show that events *are* particulars must cope with a certain disanalogy between event-particulars and object-particulars. The significance of the disanalogy is that it helps to secure the metaphysically important distinction between events and objects; and my account needs this distinction. Further, the disanalogy I have pointed out is different from the traditional claim that events have temporal parts while objects have only spatial parts.

The individuation of events is conceived differently by particularists and universalists. Particularists, like Davidson, maintain that events are fully-fledged individuals because there obtains the semantic fact about them that they can be referred to under different names and descriptions. By contrast, those who stress the role of event-*types* claim that events *qua* types are universals. For example, Chisholm points out that we re-identify events by the qualitative sameness they exhibit through their repeated occurrences. Therefore "any theory of events should be adequate to the fact of recurrence, to the fact that there are some things that recur, or happen more than once."[62] Particularists, on the other hand, cannot claim that the same event occurs more than once.[63]

The arguments for events being universals are based on *three* considerations. The *first* has to do with the repeatable character of events; the *second* is based on the fact that different properties can be instantiated in one and the same space-time portion; and the *third*

---

[62] Chisholm, R. (1970), 15.

[63] As Brand notices, a 'major problem for the Particularist theories is accounting for recurrence'. Brand (1975), 138.

explores the deficiency of the rival extensionalist view with respect to causal explanations. Let us look at them in turn.

Events are repeatables in Chisholm's view; this is another way of saying that they are in fact universals. For example, when I say "I dropped the spoon yesterday at dinner and today I did it again", the pronoun "*it*" refers to a qualitatively indistinguishable token of the same event-type. Typically, such routine actions and generic events admit repetitions; this, however, presupposes that the essence of the event-type is not particularly rich: if, for example, a special grotesque way of dropping the spoon were part of the content of the event that occurred yesterday, it might not have been repeated exactly today. So events as repeatables cannot have rich essences.

According to the repeatability argument the same event-*type* gets repeated in qualitatively indistinguishable *token*s. The temptation might arise here to take a simple solution to the abstract/concrete issue by saying that event-types are abstract while event-tokens are concrete. This would relieve the need to take events to be tropes; a conclusion that I am painfully striving towards. The simple solution, however, is not available because event-tokens are *not* concrete in the sense that the spatio-temporal position they occupy could uniquely identify them: as it will be shown by the second universalist argument, more than one event can have exactly the same spatio-temporal location. By contrast, concrete object-particulars can, in fact, be uniquely identified by reference to their spatio-temporal position. So, event-tokens are also abstract in a certain sense, therefore the abstract/concrete distinction cannot be reduced to the type/token distinction. Thus event-tokens remain ambiguous between being abstract and being concrete.

Repeatability is the basis of the property-exemplification account of events suggested by Kim.[64] This account implies that the constitutive property of events can be re-exemplified in numerically distinct

---

[64] See Kim, J. (1976)

instances. Now it is familiar that properties are named by predicates and sometimes we refer to the same property under different names. However, it would be difficult to decide, on a priori grounds, when different predicates name the same property. So the universalist position must be backed by an account of sameness of properties under different names.

Property identity is a difficult thing: 'killing' is different from 'stabbing' though on particular occasions the instance of stabbing can *be* the instance of killing. So 'Brutus killed Caesar' and 'Brutus stabbed Caesar' can be the same events. Still, the property exemplification view is committed, at least by opponents like Davidson and Bennett, to an unnecessary abundance of events: roughly, there are as many events as there are predicates *to name* their constitutive properties.[65] In the absence of an adequate criterion of property-identity one is obliged to entertain this counterintuitive position.

The second argument for events being universals stems from the fact that different properties may be instantiated in the same space-time portion. For example, if Sebastian sings a song while he thinks of his holiday then two different actions take place in the same subject at the same time. Or, if one boils water in a pot while dissolving some salt in it then two different events take place in the same substance, at the same time, moreover involving all the same molecules of the substance. Therefore events should not be taken as extensional entities characterised exclusively in terms of their spatio-temporal extension.

There may be a feeling of non-sequitur, though. Even if events are not wholly extensional entities, the property-exemplification view needs a further support. For the point is that events occupying the same space-time portion can be distinguished not only on the basis of the properties they exemplify, but also by reference to the objects they involve

---

[65] Kim's view is criticised by Davidson in his *Essay*, ch.8. (1980), by Bennett (1987) ch.5., Bennett (1988), pp.319-322.

essentially. For example, the event of salting, unlike the event of boiling, involves essential reference to the piece of salt used, though both events have the same spatio-temporal extension. Similarly, the song is essential to the action of singing while it is not essential to the thinking-of-the-holiday action. Conversely, holiday-thought is essential to the latter, but not to the former, etc. though both take place in the same subject at the same time.

This objection only shifts the problem of individuating events to the problem of individuating objects. Since now the question is this: *in virtue of what* are the objects involved capable of contributing to the individuation of events? Do they do their job as unanalysable particulars with a spatio-temporal extension? Obviously not, since in this case they would merely be proper parts of the whole spatio-temporal extension of the event, and the event cannot be individuated by reference to any proper part of its extension. So events should not be analysed solely in extensionalist terms. The other option would be to individuate these objects by recourse to their properties: so events with overlapping spatio-temporal extension could be individuated by the properties they exemplify *and* by the properties exemplified by the objects they involve essentially. In this vein we remain within the universalist position; and this is precisely what universalist arguments are meant to support.

Independent considerations can also undermine the extensionalist view of events. Arguably, events have spatio-temporal position as a feature of their *particularity*, but the indication of such position does not *individuate* a particular event. In other words, what serves as a particularizer, i.e. the spatio-temporal position, does not automatically serve thereby as an individuator as well. I shell get back to the difference between particularizers and individuators in later chapters.

Still, the extensionalist view of events is defended by some authors. For example, Quine's idea is that since events are entities occupying space-time zones their identity boils down to such occupancy. According to Quine events comprise the whole content of a space-time zone. "Each [event] comprises the content, however heterogeneous, of some portion of space-time, however disconnected and gerrymandered".[66] In Bennett's reading the "content" here "cannot mean whatever physical object is contained in the zone" because "Quine uses his ideas about events and zones as a basis for explaining what physical objects are".[67]

Bennett takes Quine to suggest, in the quoted passage and its vicinity, that "*there are only concrete events*". The reasons for such a position are intimately connected to Quine's idea of physical objects understood as four-dimensional. Whereas in my view events should be interpreted against the relatively stable background of three-dimensional objects preserving thereby the event-object distinction, or, in more recent terminology, the occurrent-continuant distinction. One of the main arguments against postulating four-dimensional objects comes from Geach: he points out that on the four-dimensional view the genuine notion of change is lost by being reduced to a variation of attributes between the different parts of the spatio-temporal whole.[68]

In particular, Geach explains how the four-dimensional view of objects conflicts with change. On this view, for example, we cannot properly say that the temperature of a poker has changed. We can only say that there are different temperatures at the different positions along the poker's time-axis. Similarly, the poker can have different temperatures at its different spatial parts: hot at one end and cold at the other. So the poker's being hot on one day and cold on the next is just like its being hot at one end and cold at the other. What we have instead of change is just a variation of attributes between the different parts of a four-dimensional whole. The upshot is that obliterating the distinction between occurrents and continuants in the four-dimensional view results in what is called the *spatialization* of change. For some critics of the four-dimensionalist view the spatialization of change is equivalent to the

---

[66] Quine (1960) 171.

[67] Bennett (1988) 104.

[68] See Geach (1972) ch. 10. pp.289-327.

loss of the notion of change: for genuine change implies that we cannot revisit the past but with spatialization we have simultaneous access to whatever is displayed along the time-axis.

Returning to the purely extensionalist view of events, one can say the following. Quine opts for *concrete* events but, first, "concrete" is not univocal since it is associated with different criteria. Second, its use in the Quinean context is particularly misleading. The zone-event is concrete as a spatio-temporal extension, but it is not concrete in the sense of singling out a unique particular. The separation of one zone from another is not governed by the principle of individuation: one can take, at will, larger or smaller space-time extensions to be zones. My reading is supported by Quine's remark that these space-time portions can be "gerrymandered".[69] While clearly, this can never happen to fully-fledged individuals: genuine individuals cannot be gerrymandered. The Quinean zones can be chopped arbitrarily; therefore their case is more analogous to cases of mass terms than to cases of common nouns denoting individual substances and dividing their references among these individuals. For example, any bearer of the name "rabbit" has determinate boundaries while "water" or "sugar" can be instantiated by any arbitrary portion of these materials. So the Quinean zones are not concrete in the sense of providing for individuation but they are undoubtedly extended. Therefore, to avoid confusion, I am inclined to label this view the *extensionalist* view of events. The extensionalist zone-view has two drawbacks. One familiar charge against it is that it cannot cope with the fact that different events can take place in one and the same zone. The other, I have just clarified, is that it cannot provide for individuation since zones are tailored in an arbitrary manner.

Equipped with these considerations one can now formulate the *third* universalist argument. It is given by Bennett who points out the

---

[69] The individuation problem of scattered objects is ignored here. I take as 'fully-fledged' individuals those that are spatio-temporally continuous and have non-arbitrary boundaries.

deficiency of the extensionalist view with respect to causal explanations. Causal explanations, whether they have the form of fact-causation or event-causation, pin the causal connection down to some causal power exhibited by the properties of the cause. But zones cannot have causal power. Although something in their content can account for such power, still the zones themselves are not specified by reference to such causal potentials as properties and relations. "On the Quinean theory, event-causation statements say only that there is some causal flow from one zone to another, i.e. that undeclared features of two zones are causally relevant to one another in a certain way".[70] Since it is not stated what these features would be, event-causation statements are, on this account, wholly uninformative and deprived of any explanatory power. They "merely say that some unspecified kind of causal flow went from one zone to another". (*ibid.*)

Similar considerations lie behind the distinction made by R. M. Martin between events and event-concepts. He suggests that "in addition to events one should recognize, it would seem, event-*concepts* as well, namely events taken under a given *Art des Gegebenseins*."[71] The latter yields events under a certain mode of presentation which can confer explanatory power on the events thus presented. For example, "marrying Iocasta" and "marrying Oedipus' mother" have turned out to be the same event but only the event presented under the latter mode could explain Oedipus self-destructive behaviour.

In sum, we may conclude that a wholly extensionalist view of events is untenable. Events are also partly intensional as to their nature, for the following reasons. Different events can be co-located in the same zone; the same event type can re-occur in numerically distinct exemplifications. And the constitutive property of the event is essential to causal explanations. But we have also seen that events are particulars:

---

[70] Bennett (1988), 116.

[71] Martin, R. M. (1975), 183.

they are space-time occupants and nameable entities that can be quantified over. Still, they are not objects of verbs in the same way as substance-particulars are. Given all these, it should now be clear that the best account of all these aspects would be to say that *events are abstract particulars*, i.e. *tropes*.

Particularism

Tropes have been delineated from accidents; we have seen that the definition of tropes given by Williams matches the two standard notions of accidents. However, the current widespread interest in tropes is motivated largely by the polemic between *universalism* and *particularism* rather than the desire to give a more refined account of accidents either in Aristotelian or in Brentanian way. The particularist stance is straightforwardly expressed in the characterization of tropes as "abstract particulars which are predicable of concrete particulars" given by G.F. Stout, an early forerunner of the trope theory.[72] For Stout the qualitative features predicable of concrete particulars are themselves particulars and not universals, this being the hard core of the trope theory. Stout's contribution to the trope-theory is appreciated by Williams, Campbell and Bacon. More recently, the standard trope-view proposed by Campbell accepts Stout's definition of tropes as qualitative or abstract particulars.

Now trope-particularism has, on its agenda, to account for qualitative features in particularist terms; and concrete substances, provided that they are not taken as unanalysable primitives, are also supposed to be

---

[72] Quoted, with approval, by Williams (1953), (repr. in: Loux, 2001) p. 63. (reference to Loux' volume) Stout's original formulation is to be found in the *Proceedings of the Aristotelian Society, Supplement*, (1923) v. 3. p.114. See also: G.F. Stout(1971b)

analyzed into constituent-particulars. As to the former goal, tropes are suggested as property-particulars; so properties and universals are construed as open classes of resembling tropes. As to the latter goal, concrete substances are conceived as constructions from property-particulars, rather than constructions from sharable and shared universals. In view of these goals it would be wrong to understand the trope theory as a kind of *nominalism*.[73]

The difference between trope-particularism and nominalism is this. Nominalism refuses to give a reductive account of the individual substances for it takes concrete substances are irreducible, primitive ontological items. The trope theory, on the other hand, has its trope-**BT** form offering a reductive account of substances in terms of the constituting tropes. Individual substances are seen as collections of co-located tropes. By contrast, nominalism offers a reductive account of properties in terms of classes of concrete individuals (class nominalism), while the trope theory retains the *abstractness* of the qualitative features and is *not reductive* with regard to the properties. Therefore the trope theory does not feature the historical debates between platonic property-realism and nominalism for the simple reason that it cannot be identified with the nominalist horn of the dilemma. Also, it does not share some of the tenets of platonic realism either.

The temptation still to associate the trope theory to nominalism arises from that the earliest predecessors of the theory are the British empiricist thinkers who actually subscribed to some form of nominalism. But what they subscribed to is *not* metaphysical nominalism about individual substances. The British empiricists insist that we perceive objects through their qualitative features. These features strike our senses in the particularized form as they pertain to individual objects and never as properties over and above their particular instantiations. For example, we never perceive redness as such, only the particular red quality of the rose, or, the post box, etc. As a consequence, redness as such does not

---

[73] For the varieties of nominalism see D.M. Armstrong (1978a)

exist as an ontologically independent item as it does, for example, for the platonists. Then the question arises how abstract singular terms should be conceived, and the standard nominalist answer is that they should be taken as names in the language. In this sense the British empiricists are nominalist about abstract reference.

This *semantic nominalism* embraced by the British empiricists creates the illusion that they are *metaphysical nominalists* about concrete particular substances as well. But this is not the case. For the nominalists take individual substances as basic entities and not as constructions out of perceivable qualitative features. While for the British empiricists they should be analyzed as the compresences of certain perceivable/cognizable qualitative features. For example, the rose is the compresence of a particular odor, colour, shape, texture, etc. The rose is what it is qualitatively for our senses, either actually, or counterfactually. In sum, it is the verificationist spirit of the British empiricists that qualify them as forerunners of the trope theory, more precisely, as forerunners of the trope version of **BT**. And if they are nominalists, they are nominalists in the semantic sense as indicated above, and not in the metaphysical sense.

For the tropists quality-particulars are ontologically basic entities. As Armstrong says, interpreting and approving Campbell, "particulars *reduce* to bundles of compresent tropes".[74] The status of these reducing entities is spelled out metaphorically by Williams: for him tropes are "the very alphabet of being". And, to put it more technically, Campbell proposes a "one-category ontology" in terms of tropes. Thus a quick move can be made from the explanatory reductive account of substance-particulars to a one-category ontology. However, a one-category ontology is burdened with the task of construing every item in the ontology, from substances to numbers, from events to propositions, relations, beliefs, etc. as tropes or compounds of tropes. The move is quick, but is it safe enough?

---

[74] Armstrong, (1989b), p. 114.

As we shall see, it is not. The trope theory need not be devised as a universal remedy for every problem of metaphysics. For example, relations seem to be stubbornly resistent to an overall tropist approach. Here I agree with Bacon and Vallicella that at least certain relations as universals are ineliminable from the ontological palette. As Bacon says, the trope theory "requires at the very least a category of tropes and a category of relations of tropes or meta-relations".[75]

The trope-account can even maintain the distinction between particular relational facts and relations proper. For example, the love-relation as a universal can be seen as clearly distinct from such particular relational facts as "Othello's loving Desdemona", or "Romeo's loving Juliet", etc. The love-relation is not the sum-total of these particular relational facts. Relations can also exist unexemplified, while it would be weird to talk about unobtained relational facts. So relations exist as abstract entities, even if nothing enters as relata to make particular relational facts.

The moral is this: while the explanatory reductive treatment of concrete particular substances in terms of tropes may be promising, an overall monistic trope ontology trying to squeeze every metaphysical item under the heading of tropes seems to me to be a misguided attempt. Tropes are abstract particulars predicable of concrete particulars. Moreover, the very individuation of tropes requires reference, in a non-circular way, to these concrete particulars. The particularity, say, of the wisdom-trope that characterizes Socrates is not to be understood as the instantiation of the universal "wisdom" being numerically the same in every instantiation. This is denied by tropists since they find it puzzling that the very same universal inheres in different instantiations. One of the goals of the trope theory is precisely to accommodate our pre-theoretical intuition that the properties are the properties *of* the given concrete particulars. Therefore it is "Socrates' wisdom" that characterizes

---

[75] Bacon (1995), p.72.

and partly constitutes Socrates rather than the independent universal "wisdom".

This being the case one might find it embarrassing that concrete particulars can reduce to bundles of compresent tropes in the explanation while at the same time the constituting tropes acquire their identity partly by reference to the particulars they make. Socrates' wisdom is his and not anyone else's, still Socrates is accounted for in terms of the tropes that are dependent on him in the way indicated. Obviously, then, such an account of the concrete particulars *and* the tropes constituting them seems to be fatally circular. This problem has already been forecast in the *Introduction* and there I have promised a satisfactory treatment of it.

I will give a final answer to this problem in the next chapter. As to the inner structure of tropes, the propositional account has been received here with certain provisio. Undoubtedly, the "Socrates' wisdom" trope can be parsed as "Socrates being wise" which in turn invites "Socrates *is* wise". But facts like this, backing the respective propositions, are ontological hybrids, being the non-mereological compounds of an abstract component and a concrete particular. And when we turn to ontological claims, hybridness comes up again: for the claims rest either on the emphasis of the abstract part, or the emphasis of the concrete part. If emphasis is on "wisdom" rather than on "Socrates", when conceiving the trope, this would have the consequence that tropes prove to be *transferable* from one particular to another. Say, "Socrates' wisdom" could be carried over to "Plato's wisdom". This position is adopted by Armstrong.[76] Thus the trope is endowed with some independence from the particular it actually characterizes. This would result in making tropes too much like universals. However, if emphasis is put on the subject-substances, these will become more independent from the structure and make a separate category beside the tropes that pertain to them. With substances thus becoming basic entities, it would be essential to "Socrates' wisdom" that it is *his*, because it is unable to exist without

---

[76] Armstrong (1989b)

him. The qualitative content will be suppressed thus in the individuation of the tropes.

Alternatively, tropes can be seen to lack an inner structure determined by the corresponding universal and the bearer substance, like, for example, a wisdom-side and a Socrates-side in the "Socrates' wisdom" trope. Instead, the claim is that tropes are unstructured and both universals and particulars are construed as tropes. Roughly, universals will be the set of exactly resembling tropes, while particulars will be the set of co-instantiated tropes. This option relies heavily on a set-theoretical construction and is adopted by John Bacon.[77]

A mixed option is represented by Simons who accepts the trope-bundle construal of substances with the amendment that a hard core with essential tropes is posited over and above the assembly of the constituting tropes, playing also the role of the individuator. This account nicely keeps a balance between qualitative trope-content and dependency on, and individuation by, the bearer-substance. Simons' theory will be elaborated in detail.[78]

As an assessment of these alternatives, I say that the transferability of tropes weakens the genuine novelty of the trope theory as an account of *particularized* qualitative features. Individuation exclusively by the bearer-substance flirts either with the bare substratum theory or the Aristotelian account. Bacon's theory inherits the problem of the *set-theoretical construction* of substances; this will be discussed later. So, Simons's treatment seems to be the most promising alternative.

---

[77] Bacon (1995)

[78] Simons (1994)

III. The Individuation of Tropes and Substances in BT. The Main Criticisms of the Trope Theory

Campbell and Bacon both espouse a purely tropist ontology despite their disagreement about the status of *relations*. Martin, Simons, and Armstrong propound a mixed ontology, recognizing substances in addition to tropes on the ontological palette. Martin accepts a kind of substratum view, while Simons amends the simple trope-cluster theory by positing a hard core of essential tropes tightly bundled by mutual foundation behaving like a substratum.[79] Armstrong's problem with the trope-cluster theory is that he finds the individuation of the tropes difficult and therefore he tends to regard only substances as genuine individuals.[80]

The major problem for mixed trope-ontologies *not* committed to primitive substances can be glossed as the problem of finding some device to meet the circularity charge, i.e., the charge, that on these views the substances and the tropes seem to individuate mutually each other. This charge can be obviated in my view along the lines indicated before.

Here I shall examine critically those main features of Campbell's and Bacon's tropisms that are particularly relevant to the bundle-of-tropes construal of the individual substances. This construal presupposes the metaphysical distinction between *occurents* and *continuants* that I have

---

[79] Martin, C. B. (1980), Simons, P. (1994). On tight bundling in mutual foundation see chapter V.

[80] Armstrong, D. M. (1989)

already defended by taking tropes as abstract entities.[81] The relevance of this point, to repeat, is that recently the traditional *abstractionist* interpretation of the tropes has been challenged and a *concretist* reading has been suggested instead. In order to restate the traditional view of Williams and Campbell some independent motivation must be brought in. As a final topic of this chapter, the main standard criticisms of the tropist ontology will be considered.

The vulnerable aspect of Campbell's one-category ontology is that he declares the trope to be "an unanalysable primitive". When it comes to the question of the individuation of the tropes Campbell appeals to this primitive character; he makes clear that tropes are unstructured, simple entities. As he puts it, tropes are not only qualitatively simple, but also, "they are categorially simple in that they are not the union of a particularizer or individuator with a (maybe universal) nature".[82] Now qualitative simpleness means that it is only one property that is featured by a given trope. This claim may be challenged though, if the spatio-temporal positions of tropes are also recognized among their features. To avoid this challenge simpleness may be defined only by reference to the constituting intrinsic property of the trope, denying thereby that external relations like the spatio-temporal position affects simpleness. So, for Campbell, a trope is not an Aristotelian individual in being a *this-such* where "this" is the deictic component and "such" refers to the intrinsic nature, but an unanalysable primitive whose individuation cannot, and need not, be accounted for. To quote: "To preserve the simplicity of tropes, one must then affirm that *individuation is basic and unanalysable*".[83]

Campbell's formulation suggests that the simplicity of tropes can be secured only by declaring that individuation is a primitive. However, if

---

[81] See chapter II.

[82] Campbell, *op.cit.*, 81.

[83] Campbell, *op.cit.*, 69.

the explanatory potential is preferred against mysterious simplicity, a less sparse ontology is more appealing. Accepting also substances and the dependence of tropes on them, tropes can be taken as entities whose individuation is derivative from the individuation of the bearer substance. One might object that this is not much advance on the original problem of the individuation of tropes, since it is now only passed on to the equally vexing problem of the individuation of concrete substances. It seems to me though that this latter problem can be handled more easily than the former.

Before coming to this issue, let us survey the various possibilities for the individuation of tropes. *First*, there is the possibility to individuate tropes by reference to the property they encompass. Since an individuator is always a particularizer as well, though not the other way round, a particular trope would be yielded whenever a given property is instantiated. Say, a green trope of a leaf would count as a particular quality in virtue of instantiating the property "green". And, if another green trope of another leaf (or, of the same leaf) were particularized also by instantiating the same property "green", it would count as the same particular trope as the first one. In this vein all the particular tropes encompassing the same property would count as the same trope. This manouvre is nothing but the re-formulation of the familiar universalist position that one and the same universal can be instantiated in many different particularized forms. So, instead of trope individuation we would get back to the instantiation of universals. But a trope is not equivalent to an instantiated universal; if it were, a common nature would be presupposed to these particular instantiations. Campbell and other tropists however vigorously deny that there are such common natures. If there were, tropes would be deprived of their individuality since by sharing the same common nature they would now be assimilated to instantiated universals. Typically, tropists find fault with universalism precisely because they find it intolerable that the numerically same universal gets multiply located by its multiple instantiation. What seems embarrassing for them is that the same universal can be present at several places and several times inhering in distinct concrete individuals. Therefore the individuation of tropes solely by reference to the encompassed property is not an option, except on pain of abandoning the very core of the trope theory. This scenario is not considered by Campbell since he is a devoted particularist.

The *second* possibility which is the only one considered by Campbell is to individuate tropes with the help of the places they occupy. Now the relational property of occupying a place could play the role of a (partial) individuator provided that the colocation of tropes is excluded. But it is hardly possible to exclude trope-colocation, since the abstract character of tropes admitted also by Campbell, rules out such restriction. Since multiple occurrence can not been excluded, it would be possible even for qualitatively "exactly similar" but numerically different tropes to occupy the same place. For example, two exactly similar colour tropes could be compresent, and, as a consequence, they could not be told apart by reference to place as a partial individuator. But, *ex hypothesis*, these tropes are different.

Taking place as an individuator is coupled with the background assumption that tropes are simple in nature. This is the version considered by Campbell. In this case having a place and exposing a certain qualitative aspect would not be distinct from each other. Take a colour trope that is simple by presupposition. If the trope is simple, then, as Campbell says, "its place must not be something distinct from its colour. Thus a shape, a colour and any '*other*' compresent trope collapse into identity".[84] But it is clearly intolerable that qualitatively different tropes collapse into identity just because their places are supposed to be inseparable from their qualitative aspects. To avoid this unwelcome consequence Campbell takes individuation as *basic* and *primitive*. Further, he treats the problem of place in the following way: he renders the place-tropes to the status of "spatial quasi-tropes" distinct from the qualitative tropes that they are compresent with. This means that whenever a bunch of tropes is compresent then, apart from the member-tropes *plus* the relation of compresence, whose status has to be decided

---

[84] Campbell, *op.cit.*, 68.

yet, there is also a "spatial quasi-trope" that belongs to all the compresent qualitative tropes.

This solution, however, is far from being satisfactory for two fairly obvious reasons. One is that the supposed spatial trope has to belong to several other tropes and so it is a shared entity rather than a genuine unshared and unsharable trope. Probably, this is the reason why Campbell calls it a "quasi-trope". But it is far from being clear how genuine tropes and quasi-tropes could be tied together by compresence. Here the vexing point is not that entities of different kinds are tied together since there are several such metaphysical ties. The point rather is this: what makes one of the entities in the symmetric compresence relation different from all the other entities of the same relation such that each bundle under compresence requires one such different entity?

The other source of my feeling of discomfort is this: provided that there are no uninstantiated tropes, every trope has to occupy a space-time region. Therefore, the spatio-temporal occupancy is an essential feature of the tropes (though it is contingent which spatio-temporal region they occupy). In view of this it is hard to maintain, with Campbell, that the quality instance tropes and their spatial and temporal quasi-tropes "are distinct entities" presumably implying that they could exist independently of each other. Maybe, the quality-instance trope and the spatial and temporal quasi-tropes are distinct in the sense that they are only contingently related: no particular spatial and temporal tropes necessitate any of the qualitative tropes. But *some* spatial and temporal tropes *are* necessitated by each qualitative trope; and in this sense they are not independent, since it is part of the nature of the tropes which spatio-temporal position they occupy. The moral is that the spatio-temporal feature of the tropes is a controversial issue.

The *third* possibility that seems to be the most promising takes tropes to be individuated by their bearer substance. The strong intuition supporting this option is that tropes cannot exist as freely floating ontological building blocks waiting to be combined into different individuals.[85] An existing trope is always syncategorematic for being the trope *of* an individual. This feature does not tell against the trope-bundle theory of substances since, as I shall show, the individuation of substances has its explanans independently from that of the constituting tropes. So we can deny the free-floating character of tropes without risking the trope-theory on a whole.[86]

The option I recommend is not available for Campbell since he adheres to a one-category ontology. As is known, individuation by the bearer substance is the standard epistemic procedure with accidents: Mona Lisa's smile or Einstein's thoughts are the sort of transient entities, halfway between being short-lived continuants and events (or, more precisely, the immediate effects of events), that can be individuated only by reference to Mona Lisa and Einstein respectively. This individuating aspect, together with the particular qualitative aspect, qualifies the accidents as tropes.

With this suggestion for the individuation of tropes we are back to the origin of the trope theory in the traditional doctrine of accidents discussed earlier. Does this imply that individuation by the bearer substance is open only to those tropes that are accidents? As I shall show, it does not. Accidents are contingent beings; they belong to the bearer substance but the individuation of the latter does not depend on these contingent features although they also contribute to the complete individual concept of the substance. Therefore with accidents the circularity charge can easily be avoided: it is not the case that accident-tropes *and* substances are individuate mutually each other.

Some tropes, however, are essential relative to the very identity of the substance they partly constitute. Now the question arises whether

---

[85] See Mertz, D. W. (1996), 25-32.

[86] According to Mertz this is a decisive objection against the trope-theory. See: Mertz (1996), 26.

essential tropes are also identifiable by reference to the bearer substance and if so, whether this can be explained without being exposed to the circularity charge. It seems to me that both questions can be answered in the affirmative. As to the *first* question, there is no separate route for the individuation of the essential tropes. Trope **BT** comprises property-particulars of both modal status.

As to the *second*, the circularity charge can be evaded if the construal of the substances on the substance-trope view is sophisticated enough, so that the substances do not turn to be the *mere* collections of tropes. One such device that will be more fully elaborated with Simons's two-tier theory is to make essential use of the *foundation* relation, more precisely, *mutual foundation*. The idea is that mutual foundation among essential tropes in the core goes proxy for the substratum such that the outcome is neither a substance with a bare substratum nor the mere collection of tropes. Rather, the outcome is an *integrated whole*, which is qualitative but *is not* identical with the bundle of its qualitative features. This function of the foundation relation goes back to Husserl. But it can perform other functions as well; for example, it can account for the fact that the collection of abstract particulars, under the mutual foundation relation, is not an abstract entity any more, but a concrete individual. This will be shown in the Vth chapter. It suffices to say here that the mutual foundation of tropes results in concrete individual substances and the individuation of tropes hinges on the individuation of these bearer substances. Are we better off now with this intermediate result?

I think we are, since the decisive point is that the individuation of *concrete* entities has resources other than the individuation of *abstract* entities. A concrete individual is uniquely identifiable with the help of its spatio-temporal location because no other concrete individual can occupy the same location. By contrast, tropes as abstract particulars can be co-located and this is the main obstacle to individuating tropes via the places they occupy: since this would have the unwelcome consequence that the various co-located tropes would collapse into one.

With tropes and, similarly with event-tokens, the indication of the spatio-temporal position operates as a *particularizing* factor, but it does not yield the *individuation* of the item in question. To be clear about the difference between individuating and particularizing, consider the following. Whenever an event is characterised as taking place at a given spatio-temporal segment, we can know that it is a *particular* event or *event-token* as opposed to the corresponding *event-type*. Say, that it is the boiling of an amount of water in a pot *here* and *now* and what is at issue is *not* the repeatable *event-type* of "boiling" in general. But the indication of the spatio-temporal position does not uniquely *individuate* the event belonging to that spatio-temporal segment, since by the very nature of events several events might take place in the same spatio-temporal segment. For example, "boiling" here and now can co-occur with "salting" here and now. Similarly, an extension-trope of a car and its shape-trope might occupy the same spatio-temporal position; unless some distortion is made on the car, its extension goes with its characteristic, well-designed shape. But clearly, the two tropes are different.

Concrete entities, however, are the unique holders of their spatio-temporal position. So the spatio-temporal position not only uniquely single out a concrete individual but also, partly individuates it. The *deictic* element of the spatio-temporal position contributes the "*this*" in the "*this - such*" of the Aristotelian individual substance. The unique spatio-temporal position of individuals excludes other individuals being partly individuated by reference to the same spatio-temporal position.

The particularizing role and the individuating role do not go in tandem, as I have said. As a further example, take bare substrata. These are propertiless ingredients of substances that can perform the particularizing function in virtue of the fact that no two different substances can share the same substratum. But, being propertiless, they are not efficient in individuating them. This is the reason why swap of substrata is possible. The distribution of particularizing substrata over numerically distinct particulars can even be just random. This problem urges us to recognize that individuation involves qualitative features apart from deictic and particularizing elements. What is, then, the role of the qualitative features? Most plausibly, only the essential qualitative features of the qualitative manifold play a role in individuation. Otherwise, if contingent features were also encountered, individuation would amount to a complete and exhaustive description of the substance; i.e. the Leibnizian complete concept of individuals. Therefore the individuation of concrete substances involves essential qualitative features *plus* the unique spatio-temporal position that accomplishes the business of particularization as well.

Now we are in the position to answer the question *why the individuation of substances is independent, in crucial respects, from the fact that these substances can be analyzed as bundles of tropes*. The answer also provides for the possibility that the individuation of the tropes hinges, in a non-circular way, on the individuation of the substance they belong to. The answer is twofold: first of all, *concrete* individual substances are the *bearers of a qualitative manifold*, while their constituting abstract tropes encompass only one property and not a manifold *qua* a manifold. Bearing a manifold of qualitative features is one criterion of concreteness implying independence. Therefore concrete individual substances enjoy independence even if they are presented in the analysis as bundles of tropes. Further, the individuation of concrete substances requires *essential* qualitative features. Thus we can claim that it is the subset of the essential features from the qualitative manifold that yields the "*such*" component of the "*this - such*". Individuation, as I understand it, does not involve the complete list of the actual properties making up the substance, but only the essential features without which the individual substance would not be *the* individual substance it is. Second, the *deictic* element, which is the indication of the spatio-temporal location contributes to substance-individuation: it plays the role of *a (partial) individuator and not simply a particularizer when concrete entities* are concerned; while abstract tropes and events cannot be individuated by reference to their sharable and shared location.

In sum, the role of bearing a manifold *and* enjoying a unique spatio-temporal location, both pertinent to the very notion of concrete entities, make the individuation of substances largely independent from the mere possession of their constituting tropes. Thus the suggestion is this: tropes are individuated by reference to the bearer substance; whereas the latter, although constituted by tropes, is individuated by reference to the set of essential tropes selected from among its qualitative manifold via *foundation, and* the unique spatio-temporal position. *These resources of the individuation of substances taken jointly are not due to the mere fact that substances are constituted by tropes.* In this vein the circularity charge has been circumvented. And the major obstacle to embracing a dualistic substance-trope view is removed as well.

My solution for the individuation of the substance-bundle rests on commitment to *essentialism,* sortal and individual. I also rely on the Kantian notion of things bearing the manifold of properties, plus the distinguishing role of the spatio-temporal location. If I were to rely exclusively on spatio-temporal location in the simple or naive bundle theory then my suggestion would be vulnerable to the retort that impure properties like having a spatio-temporal location cannot serve as individuators. To recall, having an impure property requires standing in some appropriate relation to another individual. And if the chain of individuals being in need of further individuals to their individuation never stops, we will never be in a position to say that any object is sufficiently individuated. Let alone the fact that being individuated is a precondition for a thing entering into any relation. Losonsky considers this objection stating that "impure properties cannot be the *sole* individuators of objects because an object can have an impure property only if it is already individuated".[87]

Now one way to halt regress with impure properties being in perpetual need of further individuals, is the Casullo-type suggestion that makes essential use of a privileged set of individuals, notably, the landmarks, that have only pure properties. Losonsky repudiates this suggestion because he finds privileged individuals suspect. Apart from

---

[87] Losonsky M. (1987a)

finding privileged individuals suspect, I have another worry with Casullo's suggestion. It is, to recall, that the existence of such landmarks does not follow from his account of the weak bundle theory (**WBT**). Therefore landmarks function like extra posited items, rather than the consequences of (**WBT**). For this reason it is hard to see how they could help saving (**WBT**).

Haecceistic properties like "being Socrates" make another group of impure properties that could be invoked to the individuation of the bundle. These are not vulnerable to infinite regress, still, they are vulnerable to petitio principii: with them the individuals are already presupposed to their purported reductive accounts in terms of qualitative bundles. Now this sort of charge has a particularly strong force if the bundle theory is taken in its naive form identifying directly the individual with the bundle. My account, however, appreciates the special role of the *gluing* relation or the foundation relation that is able to create the kind of *unity* that the cluster, taken *simpliciter*, lacks. Haecceistic properties are problematic not only on the ground of bringing petitio principii in **BT**; they can be discarded on their own vices, independently from **BT**. The reason I have for repudiating haecceistic properties has to do with the fact that they cannot count as genuine properties: they lack qualitative content and do not exist when they are uninstantiated.

A further kind of impure relational properties that could be considered to do the job of individuating the bundle would be the properties of *unique origin*. "Originating from this zygote", or, "being the sword made out from this piece of steel", etc., are the favorite examples. The advantage of these properties is that they do not require the prior individuation of the thing before they enter into the relation; rather, the object becomes individuated by the process of coming into existence.[88] My main objection to individuation by impure properties of origin will be spelled out in the last chapter.

---

[88] Losonsky finds this as the chief merit of properties of origin. See Losonsky, M. (1987a), 194.

As for current dualistic trope theories, Martin's version does not face the difficulty of making tropes and substances mutually individuate each other since he accepts bare substratum. Armstrong, on the other hand, takes states of affairs as basic to his ontology that is *not* the mereological sum of its components. One can have, for example, "Othello" and "Iago" as substances and "hating" as a trope without automatically having the state of affair consisting in "Iago's hating Othello". Moreover, the same constituents can combine into another state of affair: "Othello's hating Iago". Now the question arises how the "hating" relational trope and other relational and monadic tropes are to be understood with respect to the constitution of individual substances like Iago and Othello. This is not explicitly covered by Armstrong. He suggests, instead, a "thin" and a "thick" conceptions of individuals. Briefly, the thin notion of individuals is the one without the associated properties or, at best, with the minimum set of properties required for mere identification, while the thick notion of an individual is fully equipped with the properties. This distinction, however, does not explain either the individuation of substances or the individuation of tropes. As for Simons, he develops a trope-bundle construal of substances, with certain amendments and refinements and, also, tropism is suggested as a general ontological stance. But his account does not explain how the individuation of concrete substances *and* the individuation of tropes, respectively, take place.

The solution offered here has essentialist commitments as I have said: it presupposes *essentialism,* sortal and individual. And the individuation of tropes is partly derivative on the individuation of their bearer substances. Now sortal or Aristotelian essentialism says that the very identity of an individual substance *qua* token of a kind depends on its possession of sortal essential properties. Aristotelian sortal properties yield only the species; but it is reasonable to claim that some explanations explore the individual nature of substances on top of their sortal features; this will be argued in the last chapter.

There is another commitment to my solution: adopting the individuation of tropes partly by reference to the bearer substance carries commitment to the non-transferability of tropes. The assumption of non-transferability, however, leads one to the question of the status of the spatio-temporal tropes. For, if these tropes are equally constitutive of the substance together with the qualitative monadic tropes then any bearer substance gives incessantly way to another bearer substance as things move in space and change in time. But then, with another bearer, the "original" tropes would cease to exist. Say, if a piece of cloth is cut out from a curtain and is sewn onto another one, all the tropes constituting the piece of cloth, the colour, texture, shape, etc. would cease to exist and new but exactly similar tropes would occupy the place of the expired ones. In face of this difficulty it is not surprising that Campbell renders the spatio-temporal tropes to the status of "quasi-tropes". It is also hard to explain how new tropes could come into being *ex nihilo*; in any case, the question of the birth and perishing of tropes is embarrassing. Since tropes are particulars, even though they are abstract ones, they are not eternal entities like other abstract entities, say, numbers, universals, etc. The existence of essential tropes that pertain to the bearer individual for its complete life span may be explained by reference to the coming into being and perishing of the individual. More transient tropes, however, replace each other in a fairly mysterious way.

As to current trope-theories, tropes are non-transferable on Simons view. They cannot just wander off from the bearer and find another host. Armstrong, however, is concerned more with a state-of-affairs ontology. As mentioned before, states-of-affairs are compounds requiring elements that can enter into the combination relatively freely. No wonder, then, that Armstrong espouses the transferability of tropes.[89] Thus, the colour trope had by a piece of cloth can continue its existence even if the piece of cloth is sewn onto some other material. Maybe, this example is intuitively appealing. But it might be hard to accept that Socrates' wisdom wanders off from him and continues its career as *the* wisdom trope, or, one of the wisdom tropes, of Plato. In other words, the

---

[89] See Armstrong (1989b).

transferability of essential tropes is far from being acceptable. Therefore I favor the non-transferability of tropes.

Apart from ontological problems certain semantic issues arise with the trope theory. There is no general guarantee for the match between an ontology and a semantic theory. For example, while universalism is especially suitable to serve the goals of predication and abstract reference, a particularist theory like the trope theory conflicts with the basic feature of language right from the start. Just consider, if all things are particulars, individuals and qualities alike, where does the inherent generality of language come from? How can a tropist explain predication, once the predicate-trope is not an "unsaturated" entity on the trope account, requiring to be filled in with the appropriate argument, but is a "thick" trope already pregnant with the subject of predication?

In other words, the neat division of labour between the predicative role and the referential role is not satisfied if predication is equipped with a tropist ontology. For, in this case, one of the tropes already constituting the subject-term is affirmed of it by the predicative tie. This would make all predication tautologous: the predicate trope is not something independent from the very existence of the subject of predication, as I have shown before. For example, Socrates is constituted by the *compresent* bundle of tropes such as {Socrates's whiteness; Socrates's humanity, Socrates's wisdom, etc.}. Further, each of these tropes belongs to a *similarity* class of distinct but exactly resembling tropes. This is how we get Williams's "painless universals". Thus "Socrates's wisdom" trope belongs to the similarity class of {Socrates's wisdom, Plato's wisdom, Kant's wisdom, etc.}. Then, clearly, predicating wisdom of Socrates resolves into the partial *overlap* or intersection of these two classes that both contain "Socrates's wisdom" as a trope. This runs counter to the very idea of informative predication demanded by the possibility of informative language use.

Another vexing point is that the account of predication as partial overlap between two classes makes predication *symmetric*: predication becomes the intersection of two classes contributing to predication with the same role. But this violates our logical intuition that ascribes different roles to terms in the referential position and to terms in the predicative position. Traditionally conceived, the general idea of the difference is this: what the term in the referential position *refers to* is *a case of* what the predicate term expresses. Ramsey tried to obliterate the distinction by pointing out that the roles can be swapped. For example, instead of saying that "Socrates is wise", we can equally say that "wisdom Socratizes". The Ramsey-style objection against the traditional difference between particulars and universals is echoed by Mellor in his discussion of Bacon's trope-theory where predication is construed as class-overlap.

Now Ramsey's objection could be answered by pointing out the *structural* difference between individual terms and predicate terms. While individual terms are not characterized by the number of the predicates they take, polyadic predicates are characterized by the appropriate n-tuples that are structurally associated to them. Bacon approves a similar solution in order to get rid of symmetry with predication in his trope theory. He suggests the following: it can be seen that *compresence*, which is the basic relation for *particulars* in the trope theory, is an equivalence relation since it is symmetric, reflexive and transitive. By contrast, *similarity*, which is the basic relation for *properties* in the trope theory, need not be transitive.[90] Therefore the structural difference between particulars playing the referential role and properties playing the predicative role could be preserved. Moreover, it could be preserved by structural means.

Predication typically underwrites the universalist tenet that predicates express common natures: when a rose is said to be red and the post box is said to be red, too, then one and the same universal nature expressed by the predicate "red" is attributed to numerically distinct individuals. Predication, on the trope theory, would rather go with the claim that the rose has the trope of "the rose being red" and the post box has the trope

---

[90] See the 'Trope' entry written by John Bacon to *SEP*.

of "the post box being red", etc. But this is again the admission of the discomforting fact that predication is hopelessly tautological or uninformative on the trope theory. And this objection is more serious than the one about symmetrical roles.

To cope with the difficulty Campbell makes concession to Williams's "painless universals". The idea, with an example, is this: the reference of "red" can be given by any particular token of "red", either the one belonging to the rose, or the other one belonging to the post box, etc. without postulating a common nature or universal over and above the particular tokens from the similarity class. The key notion, borrowed from its use in mathematics, is the *arbitrariness* of the token. A universal is thus explained by any *arbitrary* token of it. And the invocation of painless universals helps to explain abstract reference, as Campbell claims.

So far so good, as abstract reference is concerned. Still, predication remains in need of an adequate account. Campbell is quite right in pointing out that "tropes are not, in the first instance, part of any semantic theory". Therefore he is right in insisting that in order to establish the meaningfulness of predication like "a is F" "it is neither necessary nor sufficient for there to be F tropes".[91] The separation of the ontological and the semantic issues still leaves the vexing question behind what the *semantic equivalents* of tropes are. In universalism, the match is fairly easy: predicates are the names of universal properties in logic and language, though the match is not a strict one-one correspondence. There are predicates in the language without ontological backing, as it has been pointed out by Armstrong.[92] For example, the predicate of "travelling faster than light" does not feature any instantiated property in our physical world; still it exists as an empty predicate in the language. Similarly, synonymous predicates may stand

---

[91] Campbell, *op.cit.*, 25.

[92] Armstrong (1978)

for the same universal property. However, the lack of exact match need not amount to the *lack of any semantic equivalent* or *any semantic approximation*; and the question precisely is whether tropes as ontological items have any semantic equivalents or approximations.

In his treatment of the problem Campbell applies an *ignoratio elenchi*: he replaces the highly pertinent question about the very existence of a semantic equivalent by the less pertinent question about the precision of the match as I shall explain. But the real issue that he fails to address is this: language has its resources to express recurring items in the world or in experience, while the ontological theory of tropes is motivated mainly by the concern for non-repeatable particularity; hence the inherent conflict between tropism and any semantic theory.

With language we cannot even help ourselves with deictic and indexical elements to latch onto the unique particularity targeted since these deictic and indexical elements can be combined, on other occasions of the language use, to express other particular facts and situations. Say, the indexicals "I" or "tomorrow" as *characters* pick out different *contents* on different occasions of their use. By contrast, the same trope-particular can not be used, on other occasion, to constitute another concrete individual once the bearer uniqueness and the non-transferability are agreed upon. What is worse, we cannot even say that a nominalistic semantics could be a possible semantic companion of the trope ontology since nominalism locates the generality of common nouns in language. So, the nominalist semantic answer is irrelevant to the semantic problem of tropes. Before closing this section I quote Campbell's example about the supposed loose match between predicates and tropes. Quote: "...if two predicates F and G are not synonymous, it does not follow that there must be two different tropes or tropes clusters F and G. *Being the sunrise of 27 September 1989* can involve the very same tropes as *being the three millionth sunrise*, let us suppose, although these predicates are not synonymous."[93]

Although Campbell does not spell out why he thinks that these non-synonymous predicates involve the same tropes, his reason can easily be reconstructed. These predicates are supposed to be extensionally equivalent: *the sunrise of 27 September 1989* might be the same as *the three millions sunrise* and so the idea presumably is that the content of tropes is yielded by their extension. This runs counter, however, to the accepted thesis that tropes as *abstract* entities are *quality*-instances and therefore their extensional equivalence does not turn them into the same instance. That is, the extensional overlap of the predicates expressing tropes does not guarantee the sameness of the trope-contents. Therefore the extensionalist approach to tropes, clearly decipherable from Campbell's short remark, is not acceptable.

So far we have got insight into the individuation of tropes and the individuation of their bearer substances respectively. It has been claimed that the individuation of the tropes, apart from their qualitative identity, hinges on the individuation of the bearer substance. As to the individuation of the bearer substance, this has been pointed out: given the independent resources of individuation available to concrete entities but not available to abstract entities like the tropes, the individuation of the substances is non-circular despite the fact that ultimately, for the analysis, they are bundles of compresent tropes hanging together in mutual foundation.

The main attraction of this solution is that the individuation of tropes does not remain, *pace* Campbell, "unanalysable". In fact, one of the defects of Campbell's theory is that it is unable to account for the individuation of the very items that he takes to be ontologically basic. My solution, as admitted, goes with essentialist commitments *plus* non-transferability and bearer uniqueness. In Campbell's view, by contrast,

---

[93] Campbell, *op.cit.*, 25.

the basic ontological items with primitive individuation are not the sort of dependent entities that can belong only to substances in Aristotelian manner. As the alphabets of being, tropes are around as ontological building blocks. For Campbell, on his "no-substance view, some tropes, the monadic ones, can stand on their own as Humean independent subsistents, while the others, the polyadic ones, are in an unavoidably dependent position".[94] This ontological stance, however, leads to weird consequences in the metaphysics and logic of *relations*. This is what I shall examine next.

For Campbell the main difference between monadic and polyadic tropes is not structural involving the number of the terms; rather, the difference has to do with "ontic priority" enjoyed by the monadic tropes but not by the polyadic ones. The explanation of this weird position can be traced back to his one-category ontology: according to this "the only items available to be the terms of any relations are themselves tropes" and, as is familiar, "no relations can exist ... except where all their terms do".[95] Therefore the monadic tropes yielding the terms of relations must exist prior to the relational tropes with which they enter into relation. Campbell writes: " "Monadic tropes require no bearer, polyadic ones call for at least two, which will have to be themselves tropes"... "For this reason the trope philosophy cannot treat qualities and relations as differing only in the number of their bearer, a difference which carries no serious implications as to ontic priority".[96]

Now I think that justice can, and should, be done to the *logical difference* between monadic properties and relations without claiming a drastic ontological difference involving the criterion of dependence/independence. Campbell is forced into his position only because he adopts a one-category ontology. If, however, substances are

---

[94] Campbell, *op.cit.*, 99.

[95] Campbell, *op.cit.*, 98-99.

[96] Campbell, *op.cit.*, *ibid.*

also recognized, the difference between monadic properties and relations recognized also in trope-philosophy smoothly fits into the logical and metaphysical differences standardly approved. Next I pinpoint these differences and explain why a purely tropist ontology is not feasible admitting only particular relational facts while dispensing with relations as genuine universals.

As is known, the special metaphysical problem of relations is their dependence on their terms. In *Metaphysics* 1088a Aristotle spelled out his conviction that "of all things relations are the least real" and similarly, Locke in the *Essay* ch. II. 8. said that "relations are not contained in the real existence of things but are external to them". Plato in the *Parmenides* struggled with the epistemological problem of the "knowing" relation connecting relata of different logical levels.[97] Leibniz tried to eliminate relations in favor of monadic predicates and Bradley supported his ontological monism by finding fault both with internal and external relations. So, in a nutshell, relations are associated to a whole bunch of logical, ontological and metaphysical problems. We cannot imagine a world of relations with no substances but we can conceive of a world of just one single substance without being related to other things. So relations need terms, and there is the problem of locating relations. For they are neither in any one, nor in both or all, of the relata. A special problem is that the reductive treatment of relations by eliminating them in favor of monadic properties is not feasible, as is known from logical considerations: relational propositions like aRb, that is, a's being R-related to b, can not be made equivalent to monadic propositions. For example, the relational fact expressed by the relational proposition

---

[97] Epistemic relations enjoy a special status not only in Plato's sense. Also, they are special as to the existence-requirements with respect to the relata. For example, "thinking of" is typically the kind of relation that does not require the real existence of the object of thought as a relatum because the object can have a purely *notional* existence as well. Thus one can think *of* the Golden Mountain without the latter actually existing, moreover, without being capable of existence. Such two-term epistemic relations with a missing relatum are called Brentanist relations.

"Romeo loves Juliet" is not equivalent to the conjunction of non-relational facts like "Romeo loves and in virtue of Romeo's loving Juliet is loved", etc. The abundance of literature on this topic clearly shows its metaphysical significance.

Relational facts like the one can be taken to form a similarity class. Various relata can be coupled with "love" to form a relational fact. The question arises whether it is sensible to posit a "love" relation over and above the particular relational facts of loving, and obviously the same applies to other relations and relational facts. Or, perhaps, it is better to scrunch up relations into particular relational facts. Then, in this case, the question arises what would relate these particular relational facts in order to form the appropriate similarity class. For some connection is required for the purpose of recognizing the common content of these particular claims. However, the introduction of a further connecting link gives impetus to a relation regress; while recognizing the need for a common factor paves the way to universalism. Arguably, one can hardly manage without a common factor; the invocation, however, of the threat of relation regress is somewhat unfair, since the same kind of regress threatens both the realist and the nominalist constructions of property instantiation.

The cheap but frequently applied solution, suggested first by Armstrong, is to declare that instantiation is a "non-relational tie". Now what is sauce for the goose is sauce for the gander: if instantiation as a relation can be eliminated, presumably the same applies to other relations as well. So relations in general seem to be dispensable, at first glance, over particular relational facts. What prevents me from approving the cheap solution is that there are two major complications with this suggestion.

One is the problem of changing arity. For example, the relation of "compresence" pertinent to **BT** is a relation with changing arity. While it suffices for a simple individual like a colour patch to exhibit the compresence of a colour trope, an extension trope and a texture trope, much more tropes have to be compresent in order to make a sophisticated artifact, like a computer. Now if we decided to accept only particular compresences with a varying number of relata, would not it prevent us from recognizing that these are all cases *of* compresence? *If there were no universal "compresence" with the structural feature of changing arity, recognized as such, we could not even entertain the very notion of the bundle theory of substances.* So **BT**, even the tropist variant, has the universal 'compresence' among its presupposition. For this notion presupposes that there is a common relation over and above the particular relational facts to base the theory on. No surprise then, that Bacon in his trope theory acknowledges compresence and other "metarelations" that are clearly not dissolvable into particular relational tropes.

Bacon writes: "I wouldn't go so far as to advertise [trope theory] with Campbell ... as a one-category ontology. As we have seen, it requires at the very least a category of tropes and a category of relations of tropes, or metarelations, as I have called them". Also: we are left "with ontological atoms of at least two kinds: tropes and relations (whether first-level or second-level)".[98]

The other problem that also points towards the conceptual necessity of positing relations is also *structural*. It consists in that relational tropes involve *aspectual* concurrence as opposed to simple concurrence in the subject. *Aspectual* concurrence can be explained as follows. Monadic tropes are typically identified by their bearers: within the set of exactly resembling tropes what makes Socrates' wisdom trope different from Plato's wisdom trope is the mere fact that the former belongs only to Socrates. Polyadic tropes, however, are not so easily identifiable by reference to the bearer since they do not have *just one* bearer. Rather, they obtain among more relata *in a structured way*. Thus, "Othello's loving Desdemona" and "Othello's trusting Iago" are tropes that concur in contributing Othello as a subject: both yield the relational features of the Othello-substance. By contrast, "Iago's hating Othello" is a trope that concerns Iago at the first argument place and concerns Othello only in

---

[98] Bacon (1995) ch. 5., pp. 72., 77.

the second argument place, in the object position. Therefore the trope "Iago's hating Othello" and the trope "Othello's loving Desdemona" do not yield "Othello" in the same way. The logical solution adopted by Bacon is to relativize the tropes' concurrence to argument places numbered in sequence. This is not very complicated technically, although it is more complicated than simply assigning Othello's courage trope and Othello's jealousy trope to the Othello bundle. But there remains the vexing metaphysical problem: how to treat the *orders* of these *aspectual concurrences* from ontological of view? Could the orders of aspectual concurrences be taken as particulars or are we compelled to recognize them under the heading of a *universal structure*?

Obviously, the structural aspects are not dissolvable into particular facts, therefore relations must be recognized apart from particular relational facts. At this point I part company with Campbell and join Bacon and, as a recent advocate of relations, Vallicella. It is an especially acute question with the trope account of individual substances whether the bundling relation specifically, and relations in general, are supposed to be universals *or* irreducibly relational tropes dependent on the monadic tropes they relate. If they are treated as universals, that is, repeatables, then we get a distinction between the universal of "compresence" or "concurrence" and the particular "relatedness" by compresence of, say, a given extension trope and a given colour trope making thereby an unrepeatable relational fact. The need for such a distinction is urged by Vallicella. As he points out, the distinction might collapse on the trope account: "if relations are, or are reducible to, particulars, then there are no relations as distinct from relational facts". However, "if there are relations then they must be universals", states Vallicella.[99]

Relations, from a logical point of view, are the kind of "unsaturated" entities that are not reducible to monadic properties, and the number of

---

[99] Vallicella (2002) pp.15., 16.

terms they require depend on the arity of the relation in question, though some relations have changing arities.

I have started out with the putative 'ontic' difference envisaged by Campbell. Now we can see that it produces further complications. If polyadic tropes can exist only in virtue of there being monadic tropes to sustain them, the monadic tropes serve as *foundations* of the relation. Say, two jackets stand in "*being the same colour*" relation. This means, according to Campbell, that "the monadic colour features of the jackets are thus the *foundations* of the same-colour relation between those jackets."[100]

It has to be noted here that "foundation" in Campbell's sense is not the same as the Husserlian relation of mutual foundation adopted by Simons in his two-tier theory discussed later. [101] Foundationism in Campbell's sense refers to the thesis that relations supervene on qualities; for example, "being the same colour" supervenes on the colours of the jackets. The other feature of his foundationism is its "*denial of external relations*". This denial is a vulnerable aspect of Campbell's account; I shall focus on it.

Foundationism is hardly compatible with the acceptance of external relations, since these external relations hold independently of the intrinsic characteristics of their terms. For example, spatial relations are typically external: we may replace, say, two chairs with each other without affecting any of the intrinsic properties of these chairs. While changing their location, they remain qualitatively the same. Now the foundationist commitment is indispensable for Campbell's one-category ontology because in it the relational tropes are existentially dependent on the monadic tropes as their foundations. So he seems to be compelled to eliminate what is excluded by foundationism, i.e. the external relations.

---

[100] Campbell, *op.cit.*, 101.

[101] About Husserlian foundation see chapter V. pp. 128-30.

But since the price is too high, Campbell seeks a compromise, as I show soon. I also explain why Campbell's foundationism required by his one-category ontology has unfortunate consequences for the basic relation of "compresence" required *also* by his one-category ontology. These will be my last critical points with respect to Campbell's theory.

Although foundationism serving the goals of a one-category ontology conflicts with the very idea of external relations, Campbell is well aware of the problem how disastrous it would be to embrace the doctrine that "all relations are internal". Now the notion of "internal relation" in its particular version put forward by the classical British idealists, notably, Bradley implies that such relations flow from the very nature of the terms. In other words, they flow from what is essential to the identity of these terms. This is the notion of internal relations criticized by Moore and others to the effect that it does not leave room for contingent truths, since on this notion all the truths follow from the essential features of the relata.

As opposed to this, today the main criterion of 'being internal relation' is supervenience on the properties of the relata. For example, you have to have a certain height and I have to have a certain height in order for the particular relational fact of you being taller than me to obtain. And the modal character of the properties of the relata is irrelevant: we both contingently have our given heights. So the contemporary notion of 'internal relations' carries no essentialist commitments. And, obviously, external relations are not suspect of essentialism either. These are good news for the tropists since the chief gluing relation of tropes, i.e. 'compresence' counts today a contingent external relation.

To solve the conflict of foundationism and external relations Campbell splits the typical two-fold division of internal and external relations into a three-fold division comprising also "relations which exist in virtue of foundations and yet which are in Moore's terminology *external*...."[102] That is, Campbell makes room for *external founded* relations which are founded on their terms, but are not essential to the identity of those terms. His example is the "being a cleaner shoe than" relation. Clearly, this relation supervenes on the given cleanness of the shoes as terms involved; however, these states of cleanness do not characterize essentially the shoes. In other possible worlds where these shoes both exist, they might have another state of cleanness. Apart from the category of external founded relations, Campbell also recognizes *external unfounded* relations: these can be highlighted with the typical example of spatial relations explained above.

Now changes in the criteria I have just explained has consequences for Campbell's categorizations: namely, his "external founded relations" smoothly fit into Vallicella's recent categorization under the heading "internal contingent relation".[103] Vallicella points out that the contemporary view of internal relations, as opposed to the classical view, does not require essential features and does not tie the very existence of the relata to the obtaining of certain internal relation. Rather, internal relations are those that hold in virtue of the intrinsic properties of the relata where the intrinsic properties need not be conceived as exclusively essential ones. Some intrinsic properties can be accidental to the very identity and nature of the relata. To return to Campbell's example, it is purely accidental to shoes whether they are clean or dirty and to what degrees. Still, the relation they enter into depends on the actual state of cleanness of these shoes. Therefore "being a cleaner shoe than" qualifies as an *internal contingent relation.*

The difference between Vallicella's classification and Campbell's is not merely verbal without consequences. Campbell accepts the old, classical notion of "internal relations" with the weird feature that a thing with internal relations could not be what it is apart from its multifarious

---

[102] Campbell, *op.cit.*, 111.

[103] Vallicella, W.F. (2002), pp. 3-5.

relations to some other things. This ontological inter-relatedness supports monism and works against pluralistic ontologies. And to preserve the traditional close connection between "internal" and "essential", Campbell re-labels "internal contingent relations" as "external founded relations". However, if one adopts an ontology with individual substances, the one I propose, then Vallicella's notion of internal relations applicable both to essential and contingent features of the relata seems to be more appropriate.

For these reasons I suggest a better division: according to it there are internal essential relations, internal contingent relations *and* external relations not supervening on the intrinsic features of the relata. These latter are the "external unfounded relations" in Campbell's sense. That is, the *external* relations we have got could serve well the needs of those ontologies that seek to accommodate the plurality of independent individual substances. The postulation of *founded* external relations would only be confusing from this perspective.

The upshot is that there remain only *external unfounded* relations; some of them are crucial, indeed, for the trope-ontology. Take "compresence", one of the central relations of the trope account of substances. This is typically an external relation that can be taken only as "external unfounded" relation, since it does not supervene on particular qualitative features. For example, extension tropes, shape tropes and colour tropes are typically compresent in macroscopic dry goods; but the relation of compresence does not supervene on *determinate* extensions, shapes, colours, etc. So, the basic tension within Campbell's theory is this: while his one-category ontology requires a foundationist account of relations "compresence" as the chief gluing relation does not fit into his foundationist scheme.

To summarize: apart from this weakness of being unable to provide for compresence, the other deficiency of Campbell's theory, as I have indicated earlier, is the lack of any cogent solution to the individuation of tropes. The individuation of tropes is declared by him to be an unanalyzable, primitive fact. None of these deficiencies show themselves on the *substance-trope view* that I support here.

Bacon's trope theory differs from Campbell's in the crucial respect that genuine relations are recognized over and above particular relational facts. Since I have already mentioned this virtue I comment now only on two further features of Bacon's theory: both are highly relevant to the trope-bundle view of substances. One is his answer to the question whether tropes should be associated only with fully determinate properties, the so-called "syntropic" properties, or, with the more generic properties typically construed as universals. The choice between the fully determinate properties and the generic properties as the "real" content of tropes is obviously not independent from the reception of universals in trope theory. The other feature of Bacon's theory is its set-theoretical construal of substances and properties.

As to the fine-tuning of tropes Bacon opts for fully determinate properties as the content of tropes. The best way to illuminate his view is to approach from the semantic side. Predicates with adverbial modifications yield the more specific properties: for example, while "walks" is a generic property, "walks slowly" is a specific one: every slow walk is a walk but not the other way round. This would imply, in Boolean terms, the inclusion of the set of "slow walks" into the set of "walks" *simpliciter*. However, the inclusion relation is obviated by the construal of properties as similarity-sets which is the fairly standard treatment of properties in trope-theory. According to this, the properties are sets of resembling tropes; so the set of 'slow walkings' contain similar 'slow walkings' that are both 'slow' and 'walkings' and 'slow *as* walkings'. Now the property is identified with this resemblance-set. Obviously, if "walks slowly" is a property in this sense, then walks *simpliciter* will not resemble sufficiently to members of this set and it will qualify as a different property. By parity of reasoning, if "walks" is taken to be *the* property construed by a similarity-set, then, obviously, "walks slowly" will not fit into the set. However, it is intuitively clear that Boolean inclusion should hold, and this requirement is supported by the validity of the semantic adverb dropping inference. For example, from someone's walking slowly it follows someone's walking according to the adverb dropping inference. But the construal of properties as resemblance-sets on the trope theory commits one to denying such inferences and inclusions for the simple reason that, with our example, the set of "walks-tropes" and the set of "walks slowly tropes" constitute utterly different resemblance-sets with no shared members.

In face of these difficulties, Bacon's position as to what counts as the contents of tropes is that only the "syntropic properties" do. In other words, only the fully determinate and specific properties constitute the content of tropes. Thus, "being snub-nosed" gives a trope, while "having a nose" does not; similarly, "being 50 kg" gives a trope, while "having weight" does not, etc. Now this position is more the result of a decision than a thoughtful argument: for, although it is fairly obvious that determinable properties are not the best candidates for yielding the content of tropes, it is not at all clear how to construe then the universals as resemblance sets of tropes, once it is conceded that only the fully determinate features can be the members of such sets. This point cannot be ignored by Bacon who admits the existence of certain genuine universals: for example, he admits the existence of meta-relations. But the appropriate link between the universal features and the more specific, trope-like features is missing on his account.

The problem of the relation of determinables and determinates is particularly acute with the trope theory. For most tropists dispense with universals as multiply exemplifiable entities and take recourse instead either to resemblance classes of tropes or painless universals in Williams' sense. Universals denied by the trope theory typically figure as genus or determinables that relate in some way to the species or determinates. To admit, the Aristotelian genus-species division is not quite the same as the determinable-determinate division suggested by Johnson since the latter division does not necessarily carve out reality at its joints, whereas the genus-species division supposedly does. Whereas the Aristotelian division is meant to cope with the real structure of nature, determinates are quite often the results of adverbial, adjectival, etc. modifications of simple properties. That is, determinates owe their existence to semantic moves, rather than being based on scientific truths about the world. To take our previous example, if "walking" is taken to be the simple, determinable property, then "slow walking" may be regarded as the more specific, determinate property; but this not to say that "slow-walking" is an inherent feature of reality.

Now tropes are identified by Bacon with the content of fully specific, determinate or "syntropic" properties. I have already indicated my worry that this position makes it difficult for universals to be construed as sets of exactly resembling tropes. Loux spells out a similar criticism of trope theory. He points out that while the tropists confine themselves to fully determinate properties, they still cannot dispense with shared and sharable properties, i.e. universal-susceptible determinables. Loux writes: the tropists "believe that by their very nature attributes are particulars and so can be possessed by just one concrete particular. They might concede that attributes are multiply exemplifiable entities, but would argue that, given the actual structure of the empirical world, they never get multiply exemplified".[104] Now this still might not be the ultimate truth about the nature of properties and things. As Loux observes: "Actually, this claim is plausible only in the case of fully determinate universals. It is difficult to see how one could hold that, with respect to determinable universals like *being colored* or *having shape*, things are not exactly alike".[105] In other words, not even the trope theory can dispense with features susceptible of being universals.

The moral is that a monolithic trope theory is not tenable: universals as determinables are not dispensable. This result is in consonance with my position developed earlier to the effect that relations are indispensable over and above particular relational facts. And what is true of relations, i.e. polyadic properties, is equally true of monadic properties. However, this fact about the trope theory that it has to

---

[104] Loux, M. (1998), 80.

[105] Loux, M. *op.cit.*, 88.

compromise over the existence of certain genuine universals, need not be seen as something discomforting; it pinpoints only the limits of the trope approach. Thus sharable determinable features are also included in the bundles of the individual substances. Moreover, an account in terms of fully determinate features is not only ontologically inappropriate; it carries the drawback that a fully specific construal proves to be too rigid when it comes to accounting for change and identity through time.

The set-theoretical construal of properties as resemblance classes of tropes is unable to provide for properties under various specificity. The further problem is the relativity of determinates and determinables. In particular, what counts as determinate and what counts as determinable is not fixed but is relative to the context of discourse. Colouredness and the various colours yield the typical example of this relativity. For example, "red" is a determinate with respect to "colouredness", but it is a determinable with respect to a shade of red, say "maroon". Such relativity, a fairly common feature of semantic theories, has perplexing consequences. If classification of the properties within the determinable/determinate scheme varies with the context, colour-incompatibility remains unexplained.[106] Say, when 'red' and 'maroon' are both classified as determinates, they exclude each other, while with 'red' in the position of the determinable and 'maroon' in the position of determinate they are compatibles.

Here again, there is another example of the bad fit between the ontological trope theory and the semantic requirements. To recall, the bad fit was illuminated by the problem of predication not treated adequately within the trope theory. In the present case additional meaning postulates might help to locate the semantic incompatibilities. In a similar fashion, meaning postulates can be used to reveal the logical and the semantic connection between a verb and its adverbial modification like the one that obtains between "walks" and "slowly walks". With such aids the adverb-dropping inference can be explained.

---

[106] Bacon, J. *op.cit.*, 16.

But the ontological trope theory, taken in itself, cannot accomodate our semantic intuitions.

Let us return now to the set-theoretical construal. Bacon construes both individuals and properties as sets of tropes. The two fundamental relations in his scheme are: *concurrence* and *resemblance*. An individual is the maximal set of concurrent tropes; a property or universal is the maximal set of resembling tropes. For example, Socrates ={Socrates' wisdom, Socrates' baldness, Socrates' whiteness, etc.} and Whiteness = {Socrates' being white; Aristotle's being white, the White House's being white, etc.}

Now it is an essential feature of sets that their identity condition is given exclusively by membership. Thus, sets are the same iff they have the same members and a set retains its identity as long as it has the same members. The adoption of the set-theoretical criterion of identity, however, produces serious problems when the items thus construed are empirical. The whiteness-set, and thus *Whiteness*, is constituted by several empirical individuals' being white. Let us denote the property thus construed F and the various empirical individuals equipped with that property a, b, etc. It is quite clear that the F-*ness* set or bundle depends, in its very existence and identity, on a's being F, b's being F, etc. There is no guarantee, however that a will keep on being F forever, or b will keep on being F forever, etc., since empirical items change, come into being and perish. For this reason it would be fatal to construe properties which are eternal and necessary beings with the help of empirical, contingent things' instantiating them. This drawback of the "set-theoretical construal" is explicitly spelled out by van Cleve in his criticism of Bacon's theory. Cleve writes: "...if a had not been F, then one of the tropes constituting the F-*ness* bundle would not have existed, in which case presumably the bundle would not have existed, so nothing would have been F".[107]

---

[107] van Cleve (2000), 108.

The question arises whether what applies to sets, applies equally to bundles. Cleve talks about the 'drawback of set-theoretical construal' while in the passage cited he makes mention of 'bundles'. So the question is, how *sets* and *bundles* relate to each other. In fact, none of the authors on tropes and the set-theoretical construal feel compelled to clarify this issue. When talking about the bundle theory they make recourse to the familiar identity conditions of sets and, when talking about the drawbacks of the set-theoretical construal, the terminology slips carelessly to 'bundles'. To dissolve the confusion I would say that 'bundles' as pieces of metaphysics serve proxy for concrete entities even if they are bundles of abstract features, while 'sets' are entities of logic with a clear technical meaning. It is still appropriate to talk about the 'drawbacks of set-theoretical construal' in connection with bundles since sets and bundles have the same identity condition.

The identity conditions of sets inherited by bundles infects the latter with ultraessentialism as I have already indicated before. In fact, any reductive bundle-view of particulars is infected with ultraessentialism since the identity of the bundles depends on the identity of their elements. Thus every element actually had by the bundle is essential to the very identity of the bundle. The same goes for sets: sets have their members essentially. Though the term 'bundle' is less technical than the term 'set', most authors take it for granted that they have the same identity conditions: once again, the coined term 'bundle' seems to be only a looser façon de parler for them. But when it comes to disambiguating the identity claims, the technically neat term 'set' is typically used instead. The only difference is that 'bundle' is reserved for metaphysical purposes. This special application, however, does not affect the clear-cut identity conditions of bundles *as sets*.

Let us see now, as the last topic of the chapter, what the standard objections are to the trope theory. Hopefully, none of them will be devastating for the enterprise of applying tropes to the bundle construal of substances.

The following objections have to be commented on: the *spatio-temporality* objection; the *multiple instance* objection; the *individuation* objection; and the *swapped tropes* objection. The further semantic objection to the effect that the trope theory is inefficient in explaining predication and abstract reference has already been discussed.

The *spatio-temporality* objection particularly relevant to **BT** is spelled out by Campbell. The starting point is that tropes are the kind of particulars that are both abstract and have a well-defined spatio-temporal location. Now it is difficult for a one-category ontology of tropes to provide for abstract but non-locatable existents like numbers, sets, propositions, etc,. As Campbell asks, "how could a trope philosophy accommodate non-locational particularity?"[108] That is, how could a trope philosophy explain the existence of numbers, propositions, etc? This style of objection is pertinent to trope **BT** via some modification; we can add to Campbell's question an equally vexing question that has remained unstated. Given trope **BT**, i.e. the view that concrete individual substances are made up of tropes, we could equally ask: how could a trope philosophy accommodate *concrete* particularity? The fact that tropes have spatio-temporal location does not automatically turn a bundle of tropes into a *concrete* particular.

To be clear, the characterization of tropes as items that are both abstract *and* spatio-temporal is not inconsistent; that is, the problem is not *what* specifically the tropes are. I have already clarified that abstractness can meet different criteria. Although quite a lot of abstract entities are also non-spatio-temporal, like numbers, sets, etc., something can be abstract according to other criteria as well, say, by featuring the qualitative manifold only from one aspect and being dependent on some bearer. Tropes qualify as abstract according to these two criteria.

In his purported answer to the question about non-locational abstract particularity, Campbell makes recourse to extended concepts of

---

[108] Campbell, *op.cit.*, 54.

dimensionality, like *ordering* that generates a quasi-dimensionality. Maybe, this is applicable to numbers so, that one can remain within one-category tropism. But it is hard to imagine how the non-locational feature of propositions could be accounted for with quasi-dimensionality. Propositions are not to be identified with utterances and therefore one cannot make appeal, say, to the acoustic dimension. I think the best solution is to confine the trope theory to its most promising field of application, i.e., the explanation of individual substances having qualitative features. And a big portion of the abstract realm, the traditional realm of platonic realism requires an alternative explanation. I can see no reason to entertain the notion of "Being as such" conceived typically as something utterly homogeneous.

There remains the other question though: how could a bundle-of-tropes account of individual substances accommodate *concrete* particularity? This question is connected to the so-called *spatio-temporal* objection in so far as the criterion of spatio-temporality cuts across the abstract/concrete division. For example, both the abstract tropes and the concrete individual substances have spatio-temporal location, still this shared feature alone is incapable of accounting for the emergence of concrete independent entities like substances out of the bundling of abstract dependent entities, the tropes. In fact, a standard objection leveled first by Armstrong against the bundle-of-tropes view of substances is that no bundling of the dependent tropes would yield an independent entity.[109] We can add now that no bundling of the *abstract* dependent tropes would yield a *concrete* independent entity.

So the task is to accommodate the difference, in the ontological status, of *what* is bundled and the bundle or collection *itself*. One way would be to argue that denying the role of bundling in making an independent, concrete entity out of dependent abstract entities is, in fact, committing the *fallacy of composition*. The fallacy consists in the unjustified assumption that what is true of the elements of the bundle is

---

[109] see Armstrong (1989b), 115.

logically true of their collection. Thus, if the elements of the bundle are abstract, so is the bundle itself. To highlight the fallacy, we can say, in a similar fashion, that each book in a library collection may be good in itself without the library collection being good *as* a collection. This being made clear we can claim that the bundle may have an ontological status different from the ontological status of the elements of the bundle.[110] Eliminating the fallacy, however, is not sufficient, in itself, to explain the emergence of concrete independent entities out of the bundling of dependent abstract entities. This problem will be more thoroughly discussed with the help of Husserlian *mutual foundation*.

As to the other three objections, the *individuation* problem should be settled first, since its solution has some bearing both on *multiple-instance* and *swapping*. To recall Campbell's point, tropes cannot be individuated by reference to their places, since this would have the uncomfortable consequence that co-located tropes of various natures would collapse into one. Say, a colour trope and an extension trope, if co-located, would count as one on this approach. There is the further possibility though, of individuating tropes by reference to their bearers. This suggestion faces the charge of circularity whenever substances are construed as collections of tropes. This has already been explained away by pointing out that concrete substances, even if they are constructions of tropes, have their own identity conditions different from the identity conditions of their tropes.

Thus, we have concluded that tropes are individuated via their bearer substance in a non-circular way. The question arises now whether this solution to the individuation problem matches with purported answers to the *multiple-instance objection.* The multiple-instance objection discussed by Armstrong, Moreland and Campbell is this: there is no principled constraint to the effect that only tropes with different qualities

---

[110] This argument about the fallacy of composition has been put forward by Vallicella in order to defend the bundle view. See Vallicella, (1997), 93.

could be co-located.[111] In other words, it is not the case that, say, a colour trope and a texture trope could be co-located, while two or more exactly resembling colour tropes, or two or more exactly resembling texture tropes could not. Nothing prevents a thing's having two or more exactly resembling colour tropes to be compresent. A red plastic ball might have several red-tropes on the same part of its surface and similarly, many plastic-texture tropes might be found on any arbitrary part of the balls' surface. With the positing of universals as the elements of the bundle this scenario is excluded. For a universal is the same both qualitatively and numerically in every instantiation. Thus it is the numerically same redness and the numerically same plastic-ness that make the plastic ball all over in its physical appearance. Moreover, it is the numerically same redness and the numerically same plastic-ness that make other plastic balls as well.

With tropes, however, the situation is different. The principle of bearer uniqueness secures that the exactly resembling tropes belonging to different substances are numerically distinct. But what would prevent *one* substance from having numerically different, but exactly resembling colour tropes, or numerically different, but exactly resembling texture tropes, etc.? Perhaps, an extended use of Leibniz's Principle might help to answer the multiple-instance objection. Embracing it I would say that if two or more tropes are exactly resembling *and* share the same location, and they are individuated by reference to the same bearer substance then they qualify as one trope rather than many.

In this vein my earlier solution to the *problem of individuation* of tropes affords a solution to the *multiple-instance objection* as well. But this is not the only answer on offer: Campbell has another suggestion perfectly in accordance with traditional empiricism. Campbell notes that the *causal power* of the second, third, etc., co-located trope with the exactly resembling quality cannot be told apart from the causal power of

---

[111] Armstrong (1978) vol. I., 86., Moreland, J.P. *Universals, Qualities and Quality-Instances: A Defense of Realism* (1985), quoted by Campbell, op.cit. 66-67.

the first trope with the exactly resembling quality. Therefore the supposition of these further items makes no difference to the physical description of the substance. This retort has not only a verificationist overtone: it is also the best strategy to *occamise* the theory, thereby getting rid of undesirable entities.

The *multiple-instance objection* explores the feature of tropes that various exactly resembling tropes can be co-located. Now the *swapped tropes objection* explores the putative feature that place is not essential to the identity of tropes. Therefore two tropes F1 and F2 with exact qualitative resemblance but different places can be swapped for one another. This scenario would leave everything as it is in the description of the world. One would not discern any difference before and after the swapping. I think, the swapping-scenario can be dismissed on verificationist grounds: if no difference is discernible by empirical means then there is no reason to suppose that the difference exists, even though it cannot be excluded a priori.

To meet the swapped tropes objection Campbell takes recourse to the difference in the individuation of the tropes. He thinks that there is a difference, although not detectable. As he says, "the difference between F1 and F2 is a difference of individuation only"..."Once we recognize this we can see that it is not true to say that the swap produces *absolutely* no difference in the situation".[112]

His answer, however, does not seem felicitous, particularly not in the light of his previous answer to the individuation of tropes. Since Campbell declared that the individuation of tropes is a primitive, unanalysable fact about them, it would be absurd to appeal to primitive individuation to explain undetectable differences. One unknown factor would thus be 'explained' by another unknown factor.

---

[112] Campbell, op.cit., 71-2.

I have surveyed the main criticisms of the trope philosophy. None of them proved to be decisive against my particular concern, the trope **BT**. However, a full answer to the question how to accommodate *concrete* particularity requires further inquiry into the details of the trope account.

V. Two-tier Bundle Theories of Substance. Objections to BT

Three two-tier bundle theories of substance will be discussed now; none is a tropist account. It is still worth considering them because the incorporation of two tiers in the theory captures an important insight. To anticipate, the modal problem of substances being vulnerable to change through time can be dealt with by distinguishing two tiers with different roles. In the meantime the main objections to **BT** will be critically assessed.

Interestingly enough, the theories of Castaneda, Cleve, and Casullo, while all qualifying as two-tier theories, center around different metaphysical themes and background assumptions. Castaneda goes back to the old-style phenomenalism and considers the account of substances in terms of constructions out of perceptible data. His concern is how ontological claims can be developed on the basis of some prior epistemological perspective. Casullo's two-tier account is basically perdurantist and is strongly motivated both by the temporal part doctrine of substances and Castaneda's bundle-bundle theory. Cleve presupposes a hard core and an outer fringe to the substance such that the former is credited with essential elements while the latter is credited with contingent elements. Cleve's position is basically universalist though he considers briefly the advantages of the bundles being made up of tropes rather than universals. Only Simons' two-tier theory having roughly the same structural features as Cleve's account, is explicitly *tropist*. This will be discussed in the next chapter.

The old-style bundle theory in classical empiricist spirit can be described by the slogan that a substance "is nothing but a bundle of perceivable qualities". This simple formulation, as it stands, is not able to provide either for the unity of the substances or for their concreteness, let alone other possible objections like the one about essential predication. Sophisticated versions of the theory introduce a special gluing relation. They also account for essential and accidental predication and try to bridge the gap between the epistemological perspective and ontological claims.

Castaneda's version belongs to this latter type. He starts out with "ontological guises" or "facets". These are the objects *as* presented in perception from a certain perspective or aspect. For example, the view of a house from a certain perceptual perspective is one of its facets; it is not the full and complete presentation of the house. Ontological guises are thus a special sort of *qua*-objects. They do not serve proxy for the objects themselves since they carry a certain perspectival limitation. They cannot be taken as the whole object in its reality, only a perspectival slice of it. Although Castaneda introduces ontological guises with the perceptual perspective of the perciever, they can be understood as *qua-objects* on the level of concept formation as well. This admission is clearly revealed by Castaneda's remark to the effect that ontological guises are "like Frege's individual senses or Carnap's individual concepts, or, the finite ontological guises are akin to Meinong's incomplete objects". For example, if I have the concept of a given house as *the* White House, then, what I have is the individual concept of a *qua-object* under a certain mode of presentation. Every object is, for us, the sum total of the qua-objects associated to it.

The special feature of these senses or concepts is that their content is structured: they are constituted by a set of monadic properties plus an individuating factor. Thus an ontological guise "is an entity of the form $c\alpha$ where c is the individuating operator and α is the set of monadic properties".[113] Now this structure of ontological guises resembles to the familiar representation of concrete individual substances in terms of properties *plus* some factor responsible for individuation. What is missing from Castaneda's approach, however, is, what the individuating

---

[113] Castaneda, H. N. (1977), 321.

operator actually amounts to and how it accomplishes its role. For example, in virtue of what can such an operator turn a set of sharable monadic properties into a unique individual guise? Given the problem of propertiless individuators discussed at length earlier, what makes a propertiless factor accomplish individuation?

The main merit of Castaneda's approach is that it affords an alternative to the simple classical bundle view presenting physical objects as mere bundles or collections of perceptible properties. According to Castaneda, the bundles of properties that we meet in perception are guises or facets but not the physical objects themselves. Objective claims about physical objects can be made only with the help of combining, so to speak, these guises into a *complex* of guises. Thus "physical objects are complexes of guises, not an altogether different new type of individual over and above the guises". The distinguishing feature of Castaneda's approach is that it reaches an ontological position about physical objects *via* the epistemological access to various perceptual and conceptual perspectives. In this sense it remains within the empiricist tradition broadly speaking, while offering a more sophisticated account. Formally, Castaneda's account is a "*bundle-bundle theory*": "First, our basic bundles, namely ontological guises, are composed of properties processed, so to speak, by the individuator. Second, our derived bundles, namely, physical objects, are not bundles of properties, but bundles of guises bundled up by a very special relation". [114] This special relation is, in Castaneda's, terminology, "consubstantiation". He denotes the gluing relation with this coined term presumably because he wants to emphasize that a substantial unity emerges as a result of gluing and not mere co-occurrence.

Thus a physical object is a *bundle of bundles*; more precisely, it is a *derived bundle* or a *consubstantiated* bundle. Its elements are the basic bundles; while the latter have properties as their elements. The question arises, then, whether there is a difference, apart from the purely

---

[114] Castaneda, *op.cit.*, 322.

structural one, between these two bundlings. In fact, there is. To continue with Castaneda's characterization of bundle-bundles: "...while the first stage of bundling involves internal predication, the second one involves external predication". (*ibid*) Although Castaneda does not define these predications, it becomes clear from the context that internal predication applies to properties in the core of the guise and external predication applies whenever a further property is ascribed to the core. "A guise c{P1,P2,...Pn}-s having a property not in its core just is c{P1,P2,...Pn}-s being E consubstantiated with the guise c{P1,P2,...Q}".[115] "E" refers here to external predication. On the face of it, this division functions like the division between essential and contingent predication. The former holds in virtue of the very essence of the core; the latter holds in virtue of the fact that the core has certain contingent properties.

The significance of the distinction is this: any bundle theory is plagued, recall, with the threat of essential predication. All the properties of the bundle turn out to be essential on the set-theoretical construal. In order to avoid this and to provide for the possibility of accidental predication, external predication is introduced. External predication does the job of ascribing accidental or contingent properties to the core consisting of essential properties.

But, perhaps, there is more to the distinction between internal and external predication than to do different modal jobs. Castaneda connects the epistemological and the metaphysical perspectives in a sophisticated way. The 'first stage of bundling' producing the facets and belonging to the epistemological perspective is "internal" according to him since our epistemic access to things meets internal criteria, at least for internalist epistemologies. While the second level of bundling resulting in physical things 'involves external predication' since the ontological perspective, which is presumably objective, is external to the single facets taken separately.

---

[115] Castaneda, *op.cit.*, 325.

External predication thus explained is different from, though provides for, accidental predication. Now **BT** requires accidental predication as well and Castaneda declares that 'consubstantiation' is such an accidental tie.

By contrast, Cleve finds that all predication is *essential* with the bundle theory, and, as a consequence, this theory cannot account for the identity of substances through time. Cleve explicitly develops his objections against universalist **BT**, mainly along the lines of targeting essential predication. I try to assess Cleve's objections from the point of view of the trope-bundle theory as well, thereby checking the putative merits of the trope-construal over the universalist construal. Then I shall present Casullo's defense of **BT** against Cleve's charges. As we shall see, Casullo tries to restate Castaneda's claim about the possibility of accidental predication within the frame of **BT**. To anticipate, Casullo's defense appeals to a perdurantist theory of identity through time. Let us look first at Cleve's objections before turning to Casullo's defense.

We shall see that out of Cleve's six objections the first three can immediately be answered by appealing to the *contingency* of the *co-instantiation* relation tying together the members of the bundles. These members are, in Cleve's discussion, generic properties or universals, and not tropes. In fact, we shall see that the *first*, the *second* and the *sixth* objections can successfully be met if universals are replaced by tropes in the formulation. I shall begin with spelling out the merits of trope-properties in my response to the objections. So, the trope-bundle construal has to face only the *fourth* and the *fifth* objections.

"*Objection 1.* If a thing were nothing more than a set of properties, any set of properties would fulfill the conditions of thinghood, and there would be a thing for every set. But in fact there are many sets without corresponding thing - e.g., the set {being an alligator, being purple}."[116]

Now a tropist can reply as follows to *Objection 1.*: he can point out that tropes are individuated by reference to the bearer substance and that they depend for their very existence on these substances. Therefore only those sets of trope-like qualitative features fulfill the conditions of thinghood that already pertain to substances. Further, if the possibility of trope-transfer is also excluded, then no arbitrary set of tropes can vindicate the unjustified claim of going proxy for individual substances.

"*Objection 2.* If a thing were a set of properties, it would be an eternal, indeed, a necessary, being. For properties exist necessarily, and a set exists necessarily if all its members do."[117]

Now *Objection 2.* actually splits into two claims and the difference has a bearing on the trope account. For, it is one thing to say that properties are *necessary* beings and it is another to say that sets are *necessarily* characterized by their members, whether these are properties or not. The latter claim is about the essentiality of set-membership.

As to the first claim of *Objection 2*, properties are in fact necessary existents but the same does not seem to apply to tropes. Tropes are dependent entities: they exist only in so far as the bearer substance does. Moreover, as the substance changes in time, earlier tropes perish and succumb to later ones. For example, when water is heated, the different temperature tropes with rising temperature give way to each other in succession. Therefore tropes are not necessary existents for two reasons even if their abstractness would qualify them for the status of necessary beings. One reason is the existence of the bearer is purely contingent, so that, for example, with no Socrates in this world there does not exist the "snub-nosedness-of-Socrates" trope in this world. The other reason is

---

[116] Cleve, J. van (1985), (2001), 121-22. Reference is made to (2001)

[117] Cleve, ibid.

that tropes are subject to replacement. They come into being and perish, while universals are immune from change. Therefore the problem of the necessary existence of the members of the bundle arises only with universal properties as members.

The other claim in *Objection 2.* is that sets are defined essentially by their members. This claim holds independently of *what* the members of the sets are; i.e. whether they are universals or tropes. But the crucial point for the present concern is whether any set of qualitative features gives a concrete empirical object. In fact, this part of the objection belongs more to *Objection 1.* than to *Objection 2.* For, remember, *Objection 1.* centers around the question whether a set, and hence an object, is automatically yielded by available member-candidates being around. The correct reply, I think, is that just as no states of affair, say, Fa, is automatically given by the existence of F and a separately, similarly, no ordinary empirical object is yielded automatically by an arbitrary set of qualitative features.

"*Objection 3.* Exemplification cannot be analyzed simply as the converse of membership. Redness is a member of {redness, roundness}, but it would be absurd - a category mistake - to say that the set is red."[118]

Since Cleve is not a tropist, his reply to the first three objections is this: since the elements of the bundle are tied together by the contingent relation of co-instantiation, no set will automatically yield an object unless the members are mutually co-instantiated. But it is contingent whether the members are co-instantiated. The same reply suffices for the worry about the thing's putative necessary existence, since the bundle ceases to exist if the members cease to be co-instantiated.

In order to evade *Objection 3.* concerning the conflation of exemplification and the converse of membership, Cleve explores the very same conceptual resource: "for a bundle to be red it is not enough

---

[118] Cleve, *ibid.*

that it have redness as a constituent; in addition, its members must be co-instantiated, and it must be *complete*, i.e., it must contain every property that could be added to it without generating inconsistency".[119]

This reply, it seems, misses the point of the objection as originally stated by Cleve himself. For the main thrust of Cleve's *Objection 3.* is *not* the incompleteness of the bundle but that it is a 'category mistake' to identify things with sets or bundles of properties. For things having properties is a matter quite different from sets having members. The post box is red but its being red is not the converse of the post box bundle containing redness as a member. What is missing is the step from *bundlehood* to *thinghood*; and this step cannot be made with set-theoretical resources. The bundle-construal is only the best available explanation *for epistemological purposes* but not a full ontological reduction of the individual substances.

The next three objections of Cleve, however, are more difficult to meet. Moreover, the fourth and the fifth apply whether the members of the bundles are universals of tropes. However, immunity to objection six is a chief merit of tropist **BT**, as I shall show. Let us see them.

"*Objection 4*. If a thing were a set of properties, it would be incapable of change. For a thing could change its properties only if the set identical with it could change its members, but that is impossible; no set can change its members.

Objection 5. Similarly, if a thing were a set of properties, all of its properties would be *essential* to it: not only could it not change its properties, but it could not have had different properties to start with. This is because it is essential to a set that it contains the very members it does.

Objection 6. If a thing were a set of properties, it would be impossible for two things to have all the same properties, since it is impossible for

---

[119] Cleve, *op.cit.*, 124.

two sets to have all the same members. Thus, the bundle theory requires the Principle of the Identity of Indiscernibles (**PII** for short) to be a necessary truth. But **PII** is not a necessary truth; exceptions to it are conceivable."[120]

Thus there remain three main objections to the bundle theory that cannot be so easily dismissed by invoking the *contingency of the co-instantiation* relation. To account for change and accidental predication and also to avoid commitment to the strong version of **PII** are the tasks for the bundle theories.

As to the last objection, i.e. **BT** implying **PII**, more precisely, the *strong version* of **PII**, note that it has been discussed earlier where I we made clear that this objection does not arise on the trope construal of the bundles. [121] For tropes making up different bundles can only be 'exactly similar', but never numerically the same, since tropes are unshared entities. Thus two numerically distinct individuals can be constituted by bundles of exactly resembling tropes without their distinctness being threatened.

Objection 6th has, however, its full force with universalist **BT**. To recall, it was pointed out before that the bundle theorist cannot avoid the counterintuitive consequence of **BT** that no two numerically distinct individuals can share all their pure properties by admitting also impure properties in the constitution of individual substances. The putative escape route with impure properties like spatial and temporal characteristics explores the fact that these characteristics are not fully shared by any two numerically distinct concrete individuals; so the bundle-theory could account for the numerical distinctness of the individuals with the help of pure *and* impure properties.

---

[120] Cleve, op.cit., 122.

[121] See chapter I.

Alas, this could be done only on pain of circularity: for, the bundle theorist strives at explaining individuals reductively with the help of qualitative features. In doing so, he cannot take recourse to other individuals "smuggled in" into the impure properties whose description contains reference to individual constants like "being at the Tropic of Cancer", "being born in the year of the French Revolution", etc. Thus the bundle-theorist is committed to *strong* **PII** with pure properties: he has to maintain that no two numerically distinct concrete individuals can share all their pure properties.

The intuitive falsity of this claim backed by numerous counterexamples forced the *universalist* bundle theorist to devise various defensive strategies. Now if any of these strategies could prove to be successful, the attraction of the alternative *tropist* bundle theory would be considerably diminished. However, the defensive lines surveyed earlier seemed to be vulnerable in various ways. Remember, Russell suggested that location in the visual field of the perceiver might be recognized among the constituting monadic properties of the objects. Since no two objects occupy the same position in the visual field, strong **PII** remains tenable. Opponents of Russell usually retort that visual position is a characteristic of the phenomenal individuals and not the physical objects. And obviously, **PII** is formulated for physical objects in the first instance.

Another line of defense of **BT** propounded by Casullo also focuses on the impure properties of spatio-temporal location. I have discussed it before; here I recapitulate briefly the main relevant points. Casullo's claim is *not* that concrete objects should be construed with the help of these impure properties. Rather, appeal is made to the fact that some of the spatial properties, notably those that yield the so-called *landmarks*, like longitudes and latitudes, are privileged: the vast majority of impure spatial properties ultimately derive from the landmarks which do not have all their pure properties in common with other things. The argument is not repeated for temporality since the temporal framework, unlike the spatial one, can be analyzed without such landmarks: for example, with the help of such relation like the relative temporal position, e.g. "being earlier than", etc. Still, the spatial case undermines the unjustified claim that **PII** is a necessary truth: the truth of **PII** is confined to the spatial landmarks.

What is missing, however, from Casullo's argument is a demonstration to the effect that some version of **BT** is in fact committed to this claim about the *existence* of landmarks. But I have already shown that the version of **BT** Casullo espouses is a general statement *without existential implication* about the existence of landmarks. Casullo's so-called "*weak*" **BT** (**WBT**) says: "A (momentary physical) thing is *contingently* identical to a complex of mutually co-instantiated properties".[122] Now, according to Casullo, the introduction of landmarks (developed though on independent considerations), helps to exempt (**WBT**) from commitment to the claim that "no two things in fact have all *pure* properties in common" and makes (**WBT**) "committed"..."only to the *much weaker* empirical claim" that "there exist a small number of things which do not have all pure properties in common with any other thing".[123] But no such "commitment" follows from the general formulation of (**WBT**), as we have pointed out earlier. Undeniably, (**WBT**) is *compatible* with the existence of such landmarks; but compatibility is a relation weak enough, so, that it cannot validate (**WBT**): from the mere fact that (**WBT**) is compatible with the existence of landmarks, it does not follow that (**WBT**) *is committed to their existence*. So, Casullo's (**WBT**) is not better off than other versions of **BT**.

A further defense of **BT** in vogue in the literature seeks to find explanation for the fact that numerically distinct individuals can share all their pure properties. This is based on Armstrong's conception of the so-called "immanent" universals which, in contrast to the "transcendent" ones, are instantiated universals fully present in many places and

---

[122] Casullo (2001), 140.

[123] Casullo (2001), 142.

times.[124] A special feature of these universals is that they can be at a spatial distance from themselves. For example, if redness is instantiated simultaneously by a rose and a post box, then one and the same redness is literally present in different places at the same time. The argument can be repeated for the temporal case: the same redness can be at a temporal distance from itself in successive, and also, in temporally partially overlapping, instantiations. Now the same applies, according to O'Leary-Hawthorne, to bundles of such immanent universals going proxy for individual substances: "just as a single universal can be at a distance from itself, one and the same bundle can be at a distance from itself". [125]

Immanent universals as constituents in **BT** can help evading commitment to **PII**. Thus there can exist numerically distinct bundles such that they contain the same universals in virtue of the fact that universals can literally be at a distance from themselves. Now let us assume, for a moment, that this sort of defense of **BT** is sound. In this case we are left with no criterion for the choice between a *universalist* bundle theory and a *tropist* bundle theory. For, although the latter is not vulnerable to the charge of implying strong **PII**, apparently the former can also avoid implying strong **PII**, and it can be adjusted to our intuitions. Unless there is some fatal fault with the Armstrongian notion of "immanent" universals, O'Leary's solution seems impeccable.

In fact, the notion of "immanent" universals is not so weird. It has Aristotelian roots and it embodies the insight that universals can exist only by inhering in substances. The critical point, as I see it, is not so much with the Aristotelian notion of immanent or instantiated universal. Rather, the point is that this theory with the multiple existence of one and the same universal cannot account for the *individuation* of the bundles. For, neither the multiplied but qualitatively identical universals nor the different spatio-temporal locations explain the individuation of

---

[124] see Armstrong (1978)

[125] O'Leary-Hawthorne (1995), 196.

substances. The former can, at best, be *particularizers* but not individuators. The latter can, in itself, only secure unique reference without giving an account of individuation. Therefore O'Leary's suggestion to save **BT** from implying **PII** does not meet the requirement of individuation of the substances construed in terms of bundles of immanent universals.

Let us return now to Cleve's *4.* and *5. Objections* targeting issues of *change* and *essential predication. Objections 4.* and *5.* both flow from the essentiality of set-membership. *Objection 4.* is formulated for local or piecemeal change, *Ojection 5.* is formulated for the radical change of coming into being. The main thrust of *Objections 4.* and *5.* is the shared insight that neither piecemeal change nor radical coming into being would be possible if substances were sets of properties. Since all the properties are essential to sets of properties, substances identified with these sets could not change their properties without violating their own identities and, for the same reason, no substance could have come into being with another set of properties. Right at the start it must have all its constituting properties since it is essential to sets to have the properties they actually do. Thus all the properties predicated of a substance must be predicable of it essentially right at the start.

This set-theoretical essentialism is not evaded if objects are taken as *wholes* in the mereological sense, instead of being taken as sets, says Cleve. According to mereology, wholes supervene on their parts; but then *mereological essentialism* is an analogous threat, since wholes are the sums of the parts they actually have. Therefore we are not better off if we replace set-theoretical considerations by mereological considerations.

The *contingency* of the *co-instantiation relation* seems to be of help in avoiding set-theoretical essentialism providing thus for change and the possibility of accidental predication. A closer look reveals, however, that co-instantiation is subject to double-talk. Viewed from the perspective of the single properties, it is correct to say that it is purely contingent for each property whether it becomes instantiated, and if it does, which properties it is instantiated together. But viewed from the perspective of individuals it might be argued that it is not at all contingent *what* properties constitute their identifying sets. For, with another set of properties, the individual would be different from the individual defined in terms of the "original" properties. It seems to me that this double talk is the strategy that Cleve explores to his criticism of the bundle theory. For Cleve writes: "...a given property or group of them can be co-instantiated now with one property, now with another .... it can be contingent, for example, that snub-nosed-ness is co-instantiated with wisdom .... Moreover, of any individual it will be true that it might not have existed at all, since the properties constituting it might not have been co-instantiated. But it will *not* be true of any individual that it might have existed with properties other than the ones it actually has".

So it seems that Cleve finds contingency from the perspective of the properties as ontological building blocks, but he finds essentiality from the perspective of the individual with respect to its components. This reading is confirmed by the following passage: "... this is not to say that any *individual* can change. If F and G are co-instantiated first with H and later with K, so that the complex FGH is superseded by the complex FKG, what we have is replacement of one individual by another, not change in the properties of one and the same individual. FGH is simply not identical with FGK." Similarly: "we cannot suppose that a complex whose constituents are F, G, and H might have existed with F, G, and K as its constituents instead".[126]

Although I basically agree with Cleve in that set-theoretical essentialism plagues **BT**, his approach is still embarrassing. For, how could one maintain *contingency* in case of the *bottom-up* procedure from properties to substances, while maintaining, at the same time, *essentiality* in case of the *top-down* analysis proceeding from substances to their constituting properties? There must be either some intermediate

---

[126] Cleve (2001), 124.

mysterious turning point in the "creation" of entities from instantiated property-sets or, more probably, two different issues are addressed.

I am inclined to say that the latter is the case. *Ontologically speaking*, no substance-bundle is necessitated to come into being by the mere existence of its building blocks. Just as no state of affairs is necessitated by the previous existence of its constituents: from the very fact that there exist Rome, Juliet and, in another sense, the "loving" relation, it does not follow that there comes about automatically the state of affairs of "Romeo's loving Juliet", or, the different state of affairs of "Juliet's loving Romeo", or, the still further different state of affairs of "Rome and Juliet's loving each other". However, sets are identifiable essentially by their members. In a similar vein, a substance, *epistemologically speaking*, is nothing for us but a bunch of qualitative features. In this way there arises a top-down conceptual necessity proceeding from the existing entity to its constituting items. On the other hand, the ontological stock only contingently yields these building blocks for the construal. Some sets might not be actually formed, though the possibility is there; some objects might not come about, though all the constituting elements are available.

A disanalogy arises, perhaps, at this point: while it can truly be claimed that sets are "nothing but their members tied together by the membership relation", one would be reluctant to claim, unless one is a hard-line reductionist, that substances are "nothing but properties tied together by the co-instantiation relation". Whenever such an account is suggested, there is typically the qualification to the effect that the account applies only from the *epistemological* perspective; i.e., that we can comprehend the substances through their cognizable qualitative features since this is how they make us notice them. With sets, however, it makes no sense to speak about a gap between the ontological and the epistemological perspectives.

One might object at this point that it is a metaphysical cliché to appeal to the difference between the ontological *and* the epistemological issues. But this is how we can make good of the modal difference between the *bottom-up* and the *top-down* procedures implied by Cleve's comments.

There is another modal difference one has to cope with. The set of properties constituting the substance is not homogeneous modally; i.e., some elements are essential, while the others are contingent. Moreover, these occur in a structured way. The essential properties constitute the core of the substance, while the accidental ones belong to the outer fringe. This is in conformity with Cleve's suggestion that helps to ensure accidental predication and change. Cleve suggests "to divide each complete bundle of mutually co-instantiated properties into two-sub-bundles, an inner core and an outer fringe, and then to identify individuals with cores rather than with complete bundles. One could then say that an individual has *essentially* just those properties that belong to its core and *accidentally* just those properties that belong to its fringe."[127]

In fact, this is the first sketch in the literature of a *modal* two-tiered bundle theory of substances. In its sketchy form it does not specify whether universals or tropes are the better candidates for the role of being the elements of the bundle, but the pioneering contribution is undeniable. As we shall see, Peter Simons follows the same lead and elaborates on the original idea. Later I shall spell out the pros and the cons while making further refinements in the theory.

It is clear, however, even at this stage that *modal objections* to **BT**, namely those missing the possibility of change and accidental predication, can be circumvented only by the *modal modification* of the original bundle view. That is, the bundle serving proxy for the substance cannot be treated as something homogeneous modally, otherwise all the properties that are actually the elements of the bundle have to be treated as essential to the very identity of the bundle.

---

[127] Cleve (2001), 125.

The all too familiar moral from the history of philosophy is at our disposal: philosophers, particularly those with rationalist leanings, were deeply concerned about essences and necessity, while they failed to recognize the *significance of contingency* in central issues like substance identity through time, personal identity, the possibility of moral responsibility, etc. Curiously enough it was the rationalist Leibniz who realized the significance of contingency and by introducing the notion of possible worlds he to modeled our modal intuitions of contingency and necessity.

The two-tier bundle theories that I have discussed so far were either *phenomenalist* theories or *modal* theories. As we have seen, Castaneda's two-tier bundle-bundle view of substance was not motivated by the wish to avoid modal objections. It was motivated rather by the empiricist goal to account for physical objects on the basis of their experiential facets or guises. To recall, the guises are the basic bundles comprising properties and the objects are the derived bundles that are the results of the basic bundles being bundled. While Cleve's version had, as its goal, to cope with the modal problem. This being the case it is obviously misleading then to speak about *the* two-tier bundle theories of substances since they cover different metaphysical issues, though not unrelated ones. For example, the empiricist or phenomenalist bundle theory, although without explicit modal commitment, provides for the possibility that the derived bundles serving proxy for substances are *re-identifiable* from one experiential situation to the other with the help of essential properties. The modal bundle theories, on the other hand, do not have to deny that accidental properties in the outer fringe can vary from guise to guise, since each guise is the representation of the substance from a given perceptual or conceptual perspective.

A still further metaphysical possibility is explored in Casullo's version of a *perdurantist* two-tier **BT**. I turn to it now.

Casullo separates the issues of individuation and identity across time, and takes it, that these two issues should be addressed differently by a cogent proponent of **BT**. This separation already reveals his background assumption: according to Casullo substances existing through time are not spatio-temporal *continuants* that are fully present with their essential properties *plus* some additional individuator through their whole temporal career. Rather, the thing that exists at any given moment is only a momentary entity and the substance itself can be taken only as the series or concatenation of these momentary things. In other words, Casullo espouses the so-called *perdurantist* view of concrete substances as opposed to their *endurantist* view.

As is familiar, these two labels were coined by David Lewis for denoting two different accounts for identity through time. The endurantist conception is basically Aristotelian, capturing the insight that concrete individual substances have spatial parts without having temporal parts. Accordingly, the substance is wholly present in each phase of its temporal durations. The perdurantist conception is a relatively novel one and is shared by those metaphysicians who find embarrassing how identity through time is accounted for in the endurantist scheme. For, if the "whole" of a substance, say, the "whole of Socrates", is present at each moment of his existence such that he is healthy at some moments and ill at others, sitting at some moments while standing at others, etc. then, clearly, we are obliged to ascribe incompatible properties to the same temporally enduring substance. In order to rule out the incompatibility of the properties we can take it that it is not the "whole" of the substance that is temporally located at the successive moments of its temporal existence. Rather, it is only a temporal slice of it that belongs to a certain moment and the substance itself is made up of the succession of these temporal parts. Since no temporal part is characterized by incompatible properties, the incompatibility charge is evaded. The price one has to pay for this solution is the adoption of the counterintuitive notion of substances being made up from other entities, i.e., their temporal parts or slices. As a consequence, substances do not have only spatial parts, but they have temporal parts as well. Just as the substance is spatially extended in virtue of its parts being spatially extended, in a similar fashion, it is temporally extended by virtue of having temporal parts with various temporal extensions. So substances do not make single, unitary entities; rather, they are the concetinations of slice-entities.

No space can be devoted here to an exhaustive criticism of the perdurantist view. It suffices to mention here only one objection that is pertinent to perdurantist two-tiered **BT**. The objection is this: perdurantism would be successful in handling the problem of ascribing incompatible properties to the same substance existing through time provided its notion of temporal parts were uncontroversial. In particular, if the temporal parts could be specified independently of the substance whose temporal parts they are without presupposing the prior notion of the substance. Alas, this is far from being the case. Take, for example, the temporal part or slice of Russell specifiable as "Russell-at-the-age-of-five". Now try to identify and individuate this temporal slice without reference to Russell as *the* individual. Obviously, temporal slices do not just hang around and join to form substances in succession at will. There must be already something about these temporal slices right at the start that qualifies them as the temporal parts *of* certain substances. Thus "Russell-at-the-age-of-five" cannot be *identified* save by reference to Russell himself. Moreover, the same holds for the *individuation* of the temporal slice. Unless it comprises certain properties characteristic of Russell it cannot "fit in" to the succession of temporal parts constituting Russell. Here I am thinking of genuine properties that make the salient features of Russell, either only at certain times or at every time of his existence. I do not countenance haecceistic properties like "being the temporal part of Russell at-a-time".

The upshot is this: temporal parts cannot be individuated by any other means than by reference to the substance. Still, as we shall soon see, Casullo attempts to account for the individuation of the substance in a bottom-up manner, starting with properties belonging to the temporal parts. In his perdurantist two-tier theory the temporal parts belong to the *basic* tier and it is the "whole" substance as the series of temporal parts that makes the *derived* tier. Although Casillo tries to support his account by vindicating Castaneda's bundle-bundle theory, it is not motivated by the wish to correct phenomenalism through the construal of physical objects *via* the perceptual guises or facets. Rather, it is motivated by the temporal part doctrine of substances propagated by Lewis that aims at accounting for identity through time. Clearly, these are two different metaphysical motivations, even though they apply a structurally similar strategy.

Let us see now Casullo's strategy and show why his version cannot avoid the charge of essential predication despite his avowed attempt to do so. Casullo emphatically stresses that his version of **BT** "offers *different* solutions to the problems of individuation and identity through time". [128] By contrast, endurantists account both for identity and individuation by relying on the notion of *continuants* that exist and enjoy their individuation through time. Perdurantists, however, take it that these two different functions are not, and in fact cannot, be performed by the same entity. For the vehicle of enduring existence through time is not a single enduring entity, rather, it is the concatenation of momentary things. Briefly, this is their answer to the question of identity through time. As Casullo puts it: " (2) An enduring thing is a series of momentary things all of which stand in some contingent relation R". Thus "the identity of an object through time is to be explained in terms of relations which obtain among its temporal cross-sections".[129]

What about individuation? What is the vehicle of this function? Whatever it is, given the perdurantist answer to identity through time, the 'whole' thing is not the vehicle of individuation since it does not exist through time as a single entity; rather, the temporal slices are individuated in virtue of having their own individuators. That is, each temporal slice has its individuator and presumably the individuation of the 'whole' thing depends upon the individuation of these temporal slices. Let us look at this more closely.

---

[128] Casullo, (2001), 137. 138.

[129] Casullo, (2001), 136.

Casullo: "Clearly, a proponent of **BT** cannot rest content with (2). For (2) merely reduces enduring things to series of momentary things. But now the bundle theorist is faced with the problem of showing that a momentary thing is nothing but a complex of properties. And, clearly, the solution to this problem cannot be the same as the solution to the problem of identity across time. For (i) the constituents of momentary things must be *properties* rather than *things*; and (ii) they must be related *at* a time rather than *over* a period of time." Therefore the proponent of **BT** has to come up with the following claim (using Casullo's notation):

"(1*) A momentary thing is a complex of properties which all stand in the relation of co-instantiation to one another."[130]

So, individuation is based on the *properties* of momentary things, while identity through time is based on the concetination of these *momentary things*.

Now the question arises whether the ontological distinction between *things* and *properties* can secure the desideratum of separating appropriately the issue of individuation from the issue of identity through time. Remember, the aim of the separation was to ensure accidental predication along the following lines: although a momentary thing is defined *essentially* as a set of properties yielding thus *individuation, identity through time* depends on the *contingent* entering of each of these momentary things into the series making up a substance. And the question is whether the ontological difference between things and properties can really offer explanation for contingent predication in **BT**.

Now undeniably properties as constituents are abstract, while the 'things', the 'whole' one as well as the temporary slices, are concrete. It seems to me though, that this ontological difference is not really relevant to the modal problem of accidental predication for the following reasons.

---

[130] Casullo (2001), 137.

If an enduring thing is the series of slice-things then, clearly, if the thing had some other slices than the ones it actually has then the thing would qualify as an entity different from the one identified in the non-counterfactual situation. So, in this sense, *the actual slice-things are essential to the things' identity through time*. Further, the differences between the slices can be explained only in terms of the constituting properties. Thus, after all, the individuation of the enduring thing hinges on the properties its temporal slices actually have. With different properties in the slices a different individual would be individuated. So, in this sense, *the actual properties of the slice-things are essential to the individuation of the substance*.

Contingency remains though at the level of the very *existence* of the enduring entity in question: since nothing necessitates the existence of a concrete substance, the fact that it might not have existed implies that its temporal parts might not have existed as well. But this applies to its temporal parts *together*, taken *all at once*, since we cannot make good on the claim that for *each* temporal part of a thing it is true that *it* might not have existed. For, in that case the thing *as* defined in terms of these parts would not exist either. Thus contingency cannot be explained as (roughly) the same thing's possibly having different temporal parts. It can only be explained as the *contingent existence* of the very same thing identified essentially by its actual temporal parts and the properties actually had by those parts.

Therefore I cannot make sense of Casullo's claim that "even if we grant that each *momentary complex* of properties has its constituent properties essentially, it does not follow that an *enduring thing* which contains the complex as a temporal part has those properties essentially". His only reason to support this dubious claim is, again, the familiar ontological distinction: "although momentary things are complexes of co-instantiated properties, enduring things are *not*".[131]

---

[131] Casullo, (2001), 138.

We have just seen that this is not a good reason to deny the essentiality of predication with **BT**. For the ontological status of the constituents is not a relevant factor in the context of *individuation-in-terms-of-constituents* characteristic of **BT**. The constituents of the basic bundle or basic tier might be properties as *abstract* entities, the constituents of the derived bundle, i.e. the whole thing, might be *concrete* slices. But whatever the constituents are they all fall under the *principle of the essentiality of the constituents* in **BT**. This follows from the very notion of **BT**. A bundle is always defined in terms of its constituents and replacement of any of the constituents yields another bundle.

Still, Casullo seems to take the following position. With momentary things as complexes of co-instantiated properties the essentiality of the properties can rightly be claimed, therefore he does not question the claim that every element of a momentary complex is essential to the complex. For example, if FGH is a momentary complex, then "H is an essential property of the momentary complex FGH". But Casullo thinks that "it is a contingent fact that any particular momentary thing belongs to the temporal series which constitutes some particular enduring thing".[132] That is, while momentary complexes are compositionally rigid with respect to their constituting properties and thus property-constituents are essential to momentary things, the enduring things themselves, whose direct constituents are the momentary things, are compositionally non-rigid so that the temporal parts are had only contingently. Thus any of the object's temporal parts might not belong to its constituting temporal series.

Now it seems extremely difficult to make good on this position. For how can one reasonably defend the claim that a temporal part, *qua* a temporal part *of* a substance, only contingently belongs to that substance? As one can see, Casullo wants to avoid commitment to the following claim: "If FGH is a temporal part of *a* then *a* has that part

---

[132] Casullo, (2001), 138.

essentially". According to him this should be repudiated as a "form of mereological essentialism". To admit, mereological essentialism might not be so attractive for metaphysicians. However, one need not decide about such loaded issues as mereological essentialism in order to see clearly that it hardly makes sense to speak of a temporal part *qua* a temporal part without reference to the object whose temporal part it is. Temporal parts like "Russell-at-the-age-of-five" do not just wander around spontaneously, waiting to be incorporated into a series as a temporal part of some previously unspecified individual substance. The notion of a "temporal part" may be useful though for conceptual analysis. It can help to elucidate the point that the "same" individual might have contradictory properties at different times. But the ontological independence of the temporal parts from the subjects does not follow from the analysis.

One might retort that the ontological non-independence of temporal parts from the substance plays into the hands of extreme essentialists, and, presumably, it also plays into the hands of extreme *determinists*. For it commits one to the counterintuitive claim that every concrete substance has, in an omnitemporal sense, exactly those temporal parts that it acquires in succession during its temporal life-span. Thus, if FGH is a temporal part of *a* at time *t*, it *is* (*was/will be*) always the case that *a* has FGH at *t*. Fortunately, there is no compelling reason to buy into this deterministic predicament. For the claim is *not* that *a* is individuated, right at the start of its career, by the temporal parts that it is going to acquire only later, in succession. Rather, the claim is more modest and safe saying only that no temporal part *qua* temporal part of a substance can be identified save by reference to the substance. Thus it is a trivial truth about the identification of temporal parts *qua* temporal parts; but it does not imply the dubious position that one cannot spell out such trivial truth save by yielding the "full" individuation of the substance in terms of all its temporal parts ever had. For, in this case, we would be entitled to talk about individual substances only after they have expired from existence.

However, Casullo seems to be forced to embrace this position. For one cannot consistently maintain that while the constituting properties are essential to the temporal parts of substances according to set-theoretical insights, the constituting temporal parts are *not* essential to the enduring thing as the temporal series of its parts. If the vehicles of individuation for these enduring things are their temporal parts, as is suggested by Casullo, then the "full" individuation of an enduring thing is yielded by all its temporal parts coming about in succession. From this it follows that the final and irrevocable individuation can be given only in retrospection, when the thing goes out of existence, so, that no more items could be added to its individuation. This insight should not be conflated with a deterministic position. But essentialism seems hardly avoidable: if properties are essential to temporal parts, these latter are, in turn, essential, in the very same sense, to the enduring thing whose temporal parts they are.

The moral is that it is extremely difficult to spell out contingency in **BT** unless one is prepared to accept an essential core and a contingent fringe to the substance right at the start.

With perdurantism, it is even more difficult to spell out the contingency of having a temporal part. For, in this case, we cannot refer properly to a temporal part *qua* 'temporal part' save by the prior notion of the substance it belongs to. The contingency of the temporal part of an individual would mean, in possible world semantics, that in some worlds "Russell's-being-a-naughty-boy-at-five" is a temporal part of Russell, while in other worlds, where the very same temporal part exists, it exists as a temporal part of someone else. But clearly, this is even more counterintuitive than things' existing at more worlds or having counterparts in other worlds. Therefore it seems that in these other worlds such temporal parts simply do not exist. At those worlds where this temporal part exists, it exists as the temporal part of Russell. So, at each world where this temporal part exists, it exists with Russell. But then we fall back to the position that temporal parts are had essentially or necessarily.

It seems that there is a lack of parity, from modal perspective, between ordinary *things* and *temporal parts:* the notion of a *thing* is firm enough, so that it is not dramatically shaken by metaphysical experiments such as the thing being transposed to other worlds. By contrast, the notion of a *temporal part* is fragile enough so that it is hard to conceive counterfactual situations with them.

In other words, it is extremely difficult to explain contingency in a *top-down fashion* starting with the prior existence of the individual substance. Therefore we have to take recourse to the *bottom up procedure* by presenting, in a thought experiment, qualitative constituents independently from the objects whose constituents they might be. Then we are in the position to declare that it is contingent for any of the constituents whether they co-occur in a specific bundle or not. Remember, this was the strategy applied by Cleve in his criticism of **BT**. Alas, this solution is not available in the case of *temporal parts*, for, as I have just shown, they are intimately bound up with their substances. So we can apply the thought experiment of separation only for representing how the *properties* could be bundled in various alternative ways, but not the temporal parts.

A tropist-metaphysician is obviously constrained in this respect for he cannot avail himself with independently existing qualitative constituents, not even for didactic purposes. Therefore a tropist committed to the trope-theoretical explanation of the individual substances has only one option to provide for contingency. All that he can do is to point out that concrete individual substances exist contingently. Thus it is contingent for a *whole bunch* of quality particulars serving proxy for a substance to exist at a world.

To recall: after surveying Castaneda's theory, I considered Cleve's criticism of the bundle theory and examined Casullo defence of **BT** along perdurantist lines. Briefly, Casullo claimed that contingency of predication can be secured, despite Cleve's denial, by making a distinction between basic bundles made up of properties had *at a time* and derived bundles or objects as *the series* of temporal parts. While the temporal parts are constituted essentially by the properties they have, the enduring thing as the series of its temporal parts is constituted contingently by the temporal parts it actually has. The only support given by Casullo for this asymmetry was that the constituents are ontologically different in the two bundles. They are abstract properties in the basic bundles, and they are concrete temporary things in the derived bundles. But, as we have seen, difference in the ontological nature of the constituents does not affect the essentially *essentialist* modal feature of **BT**.

Cleve's mistake, according to Casullo is that in Cleve's account the objects are directly identified with property-bundles instead of being identified with "bundles of bundles", i.e. with bundles of temporal parts. Casullo's motivation to account for identity through time meets assent. But his device is of no help in providing for contingent predication because the *bundling relation* itself has an essentialist commitment which is ultimately the same whether we are on the basic level or on the derived level. If we still have the feeling that securing contingency is to be sought with a two-tiered account then we can turn to Simons's theory. This comes next.

V. *The Bundling Relation. Simons' Two-tier Bundle Theory of Substance*

Simons's **BT** postulates *tropes* as the elements of the bundle. It has already been made clear that a trope-bundle has certain advantages over the universalist property bundle: for example, no arbitrary substance can be posited on the trope-account, since the tropes already presuppose a bearer. Further, a trope bundle is not vulnerable to the objection of implying strong **PII,** i.e. **PII** formulated in terms of pure properties. **BT** has a mixed version retaining a bare substratum for metaphysical purposes and a pure version that wholly dispenses with non-qualitative components. In the mixed case a bearer of tropes, i.e. a substratum is postulated that accounts for the unity of tropes in the substance. According to this tropes-*cum*-substratum view unity is not derived from bundling, rather it is presupposed whenever further properties are ascribed to the substance in predication. This notion of the Lockean substratum is revived by Charles Martin.

By contrast, Peter Simons' suggestion is a two-tier nuclear theory that dispenses with a non-qualitative substratum. Also, it is based on a strong bundling relation: for it presupposes a tight bundle of essentially compresent elements constituting the individual nature of the substance. This kind of substratum is not a bare particular: it is identified in terms of the essential tropes and it can be the bearer of the more loosely bundled accidental tropes. A very similar solution has been briefly suggested by van Cleve, without a full elaboration though.

To recall, substance-theories with qualitative bundles in the fashion of the British empiricists are plagued with *ultraessentialism*, since every element of the bundle is essential to the identity of the substance. Pure substratum theories, on the other hand, are *antiessentialist* since a non-qualitative substratum does not necessitate any qualitative features. These modal extremities should be avoided by a sound **BT**. So it seems that there are at least two desiderata that **BT** should meet: there is the need for *unity* that can hardly be explained as a result of some operation on the elements existing prior to bundling; and there is also the need for characterising every element of the substance in qualitative terms in order to avoid the absurd consequences of postulating non-qualitative components. Thus, whatever plays the substratum role must be both qualitative while exhibiting, at the same time, the desired unity. Martin's theory locates the qualitative features wholly outside the substratum, while the more promising suggestions of Cleve and Simons offer a qualitative nucleus with essential tropes occurring in tight bundling and a periphery with accidental tropes in looser bundling. What these notions of "tight" bundling and "looser" bundling actually amount to, will become clear in subsequent discussions. Since Cleve very briefly glosses over his suggestion we have to rely on Simons's elaboration. His two-tier arrangement tries to provide both for essential and accidental tropes and in this vein it is neither *ultraessentialist* nor *antiessentialist* unlike the rival accounts. This does not mean, however, that Simons' account is completely free from modal problems: it has a modal problem of its own, as I shall show. More specifically, what I shall show is that this account is too rigid in specifying the essential tropes of the substance in the following sense: *it excludes the possibility that a determinate of a determinable essential trope of the substance be replaced by another determinate of the same kind.*

As is familiar, the modal problem is intimately connected to change, and there are various ramifications of this issue. For example, radical change poses its own challenge to the two-tier trope-bundle view as we shall see later. Also, while there might not be changes in the essential generic features, there may be changes in their specific determinate forms. For example, Socrates is rational as a human creature through his whole career, but this rationality takes specific determinate tokens in his different temporal phases. Simons' theory has no adequate resources to tackle with this case, so, some amendments will be suggested. Further, there might not be changes at all in the intrinsic features of the substance, whether radical or piecemeal, generic or specific, still, the substance *qua* substance of a certain kind might be destroyed as a result of a mere Cambridge change. This ramification of the problem of change for substances will be discussed in the next chapter.

Since all the trope-views of substance presuppose the *bundling relation* as a gluing relation, I shall turn to this first.

The relation tying together the elements of the bundles is called "concurrence" or "compresence". With the trope-account the question arises whether this bundling relation specifically and relations in general are supposed to be universals *or* irreducibly relational tropes that are dependent on the monadic tropes they relate. If they are treated as universals, that is repeatables, then we get a distinction between the universal of "compresence" and the particular relatedness by compresence of various tropes. For example, a particular extension trope might be compresent with a particular colour trope in an object. Such compresence makes an unrepeatable "relational fact". The need for such a distinction, coupled with the acceptance of universals, is convincingly argued by Vallicella, as I have said earlier. Vallicella points out that on the trope account there are no relations distinct from relational facts since it confines itself to particulars. The admission of relations, however, amounts to the admission of universals, since relations cannot be conceived in any other way save as universals. I endorse Vallicella's position with respect to admitting universals; and I proceed with the assumption that the *bundling relation* as a repeatable *is* a *universal*.

There are two further questions that should be addressed with the bundling relation: *i*) what the arity of this relation is; *ii*) what kind of relation it is from a metaphysical perspective; in particular, whether it is internal or external, and, further, whether it is necessary or contingent. These two distinctions do not overlap since there exists a variant cutting across them: there are *contingent internal relations* as well, i.e. relations that supervene on the contingent intrinsic features of their relata.

As to *i*), there is the option of taking the bundling relation of compresence as a 2-place relation binding any two tropes in a bundle. In this case, with n tropes, we get $n(n-1)/2$ relations of compresence. These relations again must be bundled by a higher order relation of compresence and the same goes for the consequent relations, leading thus to a vicious regress. Such a vicious regress does not arise, for example, with resemblance relations. Here regress can be avoided because resemblances supervene on the intrinsic properties of their relata, and so, they do not require extra connecting links ad infinitum. This is an undeniable advantage of the so-called internal relations. But compresence *does* require extra connections, since it is a contingent external relation, at least on the standard view. So my answer to question *ii)* is that compresence, from the metaphysical perspective, is a *contingent external relation.*

One may still doubt this resolution. If the goal is to avoid relation regress, we would need, it seems, an internal binding relation. And it would be possible to derive the internal character of compresence from the nature of the tropes as relata. For example, it could be the case, by the very nature of certain tropes that they essentially co-occur. In this case the bundles would be necessitated, so to speak, by tropes that are doomed to co-occur in bundles. "Where two or more tropes essentially occur together, it is more plausible that their compresence is internal...", as Simons suggests.[133] It is worth repeating here that the current understanding of internal relations is different from the one entertained by the classical British idealists. For, according to the latter, all internal relations are essential since they flow from the nature of the relata. Now what Simons claims is that essential co-occurrence *is* internal, but there is no claim to the effect that it holds the other way round, i.e. that internal relations are *all* essential. According to the prevailing conception of internal relations this claim is false. For, on the current understanding, internal relations hold in virtue of the intrinsic properties of their relata. And these intrinsic properties can be either essential or accidental. Accordingly, some internal relations are essential, others are contingent. For example, the colour of two jackets are their intrinsic

---

[133] Simons (1994), 559.

accidental properties in virtue of which these can stand in the "being darker in colour" internal contingent relation.

In view of this understanding of internal relations *and* the role of compresence as a bundling relation it seems to me questionable that the compresence of tropes can be internal at all. For, internal relations supervene on the intrinsic properties of their relata, but *which* property of the tropes would make them inclined to be compresent? Which feature of the actually co-occurring tropes necessitates their co-occurrence? In virtue of what are an extension trope, a colour trope, a texture trope, etc., compresent in a substance? There is the bare fact that they make up the same substance, but this is precisely the fact that is supposed to be established by the compresence relation. Thus compresence cannot be an internal relation, *eo ipso*, it cannot be an essential relation either.

There could be an alternative suggestion though, according to which the tropes have the second-order relational trope of "essential compresence". This, however, is not an intrinsic property required by the current view of internal relation. It is only on the classical reading of "internal relation" represented by Blanshard and Bradley, that it involves the essential compresence of the relata. For, according to these authors, "the very existence and identity [of the particular] is bound up with its standing in that relation", i.e. the relation of compresence.[134] But this conception obviously goes with ultraessentialist commitments.

The upshot is that compresence must be considered as a contingent external relation. But the threat of ultraessentialism still emerges here since the substance is identified with the complete bundle and so we face set-theoretical essentialism. The bundle construal makes substances too vulnerable to change: if a single trope or property from a bundle is replaced by another, then this results in a new bundle, and, as a consequence, a new concrete particular. For example, when a leaf

---

[134] See Vallicella (2002), 6.

exposed to the sun warms up, then the new bundle would make another leaf. We cannot even say that the latter is a successor to the former. Thus the bundle view puts at risk the identity of the individual substances even through trifle changes. Individual substances would be "counterfactually wholly unstable", to borrow van Inwagen's phrase.[135]

Vulnerability to change is a major obstacle to the bundle-view that cannot easily be overcome and, moreover, it holds irrespective of *what* is bundled: universals *or* tropes. This problem is not related to the ontological decision what the members of the bundle are decided to be, rather it has to do with the set-theoretic idea of bundling. It holds for substances *as* bundles whether they are bundles of universals or bundles of tropes.

Let us return to *i)*, the question of arity, and explore further options beside the one already discussed. A further possibility considered by Simons is to take compresence as a 3-place relation connecting any two tropes and a place where they both are. From the point of view of our present concern its main disadvantage is that it makes the *motion* of substance mysterious. For either it ties the tropes to their places, in which case the substances cannot move at all, *or* motion is taken as the occupancy of a series of successive positions. In the latter case the motion of substance consists in the whole series of 3-place compresence relations, each involving two tropes and a given place P, being replaced by a similar series of 3-place relations, again each involving two tropes and a given place P', etc. The co-ordinated move of the series is mysterious: " What explains the fact that all of these compresence relations with P', P'' etc. not only affect all the same tropes, but that they are all generated at the same time and all lapse together, in perfect harmony? What keeps the tropes from wandering off in different directions?"[136]

---

[135] See Inwagen (2001), ch. 11.

[136] Simons (1994), 560-1.

The last option would be to conceive compresence as a *variably polyadic relation* with changing arity: the arity of the relation depends on the number of the tropes that are bundled. In this case regress cannot start, since no higher order relation is required in order to glue the lower order gluing relations. Van Cleve suggests this treatment.[137] The further advantage of this option is that there is no need to take compresence as an internal relation, in order to avoid regress, since here regress simply does not arise. In this vein the best choice for arity squares with the best metaphysical choice about the nature of the gluing relation. Ultimately we can say that *compresence is logically a variably polyadic relation, while it is metaphysically a contingent external relation.* The correct decision about its logical feature supports its appropriate metaphysical understanding.

Unfortunately, arity considerations are of no help with set-theoretical essentialism generated by taking substances as bundles of certain qualitative features. Further, if compresence is taken as a contingent external relation, as it should be, we simply do not know which tropes must be compresent in order to make a substance. The compresence relation itself is *neutral* with respect to the *modal status* of each trope making up a substance. As Simons remarks, "if some tropes are essential to their substances, and others are accidental, this is not marked in the huge relation binding them all together. And the relation does not of itself explain why when a substance changes, part of the bundle remains fixed, while other tropes of similar kind slip into the slots just vacated by their expiring colleagues".[138] All we can know for certain is that it would be highly undesirable to have all the co-occurring tropes as essential to the substance; and, equally, to have none of them as essential to it.

Phenomenologists on the continent seem to have a similar problem of essentialism in their constructions. According to Husserl some of the

---

[137] Cleve (1985)

[138] Simons (1994), 561.

'sensuous contents' present themselves as inseparable from the rest and from the whole object itself; and such contents are 'essential' to the object in this sense. Husserl reminds us of Berkeley's position with respect to the phenomenology of inner experience. Berkeley in his polemic against Locke made clear that while the concrete parts of the objects can freely be separated from it and put together again at will in creative imagination, the abstract features of the objects that are wholly dependent in their existence on the object, are not separable in this way. For example, we can imagine a man's head together with the trunk of a horse and present this monster to us in imagination. By contrast "it is impossible to form 'abstract ideas', to separate the idea, e.g., of a movement from that of a moving body."[139] Husserl uses the notion of "part" indiscriminately both for concrete, independent parts that are separable in imagination and also, for abstract, dependent parts, i.e. qualitative "moments" that are inseparable from the things since we cannot abstract them from the rest. "... a head can certainly be presented apart from the person that has it. A colour, form, etc., is not presentable in this fashion, it needs a substrate, in which it can be exclusively noticed, but from which it cannot be taken out."[140]

Now this inseparability of sensuous content in imagination parallels our modal problem. But inseparability in the phenomenological sense is simply a feature of human psychology and perception. Although it implies the essentiality of the abstract parts in the sense just clarified, it does not carry with itself commitment to set-theoretical essentialism in metaphysics. The phenomenology of perception may have its intuitive appeal without justifying though a metaphysical position.

The bundle theory initiated though first by the British empiricists is an *ontological* theory in the first instance, and not an epistemological theory, despite its epistemological origin. But then **BT** has to give an

---

[139] Husserl, E. (2002), vol. II. 6.

[140] Husserl (2002), vol. II. 13.

account of the modal status of the various ontological items that enter into bundling. It cannot just be pointed out that all of these abstract elements make an inseparable sensuous content in perception and imagination. Husserl is quite right in saying that Berkeley's reason for adopting his position with respect to the inseparability of the abstract qualitative features from the thing is that for Berkeley "this inability to exist means no more than inability to be perceived", i.e. to be perceived in a separate presentation. For Berkeley, unlike for the current tropists, the ontological position owes its force to the epistemological position.

As to Husserl, under the heading of "the inseparability of non-independent contents", he considers "instances of inseparable contents, e.g. the relation of *visual quality* to *extension*, or the relation of both to the *figure* which bounds them".[141] Although extension and figure are also physical features in their own rights, in the context of "visual quality" they figure as perceptual items. So the inseparability and non-independence of the moments stressed by Husserl is phenomenological rather than ontological. Therefore the Husserlian insight about the moments is not directly relevant to trope philosophy.

Interestingly enough, trope **BT** connects the ontological and the epistemological aspects in its historical development. Originally, it was motivated by the empiricist insight that the concrete things make themselves noticed through their salient perceivable features, so we tend to identify things with bunches of these features. Then we slip from these epistemological motivations to the ontological side; and the ontological dependence of moments, accidents on the bearer substance has already been prepared theoretically by the Aristotelian tradition. With these backgrounds in mind, the Husserlian contribution to foundation as the gluing relation should be treated with certain provisions.

---

[141] Husserl (2002), vol. II. 6-7.

Returning to the problem of compresence as a bundling relation, it consists in that it relates indiscriminately both the essential and the accidental tropes of the substance. Even the motion of the substance, let alone other changes, becomes a risky enterprise on the reading which explains motion by relating successive bundles of tropes to successive places. In view of this complication it would, perhaps, be more convenient to take substance as a basic primitive unit, the bearer of its tropes, and explain motion or change without invoking the co-ordinate succession of the series of bundles. Still, it would be too hasty to conclude that changes are best interpreted on a primitive notion of substance. If changes occur in the qualitative features of substances, as in fact they do, we must be able to say what count as identity conditions for these substances. More specifically, we must be able to explain the fact that these substances bear certain tropes without which they cannot survive, yet they can survive the loss of some of their other tropes.

There are two options here. According to one, we postulate a substratum, a hard core of substance, which is unanalysable in terms of the associated tropes. How can we then explain, for example, the fact that substances like humans perish if the oxygen tropes they breathe in are replaced by poisoning gas tropes? What feature of a featureless substratum would account for the drastic effect? Or, taking the other option, the substance is said to be the total bundle of the tropes it actually has. Then the question is this: what makes it the case that it remains the same substance after replacing some of its tropes? For example, if the colour of a piece of cloth fades, what makes it the case that the cloth preserves its identity through time, though it suffers the replacement of its colour-tropes? *In either case*, we cannot explain the effect of the replacement of tropes on the substance. For, if the substance is identified with the total bundle then we have to face the problem that *any* change or replacement is lethal to an individual substance since another bundle yields another substance. The tropes-*cum*-substratum view faces the problem that those changes that are considered as lethal cannot be explained since the destruction of a non-qualitative substratum cannot be explained in terms of qualitative changes. In sum, both the classical trope-bundle view and the tropes-*cum*-substratum view of substance suffer from the deficiency that they cannot mark off those changes that affect the identity of the substance from those changes that do not. Let us see whether this difficulty is successfully overcome by the *modal* two-tier nucleus theory.

The two-tier modal nucleus theory

Simons' two-tier nucleus theory avoids the ultraessentialist and the antiessentialist horns of the modal dilemma by ascribing to the substance a core with essential tropes and an outer fringe with accidental tropes. Instead of a featureless substratum a tight bundle of tropes serves as a core. The intuitive notion of a core works well for Aristotelian animate substances like "dog" or "human being" for these substances are the instantiations of irreducible biological kinds where the kinds mark out the essences of the substances. However, not all concrete particulars qualify as Aristotelian substances by instantiating an irreducible biological kind exhibiting their essence. So the question which tropes belong to the tight bundle is less obvious with other concrete particulars, say, artefacts, that do not happen to be Aristotelian substances. There we presumably have to appeal to function as a guide to essence.

Putting this problem aside, my main polemic here focuses on the rigid character of Simons' theory: this theory presupposes not only an unchanging bundle of the essential determinable tropes of the substance but it also presupposes the unchangeability of the *determinates* of these essential determinable tropes. This rigidity makes an obstacle, as we shall see, to explaining change.

Let us see first Simons' account of the bundling relation. 'Compresence' has the drawback, as we have seen that it cannot mark the difference between the essential and the accidental tropes in the bundle. To consider a more promising view, Simons appeals to Husserl's notion of *foundation* anticipated earlier.[142] Being a "primitive internal

---

[142] See more on Simons' interpretation of the Husserlian notion of *foundation* in Simons (1987), 292-314.

relation", Husserlian foundation can stop vicious infinite regress; and avoiding regress is crucial for any unifying or gluing relation.[143] Husserl distinguished between *weak* and *strong* foundations, and only the latter seems appropriate for the needs of a bundle theory of tropes. For the point is that a weak foundation admits the object's being founded on its essential proper parts. But Simons makes clear that it is "quite implausible to think of tropes as *parts* of their substances".[144] Therefore the trope theory can make use only of a strong foundation that excludes the objects being founded on their proper parts.

The formulations of weak and strong foundation are as follows. "An individual A is *weakly founded* on individual B iff A is necessarily such that it cannot exist unless B exists." "A is *strongly founded* on B iff A is weakly founded on B and B is not part of A".[145] Simons does not specify the ontological status of 'individuals' as the relata of foundation; i.e. whether they are supposed to belong to the same ontological level, such as particles, tropes, things, etc. or one can, perhaps, establish foundation between individuals of different levels. I take it that foundation with level preservation is at least unproblematic. Simons says that foundation relations obtain because "an object of one sort (a colour trope, say) requires an object of another (an extension trope) by virtue of the kind, or ideal species, to which they belong. Foundation is primarily a relation at the species level..." This means, with our example, that "any extension trope requires some colour trope, but it does not follow that *this* extension trope E requires just *this* colour trope C, since E may continue to exist while C is replaced by another colour trope C" of a different kind". (ibid.)

---

[143] As a suggestion to what features a unifying relation should be credited with, see Vallicella (2002), 28-34.

[144] Simons (1994), 563.

[145] Simons (1994) 559.

The consequence is that "specific foundation is compatible with individual flexibility". That is, other particulars can equally be composed of the same bundle of kinds or determinables. But for the same reason specific foundation is *not an adequate device* for accounting for individual substances in a bundle view. In fact, this can be regarded as a deficiency of Husserlian foundation.

Therefore Simons seeks to amend the Husserlian notion of foundation by suggesting that "one should distinguish between *de specie* dependence from *de individuo* dependence". In his own account tropes of both kinds of dependence contribute to the constitution of the individual substances. In familiar terminology, those tropes that are *de specie* depended are *determinables* and those that are *de individuo* depended are *determinates*. Recall that "being coloured" is a determinable with respect to the individual colours like "being red", "being blue", etc., while "being red" is a determinable with respect to one of its shades, say, "being maroon". Determinates can be expressed with the help of adverbial modification as well. Say, if "walking" is the determinable, "slow walking" could be one of its determinates. With the earlier example, the *de individuo* dependence of determinates would require that *this* extension trope E and *this* colour trope C could not exist without each other.

What Simons labels "de specie dependence" and "de individuo dependence" respectively in his work in 1994, are called "generic dependence" and "rigid dependence" in his work in 1987. The earlier terminology reveals that according to Simons the price to be paid for getting to individuals is rigidity in the bundled features.

Commenting on Husserl's notion of *foundation* in the earlier work, Simons remarks that Husserl "does not trouble to distinguish between rigid and generic dependence"..."since he holds, plausible enough, that individuals are dependent by virtue of being the kind of individuals they are".[146] Basically, the same sort of criticism is repeated in Simons, 1994.

Let us see now what is achieved by the Husserlian *foundation* relation: whether it is an improvement over *compresence* typically exposed to the charge that it binds indiscriminately essential and accidental features. Does foundation offer the fine-tuning of dependence? As it is conceded by Simons, foundation relation "works only for cases of essential compresence" and "between contingent or accidental tropes ... there is no foundation relation".[147]

Now the Husserlian foundation relation seems to be an advance on compresence since this relation actually discriminates between essential and accidental tropes. It does so by comprising the essential tropes and excluding the accidental ones. Still, in Simons' assessment, "Husserl's concept of foundation, has difficulty accounting for anything like the distinction in status between accidental and essential tropes of a substance".[148] And also: "the Husserlian solution ... overlooks the distinction between essential and accidental tropes in a substance."[149]

The real target of Simons' objection, I think, is *not* that foundation is unable to discriminate between essential and accidental tropes since it discriminates in a negative way. It embraces the essential tropes and filters out the accidental ones. Rather, the complaint should be that Husserlian foundation does not offer a solution for incorporating accidental tropes in the substance. For, it seems that such a project cannot be carried out with just *one* relation. And this is another way of acknowledging the fact that there remains as non-eliminable the modal problem of accounting for the unity of particulars in terms of the

---

[146] Simons (1987), 303.

[147] Simons(1994), 559.

[148] Simons (1994), 565.

[149] Simons *op.cit.*, 563.

relatedness of their essential *and* accidental constituting tropes. It seems that if one wants to incorporate accidental tropes as well in the substance, one must find another binding relation for them, since foundation binds only essential tropes. Simons' two-stage approach actually relies on two different binding relations, although he does not spell out this crucial point.

Husserlian foundation as a binding relation has a virtue recognized by Simons: it is that it explains how "independence can emerge from dependence".[150] This is a significant achievement from the perspective of the trope-bundle construals that are threatened by the insubstantiality of the bundles serving proxy for concrete particulars. Simons nicely shows how "integral wholes" can be formed by the "emergent property of independence". As he says "firstly, two particulars are said to be *directly foundationally related* if either is founded, whether weakly or strongly, on the other. Two particulars are then *foundationally related* iff they bear the ancestral of the relation of direct foundational relatedness to one another. A collection forms a *foundational system* iff every member in it is foundationally related in it to every other, and none is foundationally related to anything which is not a member of the collection. An object is an *integral whole* iff it can be partitioned into parts which form a foundational system".[151]

By presenting it in a technically more accurate form, this formulation basically follows Husserl's conception. We find in the original Husserlian text: "*A content of the species A is founded upon a content of the species B*, if an A can by its essence .... not exist, unless B also exists...The "definition of the *pregnant concept of Whole*"... can be given "by way of the *notion of Foundation*: By a Whole we understand a range of contents which are all covered *by a single foundation* without the help of further contents". Further, Husserl states that "talk of the *singleness of*

---

[150] Simons *ibid.*

[151] Simons *op.cit.*, 562.

the foundation implies that *every content is foundationally connected, whether directly or indirectly, with every content.*"[152]

Husserl also highlights the real nature of *foundation* by pointing out the difference between mere "aggregates" and "founded contents": "the form of the aggregate is quite indifferent to its matter, i.e. it can persist in spite of wholly arbitrary variation in its comprised contents. A 'founded' content, however, depends on the specific 'nature' of its 'founding' contents: there is a pure law which renders the Genus of the 'founded' content dependent on the definitely indicated Genera of the 'founding' contents."[153] This passage, just as others in its vicinity, reveal that Husserl is concerned with *generic* dependence. Thus, there is no room in Husserl's system for *individual* or *rigid* dependence. Other passages also show that in Husserl's thinking determinate qualities count as *infima species* rather than particularized qualities. For example, he says: "...we rightly treat the quality, e.g. the determinate shade of red, as the *Infima Species* within this genus. Just so, a determinate figure is the last difference of the Genus Figure"...[154]

In Simons's correction it is shown how independence can emerge from dependence in the Husserlian foundational system by the addition of a "supplementary principle": "*a collection of particulars, all of whose foundational needs are met within the collection, is itself independent*".[155] Thus mutual foundation can account for the emergence of independent entities out of dependent entities.

Earlier, I argued for the *abstractness* of tropes, in accordance with the standard view and in contradistinction to Simons' suggestion of taking tropes to be *concrete*. Accepting that independence can emerge from

---

[152] Husserl (2002), vol. II. 34.

[153] Husserl *op.cit.*, 38.

[154] Husserl *op.cit.*, 8.

[155] Simons (1994), 562.

dependence, my position now faces the difficulty of how to account for the fact that a collection of *abstract dependent* entities makes a *concrete independent* entity. It seems to me that the difficulty can be resolved: mutual foundation in Simons' sense can be credited with the means of turning the collections of abstract entities into concrete entities. If this can be shown as plausible enough, there is no principled objection against taking tropes as abstract while embracing, at the same time, the trope **BT** in Simons's style.

We have already seen that mutual foundation is sufficiently strong as a grounding relation so that a collection of dependent particulars like tropes makes an independent entity provided that all the foundational needs of the tropes are met within the collection. Obviously, if the collection of tropes becomes independent through mutual foundation it is not automatically guaranteed thereby that the collection itself becomes concrete. Its concreteness cannot simply be presupposed since the elements of the collection, the tropes, are abstract entities. One might object, for example, that mutual foundation does not automatically accomplish both jobs, i.e. turning the collection of tropes into a concrete *and* independent entity, since counterexamples show that there are independent abstract particulars as well. For example, the zero set is an independent abstract entity.

Still, it seems to me that mutual foundation can be credited with both functions. For the goal of mutual foundation is *not* to turn the dependent tropes into platonic independent entities, that is, to turn *abstract* entities of one kind into *abstract entities of another kind*. Evidently, the goal is to account for concrete particulars or substances in terms of their tropes. If this is agreed, mutual foundation cannot satisfy the *independence* requirement without satisfying, at the same time, the *concreteness* requirement making concrete entities out of abstract ones. If the tropist can meet Armstrong's objection to the effect that no bundling of the dependent tropes would yield an independent entity, he can also meet the related objection that no bundling of abstract entities would yield a concrete entity.[156]

The difference in the ontological status of *what* is bundled and the bundle or collection *itself* can be defended on other grounds as well. For example, it can be argued that by denying the role of bundling or mutual foundation making a concrete particular out of universals or tropes one commits, in fact, the fallacy of composition. The fallacy consists in the unreasonable claim that what is true of the elements of the bundle, i.e. that they are universals or tropes, must be logically true of their collection. But we have seen that the collection can be a concrete particular whatever the elements are. "A bundle of universals is not a universal, but a particular on any plausible version of BTI ", (= bundle theory) as Vallicella has put it recently in a somewhat different context.[157] So we find that the idea that bundling or mutual foundation yields *independent concrete* particulars out of *dependent abstract* particulars or universals can be defended on at least two different grounds.

So far we have seen that the Husserlian foundation relation explains the emergence of independence but it leaves unresolved the *modal problem* of accounting for the unity of the substances in terms of *both* their essential and contingent features. In Simons' correction essential tropes with *de individuo* dependence in the core of the substance fall under Husserlian foundation. Accidental tropes with *de specie* dependence in the outer fringe of the substance are presumably glued by compresence while depending also 'one-sidedly', as Simons says, on the essential tropes of the core.

Two points should be noted here. One is, that Simons retains Husserl's *de specie* dependence for the accidental tropes of the fringe

---

[156] See Armstrong (1989b), 115.

[157] Vallicella (1997), 93.

and stipulates *de individuo* dependence only with respect to the essential tropes of the core. The other is, that his two-tier theory needs two different gluing relations, as I have indicated earlier: *mutual foundation* in Husserlian fashion for the core, and *compresence* for the fringe in the spirit of British empiricism.

The difference between *de specie* dependent tropes and *de individuo* dependent tropes is basically the difference between determinables and determinates, as I have already said. Take, as an example, a human individual substance. Mutual foundation in the original Husserlian sense may require that *some* weight should necessarily co-occur with *some* extension in the bundle making up the human individual. But it cannot prescribe, right at the start of the individual's career, that it should have a determinate weight and a determinate extension. Mutual foundation is satisfied by the essential tie of tropes of *determinable kinds,* but it does not require that the members of the bundle be particular *determinates of determinables.*

So, foundation requires only *de specie* mutual dependence; but Simons wants to account for individual substances. In order to make the Husserlian notion of foundation meet this goal, Simons takes it that only those tropes can be grouped "into more substantial wholes ... which are individually founded on one another".[158] Otherwise he could not account for *individual* substances. Therefore he postulates a *nucleus* or core to the substance formed by the essential tropes with *de individuo* dependence. Undoubtedly, nucleus-formation falls under the principle of individuation, so the nucleus must be built on *de individuo* mutual dependence. "Since these tropes are all directly or indirectly mutually founding ... they form a foundation system ...such a nucleus forms the *individual essence* or *individual nature* of a substance".[159] Also, this tight

---

[158] Simons (1994), 560.

[159] Simons *op.cit.,* 568.

bundle is proxy for a substratum without suffering from the defect of being non-qualitative.

One would expect that the amended Husserlian account is able to provide for *contingent predication* and *change*, these being the vulnerable aspects of the other bundle theories. Let us see now "how contingency and change can be explained" on the amended account, these being two related desiderata. As to the first, Simons says that the nucleus "will usually not be a complete substance, since there are further, non-essential properties that the substance has. The nucleus will require supplementation by tropes of certain determinable kinds, but not require particular individual tropes of these kinds: its dependence will be specific, not individual. The other tropes it has, and which may be replaced without the nucleus ceasing to exist, may be considered as dependent on the nucleus as a whole as a bearer ... Their dependence is partly one-sided, for while these accidental tropes depend on the nucleus for their existence, it does not depend on theirs, though it requires some tropes from that family".[160]

We have got, it seems, two items each governed by its own symmetric relation: *mutual foundation* for the essential tropes of the nucleus and *compresence* for the accidental tropes of the periphery. And the two items are connected by the asymmetric relation of *one-sided dependence*: for to link any two accidentally compresent tropes we need their common dependence on the tight bundle which makes the nucleus. So, to account for the presence of accidental tropes in a substance-bundle one needs some formally *asymmetric* relation: it is one-sided dependence, which, however, is only "partly one-sided" because the nucleus also "requires" some accidental tropes. Now the question arises what sense one can give to "partly one-sided dependence". Although the nucleus requires some trope from the family of accidental tropes, it can exist without each of the particular accidental tropes it actually has. Thus the requirement for accidental tropes is considerably weak. But

---

[160] Simons *ibid*.

evidently, this is not the preferred reading, since it would diminish the putative merits of the modal two-tier theory. On a stronger reading the joining of accidental tropes of certain kinds to the nucleus is somehow *necessitated*. In this case the result is not full ultraessentialism, still, what we get is *not genuine contingency either*. "Partly one-sided dependence" puts us into the following predicament: while it is easy to argue that the essential components *must* be connected in the nucleus, it seems difficult to flesh out the desideratum that accidental tropes be joined to individual substances as their constituents without making unwanted modal claims about their necessitation.

Let us look at the other desideratum, i.e. how *change* can be explained on this account. Simons seems to imply that all the *de individuo* depended essential tropes are within the tight bundle right from the start, while changes in the "looser bundle" concern only the accidental tropes. This *static* position does not provide for the possibility that the substance acquires *new determinates* of its essential tropes and drops old ones. For example, it does not provide for the possibility that the particular form of Socrates' wisdom, humour, etc. changes from youth to maturity: Socrates is supposed to have exactly the *same determinates* of his essential determinable tropes like wisdom, humour etc. through his whole career. We arrive at this uncomfortable consequence because individual foundation is *not* flexible; as Simons himself admits, only "specific foundation is compatible with individual flexibility". In other words, the two desiderata cannot be fulfilled simultaneously on his account: either the *de individuo* dependence yields individuation, in which case there is no possibility for change in the determinates, or, change is provided for, but only in case of determinable accidental features not yielding individuation.

So it seems that Simons' improvement on Husserl's foundation by ascribing a distinguished role to *de individuo* dependence and thus making the foundation relation fit for the individual substances comes with a high price. It squares badly with those changes in the determinates of essential determinables that are reasonable to be permitted even within essentialist frameworks.

The roles ascribed to *de specie* dependence and *de individuo* dependence in Simons' version have, as I see it, *three uncomfortable consequences*. *First*, suppose with Simons that only the *de individuo* mutually depended tropes are essential for the substance. So, what is essential is only that the given particular determinates of determinable kinds co-occur. For example, that a given height, a particular snub nose etc. should form the nucleus of a given human individual. But on this account it would not be essential for the very same individual that it should exhibit the determinates *of exactly those kinds*. It would not even be possible to spell out the clause that the nucleus is completely exhausted by those determinates that are ascribed to it: i.e., that no determinates *of other kinds are required*. Further, if the determinables are not essential for the nucleus, then how can we explain the fact that other determinates *of the same determinables* have the capacity to individuate other individuals *of the same kind*, and the same individual *at another time*? For example, if I put on some weight why does this new determinate fill the bill if not for the obvious reason that it is a determinate of an *appropriate kind for me?* It seems that the *de individuo* essentiality of determinates must be coupled with the *de specie* essentiality of their determinable kinds. Strictly speaking, essentiality cannot be restricted to the individual level.

In this respect I part company with Armstrong who denies that there are determinable universals and he insists that there exist only determinate ones.[161] For example, according to him there is no Redness as a primitive universal over and above the determinate shades of red forming resemblance classes. This doctrine of Armstrong has to do with his repudiation of primitive universals in favour of immanent universals that exist only in so far as their instances do. On his construal universals are ontologically complex, because the resemblance classes of determinates are proxy for them.

---

[161] See Armstrong, D. M. (1978), vol. II.

The special problem of the determinables in the trope theory follows from the claim of the tropists that the tropes never actually get multiply exemplified. However, this is true only for fully determinate universals, as Loux rightly observes. For example, the special shape of Socrates' nose is not shared by anybody else; the faded colour of an old cloth, again, has no exact replica in another substance. But the same does not hold for the determinables of these determinates: determinables like "being coloured" or "having shape" are such that things are exactly alike in these general respects.

Once this correction is accepted, we are freed from the unwelcome consequence of conceiving the nucleus as exclusively based on *de individuo* mutual dependence. We cannot count only on the essentiality of the determinates while ignoring the essentiality of the determinable kinds. Determinates are *of* determinables and if a determinate shape is essential to a concrete particular than the determinable "having shape" must be essential to it, too. The essentiality of the determinate implies the essentiality of the respective determinable. Note, however, that the contingency of a determinate has no modal consequence whatsoever. For example, the determinate shape of a piece of wood may be contingent, while "having shape" is not contingent to it.

In sum, we cannot separate determinates from their determinables in order to adjust the trope theory to individual substances. Once we entertain modal claims about the determinates, we cannot do this unless we make essential reference to their determinables. Therefore, if we say that a given collection of determinates is essential for a concrete particular then it must be also essential for it that it has the determinates *of* certain determinable kinds.

Second, there is a further unwelcome consequence of Simons' account that requires amendment. The *de specie* depended tropes are regarded as accidental tropes. This characterization relegates certain types of forms taken up by substances in some of their phases to the status of contingency. But it is an undeniable fact that certain forms become possessed by certain substances just because they belong to the very nature of those substances. For example, caterpillars become butterflies because they are genetically programmed to develop into other forms. But this is not a contingent feature, since these forms are essentially connected to the nucleus of the caterpillar-substance. Obviously, acquired "form" is used here in the Aristotelian sense as constituting the nature of the substance. Recently, Stone has applied the same example to the consideration of how genetically programmed changes can be consistent with the survival of certain animals under different essential sorts.[162] This means, for our present concern, that since there may be changes in the essential sorts of certain particulars, a wholly static approach to the modal features of particular substances is not tenable.

In fact, the possibility of substantial change poses a challenge for Simons' nucleus theory by producing counterintuitive consequences. For, in this two-tier theory the accidental tropes are dependent on the nucleus as the bearer substratum. The nucleus also encapsulates the object's essence by being qualitative rather than "bare" as in the traditional substratum theories. Now a substantial change goes with the loss of the essence, in this case with the disintegration of the nucleus. But the nucleus, in its other role, is supposed to bear the accidental tropes which would be left without support as a result of a substantial change. For example, if a man suffers a serious accident causing brain damage so that he can perform only his biological functions by being put on machine, he is no longer a "man" by his essence. But he still retains a lot of his accidental features in virtue of his nucleus supporting these features. For example, he might retain the colour of his skin, the size of

---

[162] Stone, J. (2002), 221. Here Stone considers a "difficulty" for "sortal essentialism" being committed to the following claim: "when the inner principle that explains a thing ceases to explain it, the thing is no more". Now "caterpillars are genetically programmed to develop into an unformed insentient mass ... On the strong reading of 'caterpillars are caterpillars', individual caterpillars must cease to exist when they devolve into the unformed stage even though the same genetic constitution guides the remainder into another sentient configuration."

his body, etc. Whether his survival should be conceived as survival under another substantial form or whether his bodily continuity simply supports the continuity of his having his accidental properties may be a moot point. The relation between *survival* and *essence* will be considered in the next chapter.

What is important, however, for our present concern, is that once substantial change is allowed, the double role of the nucleus can no longer be performed together. That is, the nucleus can no longer perform its bearer-substratum role provided it ceases to function in its role of yielding the substance-essence. Therefore substantial change must lead to the complete disintegration of the object. As Denkel puts it, "a logical consequence of Simons' theory is that the properties of an object that undergoes substantial change are left without support for their existence....Therefore, on such a view, substantial change disintegrates a concrete thing completely". "Since such a logical consequence never obtains in reality, the theory that entails it must be rejected".[163]

The double role of the nucleus is not without merits though: it offers alternative to the bare substratum view and the ultraessentialist one-level bundle view. Moreover, it is ontologically benign, provided that substantial change is not on the explanatory agenda.

Lastly, there is Simons's claim to the effect that all non-nuclear tropes of the substance depend on the nucleus at the *specific* and not the *individual* level. Since *accidents* are typically among the non-nuclear tropes of substances Simons' claim should apply to them. Elsewhere he treats accidents as trope-like entities: "A smile is an accident of its face, a headache or a thought of its bearer, a quality-instance of the object it qualifies".[164] Although a tropist might object here that quality-particulars do not instantiate any further quality distinct from the given trope and so

---

[163] Denkel, A. (1997), 601. footnote 10.

[164] Simons (1987), 306.

would refrain from talking about "quality instance", this issue belongs to the fine-tuning of tropism. It suffices to say here that Simons treats accidents as tropes.

Accidents depend permanently on the bearer and Simons' treatment of non-nuclear tropes suggests that only the *type* of the accident characterizes the bearer substance, but not the particular accident it has. So, the particular smile Mona Lisa has need not be had by her; only a smile as an accident-type belongs to Mona Lisa. Similarly, the strange claim would be that the thoughts Aristotle thought once must be understood such, that only some sort of thought appropriate to the human mental level is required to be had by Aristotle and not the particular thoughts he entertained and of which he gave us manifestations. But this position is hardly tenable. Therefore one must concede that the non-nuclear tropes actually affect the substance on the individual level as well.

On a general assessment of the pros and cons, Simons' modal two-tier theory of substance fares better than any of the rival accounts. It combines aspects of the bundle theory and the substratum theory in such a way that a hard core playing the role of the substratum is specified which can yield the subject for predication. It can do so by virtue of its *unity* in the mutual founded-ness of its constituting tropes. However, Simons' account for the essential and the accidental tropes of the substance in terms of a fixed collection of *de individuo* dependent essential tropes and a changing collection of *de specie* dependent accidental tropes has unwelcome consequences, as we have seen. In the first instance, the most serious drawback is that the nucleus of an individual substance cannot either drop or acquire tropes during its lifespan by replacing one determinate trope of a determinable kind by another determinate of the same determinable kind. For example, if the nucleus of young Socrates contains a wisdom-trope, it cannot be replaced by another wisdom-trope that is more appropriate for the mature Socrates. And the same holds for his bodily extension trope, etc.

In fact, all accounts of the substances in terms of the constituting properties or tropes square badly with change. Still, I think that once a two-tier theory is available it can be turned more flexible, even if it goes against certain embedded insights. For example, what tropes are essential and what are contingent in a given phase of a substance can be fixed with the help of time-indexed properties without implying that any such distribution of the modal properties applies for the whole career of the substance.

Presumably, some essential qualitative features apply to the substances at any time during their existence; notably those, without which they would not exist *qua* substances of certain *kinds*. But the other, time-indexed features, either essential or contingent, allow for *change*. A flexible account like this that I only anticipate at this point represents no greater threat to the identity of substances through time than a rigid account ignoring changes in the determinates of determinable tropes.

As we have seen, neither substantial change, nor moderate change in the determinates of the determinables, nor the effect of individual accidents on the nucleus get explained in this scheme. All these cry for a place in the trope bundle theory. In the next chapter we shall see what supplementary theories are invoked in order to satisfy these demands. In particular, we shall see how Ehring and Simons try to combine the trope-bundle account of substances with perdurantist theories of identity through time. Although I have already spelled out my reservations with perdurantism, it is worth considering its fit with the trope **BT**.

Further, we have seen that in the nucleus theory substantial change results in the complete disintegration of the substance. In the next chapter I shall show how trifle change like mere Cambridge change can produce the same result under the assumptions of sortal essentialism. To anticipate, I will not use the case of Cambridge change to undermine sortal essentialism. Rather, I will argue that Cambridge change should be placed in a new perspective.

VI. Change, Temporal Parts and BT. Cambridge Change

The challenge to **BT** posed by change might urge one to consider the possible application of the doctrine of temporal parts to **BT**. The idea basically is that the doctrine of temporal parts yields a promising account for the identity of substances through time. We have already seen Casullo's attempt to turn the two-tier bundle theory of substances originally put forward by Castaneda into a perdurantist two-tier account in terms of temporal parts; and I have already made my critical remarks with respect to this doctrine.

Now the crucial question is whether, aside from those critical points, this doctrine could still be used efficiently to evade the charge of Cleve and others that **BT** cannot cope with change. For, if a substance is defined by the constituting tropes or universals as **BT** suggests, change in the constituents results in change of the substance. This follows from the *principle of constituent identity*. However trifle the change is, another collection of tropes or universals yields another substance. But this tells against the persistence of substances *qua* the particular individual they are and also, it tells against the principle of permanence required by the Kantian metaphysics of experience. This bunch of related problems can be described as the problem of how to conceive "identity through time". The locution implicates the desire to secure somehow the identity of the things despite minor changes in time. So "identity through time" actually covers putative identity not affected by insubstantial changes through time.

Some think that tropist **BT** fits better with the doctrine of temporal parts than universalist **BT**. The worry is that incorporating the temporal part doctrine into universalist **BT** has the shortcoming of giving asymmetrical treatments for changing objects and unchanging objects. While the changing objects would be construed as sequences of temporally restricted bundles, and so the object would be conceived as the bundle of these short-lived bundles, no *bundle-bundle account* is required in the case of unchanging objects. These latter have no temporal parts because the same object is wholly present in successive times. Therefore a *one-level* bundle account would suffice for them. So this difference between the changing relata and the unchanging relata in the bundling affects universalist **BT**.

According to Ehring this problem applies only to the *universalist* **BT** where the members of the bundle are instantiations of universals. The objection is not relevant for the trope-bundle view, because here both the changing and the unchanging objects are analysed with the same structure. As Ehring says, both "consist of R-related bundles of exactly similar momentary tropes".[165] Here the R relation is some contingent relation that connects up the members of the sequence to form a whole.

The putative advantage of the tropist **BT** over universalist **BT** from the perspective of change lies in the fact that the *momentary nature* of tropes is already part and parcel of the trope-bundle view. This is a feature that already puts the substance into the frame of change. Starting with built-in change, not a Heraclitean disorderly flux though, seems to be a better tactic than taking pains to smuggle in change somehow into a Parmenidean scenery.

The question arises how "momentary tropes" should be understood. Obviously, if time is included as the trope's constituent, then the simple nature of tropes is abandoned and the structure of the trope needs some explanation. The same applies for the spatial tropes. Further, the

---

[165] Ehring, Douglas (2001), 164. In fact, Ehring's defense of tropist **BT** along the lines indicated is not quite persuasive. For, it is hard to imagine what would count as an "unchanging object" to which the trope-bundle account would be applicable. In my view only abstract particulars like propositions, geometrical figures, etc. are *unchanging* objects, but since these are abstract objects, there is no point in construing them as bundles of *momentary* tropes. If, however, enduring tropes are also allowed, then tropist **BT** is not elegantly homogeneous any more.

incorporation of the spatio-temporal position as a constituent of the trope burdens the trope theory with the task of giving an adequate account of space and time which is too high a standard for the trope theory to pass. No wonder, then, that Ehring stays with simple tropes that are "time-indexed" without including, however, time as a constituent.

The consonance of temporal parts theory and *tropist* **BT** is summed up by Ehring as follows: "I conclude that for bundle theory and the temporal parts theory to be mutually consistent, the bundles of bundle theory should consist in tropes and include the co-instantiation relation itself and that that relation is a momentary trope. Only then can the bundle theorist take object persistence to be a matter of a relation among temporal parts, even if those temporal parts overlap with respect to enduring tropes."[166]

So Ehring's provisions comprise the tropehood of the co-instantiation relation *and* the momentary nature of tropes. First, the tropehood of relations in general, and the tropehood of co-instantiation in particular, ensure that one can stay within a purely tropist **BT** without invoking universals. Second, these co-instantiations are momentary, so that they incessantly give way to other co-instantiations and presumably each such co-instantiation forms a temporal part. As to the first provision, I have already pointed out that in the case of fundamental relations like compresence or co-instantiation, the tropes need to be backed by universals since no account can be given about such fundamental relations exclusively in terms of tropes without reference to the respective universal. As to the second provision I note that the significance of the temporal part doctrine as a purported account of persistence is considerably diminished by Ehring's admission of an "overlap with respect to enduring tropes". His admission presumably is that substances can persist in virtue of consisting partly of enduring tropes that are invariant through change. So persistence is secured by the

---

[166] Ehring (2001), 168.

enduring tropes. But in that case it is hard to see what role the temporal part doctrine would play in explaining persistence through time.

Therefore I take it that persistence requires enduring items and not just the concatenation of successive items. Maybe, momentary things are well explained within the perdurantist frame as complexes of properties in momentary co-instantiation. But the crucial point far less accounted for adequately by perdurantism is what makes an *enduring* thing out of the series of momentary things. According to perdurantists it is the fact that all these momentary things stand in some contingent *R*-relation. Thus the very existence of enduring things depends on this unspecified relation, and it does not suffice to say that momentary items cast as "temporal parts" are ubiquitously around. For, in order to turn them into parts *of* an integral whole, the gluing relation should be sufficiently strong. It should be so strong, I suspect, that the prior unity of the *thin* thing should already be presupposed.

The fact that tropes are momentary entities and even most of the enduring tropes last shorter than the object itself, makes the trope **BT** eligible as a theory of change. But it does not follow that persistence should be accounted for in terms of temporal parts. All that follows is that change and variance are already built-in features of the tropist **BT**, while they are not built-in features of the universalist **BT**. In this respect I agree with Ehring that a tropist **BT** admits change. But no compelling reasons have been afforded to buy into the temporal part doctrine.

The main deficiency of the temporal part doctrine, as I said earlier, is that the notion of temporal part makes no sense without the prior notion of the substance as an integral whole. Therefore integral wholes cannot be analysed reductively through their temporal parts. These parts can do some job for the analysis of change, but with the provision that they can be specified only by reference to the thing whose temporal parts they are. "Russell-at-the-age-of-5" is individuated by reference to the person Russell whose personality does not dissolve into the temporal sequence of momentary or short-lived entities. So the endurantist insight about substances as integral wholes existing through changes cannot be ignored. This is not to say that all the temporal parts belonging to an object through its complete life span already belong to it right at the start in an atemporal sense that accounts for its "wholeness". When endurantists speak about the "whole" object's being present through changes, they speak in a misleading way. Rather, the real claim should be that it is the object in a "thin" sense that yields unity. It alone is able to unite the distant temporal parts as making up the *Gesamtleben* or totality of life. Since the *Gesamtleben* comes about in succession, there is no locus for a prior unity in it. There is the possibility though of taking unity as an *emergent* feature, but this suggestion hardly works for substances. Therefore one should adopt the notion of a thin object which already enjoys unity prior to the acquisition of its full biographical contents in succession.

The temporal part doctrine of substances is motivated by the preference for process ontologies over substance ontologies. However, one does not have to commit oneself to process ontologies across the board in order to espouse a more dynamical variant of trope **BT**. For example in a dualist framework suggested by Simons continuants can be viewed "as invariants among occurrents under equivalence relation".[167] To put it less technically, the continuant is the thing that emerges, by the thread of its invariant features, out of the flux of all sorts of changes and events in which it occurs. For example, Napoleon is re-identifiable as a substance or continuant; he can be traced through various battles, political, private, social etc., actions and events happening at different places and times. All these occurrents are saliently united by the very fact that they make up the totality of Napoleon's life. The advantage of this approach is that while it explores the role of occurrents "vital to continuants" in explaining change, it does not need to take recourse to the dubious doctrine of temporal parts in accounting for the persistence of substances. For now the vehicles of change are the temporal parts of occurrents vital to substances and *not* the putative temporal parts of the

---

[167] Simons, P. (2000)

substances themselves since, in a dualist framework, only occurrents have temporal parts but not continuants. For example, "temporally specific existential propositions about continuants, such as *Napoleon existed in 1815*" could be "made true by associated temporal parts of occurrents vital to [his] existence, such as (in Napoleon's case) heartbeats, respiration, digestion, in 1815".[168] So we do not have to appeal to the temporal parts of Napoleon in order to explain change, for he does not have any, strictly speaking. But we make recourse instead to the temporal parts of those occurrents that are vital to his existence, such as the events of his bodily functioning or the episodes of the Napoleonic Wars. For occurrents have, by their very nature, temporal parts, while continuants lack them according to the dualistic conception. Traditional dualism is thus tailored to the needs of accounting for change in the substances.

Recently Simons has defended the good match between the tropist **BT** and the relatively novel doctrine of continuants as invariants among occurrents. If his defense is successful, then tropist **BT** can be saved from the familiar charge of being unable to provide for change. Ehring and Simons both recommend tropist **BT** rather than universalist **BT** as the preferred account of substances. However, their metaphysical motivations for tropism are different. Whereas Ehring regards momentary tropes as the vehicles of change, Simons appreciates tropes as items in a sparse and nominalistic ontology yielding also the truthmakers for non-existential propositions about particulars. Change and persistence are explained differently: Ehring follows Casullo's lead in construing enduring substances as bundles of temporal-part bundles - a doctrine that has already been repudiated here. While Simons dualistic stance permits him to explain change with the help of the temporal parts of occurrents vital to continuants.

Now the price paid for avoiding the doctrine of temporal parts with continuants is to view occurrents as in a sense "ontologically more

---

[168] Simons, P. (2000), 149.

basic" than continuants. Basicness means that the occurrents vital to continuants already form a "natural whole" according to Simons and the continuant is represented as the "unique abstractum or invariant" in this whole. Further, "causal connections" are said to be responsible for the formation of this "natural whole". Thus continuants are represented as derivative from occurrents.

This conception, attractive it may sound, has its shortcomings. For example, there is the logical possibility not to be ruled out on a priori grounds that the same set of occurrents involves two or more different continuants largely in the same position or role. For example, twins can live so closely to each other that the same set of occurrents can be associated to their total life including birth and death; moreover, the same type of causal connections could be at work with the same shared occurrents. For example, if the twins play tennis, they participate in the same games and both become tired as a result of the exercise, etc. But obviously, this would not turn them into the same "unique abstractum" or individual. It would simply make it a bit more difficult to separate them in their respective biographical accounts. So the set of shared occurrents underdetermines, so to speak, the identity of the continuants. Mere participation in the same set of events with the performance of the same roles does not uniquely rule out an identical individual since "participation in the same set of events with the same roles" is a rather loose constraint. Say, if you and I always go to the same parties and social events, it might indicate that we belong to the same social circle without supporting the unjustified claim that we make up the same individual. Therefore it seems difficult to derive continuants from occurrents in the suggested way unless further constraints are introduced. But those further constraints presumably would not be of any help either in the putative derivation of continuants from occurrents; since, as I suspect, those would be constraints to the effect that essential reference has to be made to the continuants whose prior existence is thus presupposed. For example, statements about *origin*, like growing from a given zygote, or made out of a certain chunk of wood might help to identify uniquely a continuant but not merely by singling out the respective occurrents of "*growing*" and "*making*". Rather, what is vital to identification is the essential reference to *further continuants* like a given zygote and a given chunk of wood as essential continuants in the occurrents of birth and creation.

In short, even if continuants are invariants among occurrents they cast this role in virtue of further continuants that supply the points of reference for them. No surprise, then, that this insight is implicated in one of Simons' remarks: "In particular *if we fix a frame of reference*, the temporal parts of the total life give us something which is identically the same at different times of its existence, yet which lacks temporal parts of its own and is thus a continuant".(italics mine) [169] In other words, a frame of reference must be presupposed for the identification of the temporal series forming a whole. And a frame of reference typically supplied by a co-ordinate system, or a calendar, or the latitudes and longitudes, etc., is an individual constant rather than an occurrent. Thus something fixed and relatively *permanent* must be presupposed even by the account that purports to represent continuants as entities emerging from the flux of occurrrents. The conception of dispensing totally with continuants and supplying the frame of reference by the derivation of other continuants from occurrrents is flawed. Moreover, the series of occurrents does not single out a unique continuant to which the series belongs unless the owner-continuant is already identified. The basic deficiency of the temporal part doctrine is not removed by the doctrine of continuants as invariants among occurrents. Rather it is repeated in a more sophisticated form.

Further, the same objection can presumably be repeated for the "causal connections" that are said to play a role in forming a "natural whole". So one *cannot* dispense with further continuants in the derivation of continuants from occurents. For the relata in causal connections, i.e. the events, are typically described as changes in the property instances of continuant-particulars. For example, the expansion of metal by heating is a change in the metal's extension, molecular state,

---

[169] Simons *ibid.*

etc. In short, events are identifiable by reference to the continuant-particulars whose properties get replaced through these occurrents. Maybe, the particulars of microphysics undergoing change do not exhibit "thingness" in the way medium size dry goods do. But they still exhibit thing-ness, whatever thin it might be, that is still distinguishable from their behaving like occurrents. In sum, the ontological derivation of continuants from occurrents is a misguided attempt, since at each point of the derivation some further continuant must be introduced.

The role of the continuant is to yield permanence and fix the background against which change can be meaningfully described. I have started my account of substances with the appreciation of the Kantian permanence condition and the substances were claimed to be the main vehicles of this permanence. Without the permanence condition no coherent account of experience is possible. If speculations about substance ontologies *versus* process ontologies can reach a position at all, they can reach the metaphysical insight that substances are the vehicles of the permanence condition vital to the possibility of experience.

Before closing the survey of the notion of continuants as invariants among occurrents, let us see how this notion fares when coupled with the tropist **BT**. Simons in (2000) repeats basically the same account of his two-tier trope **BT** that he already put forward in (1994). In both works he specifies *de individuo* dependence or *generic* dependence among the individual tropes making up the nucleus, and *generic* dependence or *de specie* dependence for the determinable tropes of the periphery.[170] Therefore, one can raise the same objections concerning his later paper that I have developed with the earlier work. The objections weigh even stronger with respect to the later paper attempting to show the coherence of trope **BT** with a theory of persistence through time, since the earlier work has completely ignored the problem of persistence. These

---

[170] See Simons (2000), 148. and compare it with Simons (1994)

objections, both mine and Denkel's, target the rigid, non-flexible nature of this two-tier tropist **BT**.

Recall that Denkel has pointed out the following discomforting consequence: the accidental properties of the substance would be left without ontological support in case of essential change when the qualitative nucleus incorporating the essence and playing also the role of a bearer-substratum would be lost. But clearly, a concrete thing does not completely disintegrate just because its substratum gets lost. For example, a destroyed statue having lost the essential status of a work of art, still continues to support, in its physical form, a great many of its accidental properties like being made up of marble, having a certain size and weight, etc.

Apart from substantial change, change in the determinates of determinables also seems to be problematic on Simons' account. Therefore I have spelled out my discontent with the nucleus being based exclusively on *de individuo* dependence, for it rules out change in the determinates. This is clearly counterintuitive since, for example, the determinate wisdom Socrates has at an age, is surely replaced by another determinate of the same kind at a successive age. He would never have been properly called "wise" had he always exhibited exactly the same wisdom. So, Simons's account cannot cope either with the survival of accidental tropes after substantial change, or with change in the determinates of essential determinables in the nucleus.

We can reasonably expect that the application of the relatively novel conception of continuants as invariants among occurrents to the tropist **BT** yields some solution to persistence through time. The question is whether it can improve on the deficiencies that I have repeated here.

Under the pressure of coping with change, the trope theory is slightly modified by Simons. He de-occamises the ontological scene by introducing the distinction between "continuant tropes" and "occurrent tropes". With this suggestion the traditional understanding of tropes as momentary entities becomes questionable. For now " if a body or other continuant continues unchanged over a period in some respect and a trope is the truthmaker for the proposition that it is so, then the trope is itself a continuant"... [171] And "occurrent tropes" are invoked as the truthmakers for propositions about events. For example, the event of "collision" requires the respective occurrent trope of collision. Although the occurrent tropes are momentary, once "continuant tropes" or "enduring tropes" are admitted, tropes cease to be essentially fleeting entities. The introduction of "continuant tropes" deprives tropes of one of their essential features; i.e. their being momentary entities that has proven to be their virtue in accounting for change in the substance. Moreover, such continuant tropes are recognized as elements of Simons's trope **BT**. For, Simons says in the very same passage, that the nucleus-bundle "consists entirely of continuant tropes".

Now if this is the modified conception, it cannot be considered as an improvement over the rigid conception of the nucleus. For here again, no change is tolerated in the determinates of the determinable nucleus-tropes of substances. The postulated continuant tropes that make up the nucleus are unchanging items. For example, if being rational and being corporeal are essential properties in the nucleus of humans, then humans are supposed to exhibit the same determinates of rationality and corporeality through their whole career.

A further problem arises from the fact that the notion of continuant as "invariant over occurrents" is supposed to be applicable now to the so-called continuant tropes. As Simons himself clearly perceives, "it is much harder to see what could be the relevant occurrent basis over which the continuant tropes could be invariants"...[172] Now the point is that continuant tropes are not identified against the background of occurrents; it is only the "higher level entity", i.e., the substance-continuant that can be traced through the occurrents, but not its constituting tropes. Moreover, the duplication of the continuant items

---

[171] Simons (2000), 150.

[172] Simons *ibid.*

threatens the ratio essence of the trope bundle theory. As Simons himself acknowledges: "but if the substantial continuant is itself an invariant over occurrents then the need to constitute it out of a bundle of tropes is either wholly lacking or its urgency is greatly reduced".[173]

It would perhaps be more accurate to say that in this case it would be unreasonable to construe the substantial continuant out of a bundle of *continuant* tropes as opposed to construing it out of the usual *momentary* tropes. It would be an overkill to discard trope **BT** just because the idea of *continuant tropes* does not fit into the scheme. It was the prospect of a harmonious match between trope **BT** and the notion of continuant as "invariant over occurrents" that Simons was out to defend. Unfortunately, his own suggestion about continuant tropes has presented an obstacle to the happy alliance.

For these reasons I take it that the alliance works only with the usual conception of tropes as momentary entities. Restating the usual conception may be promising from the perspective of accounting for change and persistence through time. So, the insight should be that trope **BT** coupled with the notion of a continuant as an "invariant over occurrents" does not require enduring items at the level of the constituting tropes; it requires an account of endurance only at the level of individual substances.

The advantage of Simons's approach is that it dispenses with the temporal part doctrine *of* substances. For the notion of continuants as invariants over occurrents makes this doctrine superfluous. The vehicles of change are the temporal parts of occurrents vital to continuants rather than the temporal parts of these continuants themselves. This seems to be a better account of persistence and change than the one suggested by Ehring. Recall that Ehring explains change by temporal sub-bundles connecting up to the substance-bundle. In short, he applies the temporal part doctrine of substances to trope **BT**.

---

[173] Simons *ibid*.

There is a further feature of Simons's account not yet discussed. Simons feels the need to modify the relation of *mutual foundation* in trope **BT** in order to make it fit for change. He does not find it sufficient to replace the temporal part doctrine of continuants by the doctrine of continuants as invariants over occurrents; the gluing relation needs to be revised as well. Let us look at this revision.

Simons explains that mutual foundation may be conceived as *diachronic* because "the mutual need of tropes does not entail synchronicity: a trope may require another non-simultaneously". The original idea of "essential dependence, of which tropehood is a genus, is neutral as to time and space." But one can accommodate change by a "transtemporal trope bundle", he says, since "in principle there is nothing to stop the existence of one thing demanding the existence of another at a timelike separation from it."[174] So the suggestion is that *diachronic mutual foundation* among the tropes constituting a substance explains change and persistence.

Now let us see whether the very notion of "diachronic mutual foundation" can consistently be maintained. The "neutrality" of mutual foundation (mutual essential dependence) claimed with respect to "time and space" suggests that this notion is purely logical or conceptual. But it cannot be so because the tropes entering into mutual foundation exist in space and time and mutual foundation specifies their existential condition with respect to other tropes also existing in space and time. So the spatio-temporal aspect must have a metaphysical significance as well.

Now mutual foundation for these items requires *compresence* in the traditional synchronic version, where the question of temporal order does not arise. But obviously the question of temporal order arises with respect to the diachronic version. Simons has explained earlier, following Husserl, that an item A is "strongly founded" on item B iff "A

---

[174] Simons *op.cit.*, 154.

is necessarily such that it cannot exist unless B exists" and "B is not part of A".[175] As a consequence, mutual foundation requires that necessarily neither items can exist without the other and neither is part of the other. Now let us see whether one can apply this definition of mutual foundation to its putative diachronic version. In the diachronic mutual foundation of A and B, the timelike separation of the items must be part of the definition. Therefore A's being founded on B would require also that B must exist prior to A. And B's being founded on A would require that A must exist prior to B. Thus mutual foundation in the diachronic version would require that both items should exist prior to the other which is clearly incoherent. So the very idea of "*diachronic mutual foundation*" is incoherent.

To cope with the difficulty the notion of mutual foundation should, perhaps, be revised for the diachronic case. But it is hard to conceive what revision would be proper; let alone the fact that the notion of mutual foundation is clear in the original definition and it is well-entrenched in our conceptual practice. Or, another option would be to seek some other, equally strong gluing relation for the "transtemporal bundles", but there are no available suggestions so far. Maybe the best option would be to return to the classical conception of tropes according to which these are momentary entities. Then change would somehow be necessitated by the very nature of tropes. For, in this case, even the permanent qualitative aspects of the enduring things would be constituted by the succession of exactly similar tropes of the same kind. And the transient qualitative aspects would be constituted by the replacement of a token of one kind of trope by the token of another kind of trope. In this vein it would be relatively easy to find the conceptual place of change, for there would be no need of a drastic revision of **BT**. If a trope-bundle is, by its very nature, momentary, the only difference between unchanging things and changing things would be that the former would consist of related bundles of exactly similar momentary

---

[175] See chapter V. pp. 128-30.

tropes of the same kinds, while the latter would consist of related bundles of momentary tropes of different kinds. Moreover, if one starts with momentary tropes that can be "exactly similar", the further advantage is that gradual, piecemeal change can also be accommodated for in terms of "less than exact" similarity admitting grades.

This suggestion also scores well with respect to the objection cast against Simons's two-tier trope **BT**. For, according to Simons's theory, the nucleus as the individuator *and* the bearer of the essence of the substance consists of tropes that are both *unchanging* and *determinate*. But I have already pointed out that the determinate tropes of certain essential determinable kinds give way to other determinate tropes of the same essential kinds during the dynamic life career of individuals. Permanence in determinables while change in the determinates can be well explained on the present suggestion that differs from Simons's. My suggestion provides for intuitively appealing cases. For example, rationality is an essential human trait, but it is exhibited in different determinate tokens in the different phases of humans. Say, your rationality-token in youth is such that it urges you to compete with your schoolmates. And your rationality-token in maturity is such that it recommends to you to co-operate with as many people as you can in order to avoid conflicts. You are rational throughout your whole life, but evidently, with very different determinates. If one retorts that I have deliberately picked out a flexible concept, the answer is that quite many essential features are flexible precisely in the way indicated.

At this point the question arises whether the desideratum of capturing the sortal essence is not in conflict with the desideratum of capturing the individual *qua* the particular individual it is. For essences are shared and sharable. What makes, then, the rationality Socrates exhibits only *his* in a privileged way and not mine or yours? This complaint could be nicely circumvented by the trope-theoretic account in the following way. While the *exact similarity* of tropes of certain *kinds* provides for the *sortal* essence, the *bearer uniqueness* of each trope making an individual ensures that the individual is to be taken *qua* that particular individual and not simply a token of the kind. But, perhaps, the very idea of bearer uniqueness is parasitic on a further item: it seems that *individual* essences are required as well in an explanatory scheme. In the last chapter further arguments will be presented in favour of postulating individual essences on top of sortal ones.

In sum: assessing the two accounts that aim at combining trope-**BT** with change and persistence I find that neither is completely satisfactory in itself. Rather, a certain combination of the two suggestions seems to be the most promising. On Ehring's approach change is already a built-in feature of trope-**BT** since he underwrites the momentary nature of tropes. Now these momentary tropes do not have to be supposed as making the temporal parts of substances; they make the substances themselves. There is no need to postulate temporal parts once the transient nature of tropes already does the required job. If temporal parts play a role they can play a role as the temporal parts of occurrents vital to continuants. As Simons points out, even temporally specific existential propositions about continuants, such as *Napoleon existed in 1815*, can be accounted for without introducing temporal parts of continuants or substances. For, in such cases the occurrents vital to Napoleon have temporal parts in *1815* like, for example, the events of the Napoleonic Wars in that year, or, simply, the events of his bodily functioning in that year, etc., and these temporal parts of the associated occurrents yield the truthmakers for the temporally specific existential proposition about *Napoleon in 1815*.

Note, however, that the notion of occurrents that has to be associated with a continuant is loose enough so that it cannot give identity conditions for continuants participating in the same set of events. But these occurrents are appropriate for yielding a temporal frame of reference for temporally specific existential propositions about continuants. In sum, the explanation of change requires only the temporal parts of the occurents vital to continuants *and* the momentary nature of tropes making up substances. As to persistence and permanence, the postulation of enduring tropes is hardly desirable, for it would make trope **BT** superfluous. The need for the enduring items can be satisfied on the level of enduring substances rather than on the level of the constituting tropes.

The last worry about trope-**BT**'s eligibility for a theory of change and persistence is the one spelled out by Denkel.[176] As he notices, accidental tropes in the periphery of the substances would remain without support in case of radical change when the nucleus is destroyed. Denkel finds this consequence of Simons's theory counterintuitive, since concrete substances do not completely disintegrate once they stop having their essence. The accidental tropes quite often remain supported, whatever the ontological status of the successor entity is.

The problem indicated by Denkel is not specific to a two-tier trope theory. What Denkel has pointed out is the crucial problem of change in the essential substances sortals. Now according to the revived Aristotelian sortal essentialism, a particular substance exists *qua* the instance of its substance sortal as long as it satisfies the sortal essence. This essence may be lost by the thing's ceasing to satisfy the essential substance sortal it satisfied before. Say, a man has belonged to the substance sortal "Man" but has suffered brain damage and so now he is a man "in name alone". Although he has not completely disintegrated as a physical entity, he is not a "man" any more according to sortal essentialist insights. A two-tier trope **BT** can do here no more than prescribe some other bearer for the surviving accidental tropes. The bearer can be another nucleus provided that the whole entity would fall under another substance-sortal, say, human Body, or the surviving entity can somehow be classified even if not in essentialist terms.

Change in the essential substance sortal can also be provoked in a tricky way. Not only "real" drastic changes like accidents with brain damage can incur change in the modal status of the substance. Surprisingly enough trifle Cambridge events can also bring about such

---

[176] Denkel (1997)

changes. As the last problem of change, I examine here the possible modal effects of Cambridge events.

The best way to introduce the problem is by reconsidering the ancient puzzle of Chrysippus. The stoic Chrysippus raised the issue whether Theon, the proper part of the man Dion, consisting of all of Dion except Dion's left foot, can survive the amputation of that leg provided that the operation is not lethal. Chrysippus is reported to have decided that it could not, but he offered no reason to support his position. Recently Burke has attempted to justify Chrysippus's answer by appealing to Aristotelian sortal essentialism. Briefly, Burke's explanation for Theon's destruction is that if it continued to exist, it would become indiscernible from the man Dion in all possible respects, and so it would begin to satisfy the substance sortal "man", undergoing thus a "sortal change". However, no survival under another sortal is permitted by sortal essentialist insights. Sortal essentialism says that things persist *qua* tokens of certain essential sorts; things exist as long as they satisfy the requirements of falling under the sortal.

The conclusion of the puzzle sounds rather counterintuitive. After all, why would Theon, the undetached proper part of Dion, perish by becoming placed at a greater distance from Dion's left foot? The change that Theon undergoes is a mere Cambridge change that is not a real alteration in any of its intrinsic properties. But sortal essentialism forbids survival under another sortal, and thus we have to face the counterintuitive consequence of the mere Cambridge change that Theon undergoes. So Cambridge change poses a challenge for sortal essentialism.

Even more recently Stone has suggested to explore the constitution relation in order to dissolve the puzzle: he takes it that Theon can survive as the *constitutor* of Dion, for now, after the amputation, it in fact bodily constitutes Deon. Thereby the drastic effect of Cambridge change that shows itself under the sortal essentialist principle is mitigated.

To anticipate, here I shall point out that the constitution relation *cannot* serve as a protective buffer between sortal essentialism and

Cambridge change. My reason is the following: Theon's putative survival in whatever form, say, the form made possible by constitution, presupposes that an essential property of Theon is lost by Cambridge change. Theon ceases to be a proper part of man which was essential to him, as I shall point out, though not a feature that makes a substance sortal. And the loss of an essential property while the thing continues its existence is denied by any form of essentialism, even the one that Stone embraces.[177] The moral will be that the metaphysical consequences of Cambridge changes should not be underestimated: substances and their proper parts are vulnerable to such changes by sortal essentialist insights. Further, Chrysippus's puzzle represents a host of background problems; these, and the various metaphysical motivations that pertain to the puzzle, will be considered as well.

Let us focus now on the arguments. In his attempt to deal with the putative conflict between Cambridge change and sortal essentialism put into focus by Chrysippus's puzzle, Jim Stone has made the following claims[178]. First, the "brittle" form of essentialism which Burke deployed previously in his approach is implausible since it entails that trivial changes in the relational properties of objects can lead to the destruction of these objects. In the puzzle, for example, Theon, the proper part of the man Dion consisting of all of Dion except Dion's left foot, is destroyed according to Burke by being separated from that foot by amputation.[179] As Stone sees it, accepting that such merely relational changes, i.e. Cambridge changes have lethal effects for the objects would reduce essentialism to absurdity. Second, he claims that one can avoid such unwelcome consequences by appealing to the constitution relation thereby granting the survival of Theon as a constitutor of Dion. This suggestion, though irrelevant as a solution to Chrysippus' puzzle, as

---

[177] See Ujvári, M. (2004a), (2004b)

[178] Stone, J. (2002), 216, 222.

[179] see Burke (1994), 134.

Stone admits, still has its main advantage that the constitution relation mitigates the effect of Cambridge changes for sortal essentialism.

Stone writes: "Once we shift to the view that post-amputation Theon merely constitutes Dion, however, the brittle form of essentialism that Burke deploys becomes less implausible. As it is false that Theon becomes a man if it survives the separation from Dion's foot, Theon is not destroyed by a mere relational change after all. Now we can insist, without reducing essentialism to absurdity that no proper part of a man can survive by becoming a whole man. In effect, the constitution relation provides a protective buffer between sortal essentialism and Cambridge change. "He says later: "Burke's alternative ... without the constitution relation as a buffer, is rendered untenable by Cambridge change." [180]

In what follows I shall elaborate my point that the constitution relation cannot serve as a protective buffer between sortal essentialism and Cambridge change. To repeat, Theon's survival as a constitutor presupposes that an *essential property of Theon is lost by Cambridge change*. For, being a proper part of a man is essential to Theon, as I shall show. It loses that feature by the amputation, although that feature does not count as a substance sortal. And the loss of an essential property while the thing continues to exist is ruled out by any form of essentialism.[181]

If sound, what this shows is that it is time to revise the standard picture according to which Cambridge changes are too insubstantial to play a role in essentialist considerations. My argument does not presuppose the disapproval of appealing to the constitution relation. I do not take a stand on this issue between Burke and Stone or the rest of the philosophical community. All I am presupposing is this: pre-amputation Theon *was* a proper part of a man, so, not a man, that is, a "non-man".

---

[180] Stone (2002), 222.

[181] I am grateful for valuable comments and criticism of an earlier draft of this paper to Robert Kirk, Stephen Barker and Robert Black.

More precisely, it was a *non-man essentially* which is clearly accepted and argued for by both Burke and Stone. Now undeniably Theon loses, by the amputation, its property of being the proper part of a man.

Before coming to my claims, the locution "being the proper part of a man" needs to be addressed briefly. Burke states his argument in terms of 'persons', not 'men'; Stone reformulates the argument in terms of 'men' admitting that "nothing of philosophical importance hangs on the simplification". Again, later Burke spells out his premises in terms of "proper parts of men" while characterising Dion as "a whole-bodied, human person" whose "part is Theon".[182] In view of these formulations I take it that the suggestion is the following: Theon as a proper part is to be identified by reference to the person Dion in virtue of the latter's having a human body. Traditionally, a special unity is ascribed to persons; for this reason it is presumably more appropriate to talk about proper parts of 'men' rather than to talk about proper parts of 'persons'.

After these qualifications I shall show, first, that being the proper part of a man is an essential property of Theon. Second, I shall explore the consequences of the loss of an essential property for the connection between Cambridge change and essentialism. The original motivation for the problem, i.e. the attempt to solve Chrysippus's puzzle will be ignored here.

While agreeing on the pre-amputation phase, Burke and Stone diverge on the post-amputation phase, along the lines that I have already indicated. I take it that *no survival is possible for Theon, but not for the reasons given by Burke*. Let us see first more closely how Burke and Stone conceive the problem. According to Burke if Theon survived the operation, it would survive as a person since by becoming qualitatively and compositionally identical to the person Dion, personhood can not be denied of it. But Theon's survival is overridden by sortal essentialism according to which the general sort of a thing is essential to its identity

---

[182] See: Burke (1994), 129., Burke (2004), 242., Stone (2002), 217.

and, as a consequence, if a thing ceases to fall under a general sort marking out its essence, it ceases to exist.

Now the change suffered by Theon qualifies as a sortal one in Burke's view, but the reason he gives does not center around what is actually *lost* by the change; but rather, it is explained counterfactually as to what *would be* gained by a "sortal change". Evidently, the change cannot be a sortal one according to what is actually lost since Theon, the "torso" not falling under the form Man, belongs to the *complement* of the essential substance sortal Man. Clearly, complements of substance sortals are not themselves substance sortals. Therefore things in that range have no substance sortal, though they have the property of falling under the complement of a substance sortal essentially, due to the essentiality of the general sort. So "sortal change" with Theon can only be explained counterfactually: it would acquire the substance sortal Man if it continued to exist.[183] Since no substance sortal can be acquired, then, true to sortal essentialist insights, Theon is done in by a Cambridge change.

Stone rejects the supposition that Theon is a man after the surgery if it survives, and considers as an option Theon's survival by appealing to the constitution relation: thus Theon survives as a mere constitutor of the man Dion. (This option is not available to Burke for he rejects coincident objects.) By invoking the constitution relation Stone purports to mitigate both the extreme brittleness of sortal essentialism and the *force* of Cambridge change. So, in his solution Theon is not done in by Cambridge change after all. In Stone's version of essentialism which he

---

[183] Burke explains 'sortal change' in the given case as follows: 'I say that Theon undergoes a "sortal change" (a change in sort) because the change it undergoes is one that would result in its beginning to satisfy, if it continued to exist, the substance sortal "person"; (3) in saying that the relational change results in a sortal change, I am relying on my third assumption. that Theon is a person after the surgery, if it exists after the surgery, as well as on my first assumption, the maximality of person, which provides the basis for denying that Theon is a person before the surgery.' (1994), 138. footnote 20

calls "relaxed essentialism" "men are essentially men" expresses the thesis that nothing in the set S of things having the feature of being explained by the form Man can become a member of the complement of that set and survive. For example, if a man loses his mental abilities, he will be a man "in name alone" since he is no longer explained by the form Man. Its proper place will be in the complement of the set Man as a "non-man". By the same token, members of the complement of the set determined by the form Man cannot survive under the form Man. For, "non-men are essentially non-men" "expresses the thought that nothing in the complement of S can become a member of S and survive".[184] So, a "torso" cannot become a whole man by amputation and survive.

Stone's version of sortal essentialism "requires no exception for proper parts of men", as he says. So, proper parts of men are members of the complement of the set determined by the substance sortal Man and presumably the same applies to proper parts of other things falling under a substance sortal.[185]

So, Stone seems basically to accept, with the above qualifications, premises 1) and 2) of Burke's reconstructed argument, that are:

"(1) The concept of a man is maximal; proper parts of men are not men."

"(2) Men are essentially men (thus non-men are essentially non-men)".[186]

Stone rejects only premise (3): "If Theon survives the separation from Dion's foot, then Theon will be a man".

---

[184] See Stone (2002), 220.

[185] See Stone (2002), 221.

[186] See Stone (2002), 217. and Burke's repeated suggestion of these premises: Burke (2004), 2.

Before coming to my reading, I suggest a restriction as to what counts as "essentially non-men" since negative properties have always been found suspect. Philosophers from Duns Scotus through McTaggart, up to D.M. Armstrong, refused them for various reasons. One of the worries is particularly acute with *essential negative properties*. How do they contribute to the characterisation of things which is part of the duty of essential properties? Fortunately, Stone provides us with a clue as to what counts as "essentially non-man". We just have to spell it out explicitly in the form of a restriction.

The restriction is plausible enough and has a bearing on my argument. It is that *only proper parts* of men are to be taken as members of the complement of the set determined by the form Man *plus* cases of whole men being man "in name alone" for some reason or another. Without this restriction the notion of an essential negative property would become trivialised. For example, every animal except men in the domain of animals has the property of being non-man and, by the essentiality of the sort, has this negative property essentially. Also, every animal of a given sort lacks essentially the property of belonging to any other sort of the domain. So, for example, a dog is essentially non-cat, essentially non-horse, etc. Moreover, if we take a wider domain with medium-size macroscopic concrete objects both animate and inanimate then, clearly, objects of that domain will have a host of essential negative properties that are supposed to play a role in their characterisation, as essential properties typically do. To avoid such counter-intuitive consequences and also to be in line with the use of "complement of general sort" in the given context by both Burke and Stone, I take it that only proper parts of things falling under a general sort, *plus* the whole thing which is literally "whole" but fails to satisfy the general sort for some reason, qualify as members of the complement.

One further note is in order here. My reading of how Cambridge change affects essentialism does *not* focus on the post-amputation phase; rather, it focuses on what property of Theon *is lost* by the change. While Burke argues counterfactually, I argue on factual grounds. If Theon survives the amputation in whatever form it does, this very fact casts a new light on its property of being the proper part of a man, hence its property of being essentially non-man. For now, after the amputation it is the case that it *was* a proper part of a man but it lost this property. Clearly, no one can deny this step.

Now the crucial point of my argument is this: the property of being the proper part of a man *is an essential property*; and if it is lost by a change then an essential property is lost by a change. Further, if the object is supposed to continue its existence, this contravenes the basic essentialist insights. To support my contention one can proceed by observing that Theon's being a proper part of a man is the property *in virtue of which* it is essentially non-man. This seems to be uncontroversial again on the basis of Burke's premises 1) and 2). So, Theon's being a proper part of a man is its essential property, though not a sortal one. This is its essential property lost by a Cambridge change while it is supposed to continue its existence under whatever form it does. But this is clearly unacceptable on essentialist grounds, because no thing can survive the loss of an essential property.

So Theon perishes in a Cambridge change, and this result of mine matches with Burke's result. However, the essentialist consideration I deploy to this conclusion is different from Burke's consideration. And it has, perhaps, the advantage that it cannot be challenged by invoking the constitution relation. For, as I have argued, once an essential property of a thing is lost, no survival is conceivable under any form.

My argument partly vindicates Burke's point to the effect that a Cambridge change actually affects Theon's essential property. However, what it affects is not a new substance sortal putatively acquired after the change, and this point has to be conceded to Stone.

But this is not the end of the story: we have to be able to exclude other reasons for Theon's being essentially non-man; otherwise we cannot prove that its being the proper part of a man was *the* essential property. For example, since I have claimed earlier that only proper parts *and* defective wholes are in the complements of essential substance sortals, the question arises whether Theon could survive as a defective whole, preserving thus the property of being essentially non-man. This would be a possible way of avoiding my conclusion. However, Theon could not turn into a defective whole by the change, and thus qualifying again, after the amputation, as essentially non-man, since Dion with the same defect does not qualify as such either.

A further possibility to undermine my approach would be the following. Theon survives the operation as our commonsensical intuition would demand, so that we do not have to face the challenge of Cambridge change for sortal essentialism as I insist. The survival, however, is grounded in the fact that Theon is an aggregate of mere flesh and bones, blood, cells, etc. This aggregate can be individuated solely by reference to such parts and the intrinsic properties involved in having such parts. Since Theon remains the same after the surgery in terms of *this* individuation, nothing actually happens to it in a Cambridge change. Theon's principle of individuation is always different from Dion's principle of individuation. While Theon is individuated mereologically, Dion's individuation presumably depends, within the constraints of his sortal essence, on his individual essence as well. Individual essences will be advocated in the next, final chapter. In this vein, having a head, two arms, a body, but only one leg, etc. are essential to Theon's identity; whereas the having of exactly these parts or any other ensemble is not essential to Dion, the man. So Theon's being a non-man, and being essentially a non-man are explained by the fact that what are essential to its identity are not essential to a man's identity.[187]

Now I do not think that Theon's being essentially non-man can be explained in this way, i.e. its being an entity individuated mereologically without reference to such relational property as being the proper part of a man. My reasons for denying this option are the following.

1. If Theon could be individuated mereologically the implication of this would be that Theon's identity would become extremely

---

[187] This suggestion was made to me by Stephen Barker.

fragile. Mereological individuation brings with it excessive rigidity. If, for example, Theon loses a drop of blood during the operation which is very much plausible, Theon dies *qua* the entity mereologically individuated in terms of the parts it *actually* has and the intrinsic properties involved. But even if the surgery is carried out in ideal conditions, Theon with its biological functions is in constant flux as to its metabolism, breathing, etc. As a biological entity, it dies every moment and is born in every moment if its identity is viewed from a mereological perspective. Mereological individuation may work well with abstract entities, like sets and classes but it is not the best guide to the individuation of living organisms. Therefore, Theon cannot qualify as essentially non-man by being mereologically individuated. My point is supported also by Burke.[188] On the mereological approach, then, Theon would die in every moment; on my approach, it would die only once.

2. There is also a positive reason as to why Theon should be identified by reference to its relational property of being the proper part of a man. The insight is this: although Theon performs many of the biological functions that humans do perform, its essential feature cannot be being a man, only a non-man. For, if exception were made for proper parts, then, clearly, instead of one man there would be a host of men: all-of-me-but-my-pinky-tip would be me as a man; all-of-me-but-one-hair-plucked-out would be me as a man, etc. Or, what Burke coins as the "many-thinkers problem", proper parts of human thinkers would themselves be human thinkers which is clearly far from the "commonsensical view". Therefore, it would be highly counterintuitive to de-occamise the identity of such entities; but mereological individuation is not a good option either, as we have seen. So the best available option is to individuate Theon as a proper

---

[188] Burke in (2004) footnote 6. states explicitly that Theon is not mereologically rigid. Here he considers another part of Dion called Adam. What the latter actually is, is irrelevant for the present concern; what is relevant is that Burke says: "Adam (unlike Theon) is mereologically rigid"…

part of a man and the main contentions are nicely captured in Burke's premises 1) and 2), underwritten also by Stone.

So I take it that Theon's being a proper part of a man was its essential property, and that Theon was, before the amputation, essentially non-man in virtue of this property.

Now to grant Theon's survival with the loss of this property would generate serious problems. Consider: if Theon can lose its property of being essentially non-man, this means, from the perspective of its diachronic identity, that having this property only in one phase of its career, the property qualifies only as a phase-property (though not a phase-sortal). But phase-properties are typically had contingently: so Theon *contingently* has the property of being *essentially* non-man (since it has it only in one phase but not through its whole career). Uncomfortable as it is, there are two options at this point. One can make concession to the time-relative reading of essential properties; but this is to make a drastic enough revision in essentialist commitments. Or, alternatively, one can argue that since Theon only contingently has the feature of being a non-man after the amputation it must have had it contingently in the pre-amputation phase as well. That is, Theon is contingently a non-man through its whole career; but this is to produce an even more scandalous damage to essentialism. For if members of the complement of the set Man are members only contingently, then, members of the set Man itself will be members there only contingently; and this violates the essentiality of falling under a general sort. These are the ensuing complications if survival is supposed under any form.

So the upshot is this: if a proper part of a substance ceases to be its proper part, say, as a result of a Cambridge change, then, under whatever form it survives, it loses its essential property of falling into the complement of the set determined by the substance sortal. And this clearly conflicts with the basic essentialist conviction that no essential property can be either lost or acquired while the object continues to exist. The only possible option left for admitting the survival of Theon say, under the constitution relation, would be to embrace a time-relative notion of essential properties, but I am not sure whether this is the kind of relaxing essentialism that Stone has in mind.

Let me note here that the post-amputation phase with Theon's surviving as a constitutor of Dion is not problematic on essentialist grounds. Evidently, pre-amputation Theon was not a constitutor of Dion as a whole, for the latter was more than Theon. The move of becoming the constitutor of Dion by amputation causes no problem for sortal essentialism, because any object is only contingently related to its actual constitutor and contingent properties, including relational ones, are permitted to be acquired or lost without the destruction of the object. *What is not permitted, however, is to lose, in a Cambridge change, the property of being essentially non-man, and acquire instead the property of being the constitutor of a man contingently.* I say "instead" because it is precisely the expiration of the property of "being essentially non-man" that would vacate the slot for the property of "being the constitutor", provided Stone's suggestion were accepted. Since this step is not permitted, therefore the constitution relation is *not* "a protective buffer between sortal essentialism and Cambridge change", contrary to Stone's claim.

Cambridge changes raise an interesting issue about essential properties being affected by change. It is widely held that such changes are relational changes that are not real alterations in the intrinsic properties of the subject.[189] Such changes are typically located in the "other" relatum: for example, Sam becoming envied by his neighbours consists in changes in the psychological attitudes of his neighbours towards him. Since it is difficult to ascribe such events to the substance, to Sam in this case, some authors try to dispense with Cambridge events. As Brand remarks, "one way to proceed in these cases is to distinguish

---

[189] About "real change" and "intrinsic property" see Vallicella (2002).

between relational and non-relational changes, and restrict events to non-relational changes".[190]

It seems to be a natural suggestion that Cambridge changes, since they do not involve the constituting properties of the substances, cannot be essential to the substances. If Cambridge-changes are located in the "other" relatum, they do not affect the constituting properties of the substance. But, then, how do they affect the substance at all? How is Sam as an individual substance affected by the growth of his neighbours' envy towards him? As we have seen Cambridge changes can still have important metaphysical consequences. They can incur sortal changes. [191]

The main difficulty in the very notion of Cambridge changes is that while being essentially *relational,* they are viewed from the perspective of a substance as the bearer of a set of monadic properties. Typically, predication with monadic properties ascribes a special role to the subject; while Cambridge changes are located in the "other" relatum. *As relations, Cambridge changes supervene on one of the relata, while being expressed from the perspective of the other relatum they do not supervene on.* For example, the envy supervenes on the neighbours' psychology but the event is expressed from the perspective of the passive partner, Sam.[192] Still, as we have seen, Cambridge changes can be evaluated modally from the point of view of the relatum they do not supervene on, as we have seen with the case of poor Theon.

---

[190] Brand (1975), 147.

[191] Weberman, D. (1999) also stresses the importance of Cambridge changes. He argues that some relational changes are real changes, especially those in the artworld and the the world of history, social phenomena, etc. which lead to *emergent entities*.

[192] Perhaps, a finer distinction has to be made within Cambridge events in terms of that whether they supervene on both relata, although they do not equally concern both. For example, Xanthippe's widowing does not supervene only on Socrates death but also, as a presupposition, on Xanthippe's being a female married to Socrates as her last husband. This example is due to Geach.

Chrysippus's puzzle raises a number of important metaphysical issues: the question of the identity of substances through time; the relation between substances and their proper parts; the application-conditions of essential substance sortals; the problem of coincident objects; the relativization of identity to time or to sortal concepts, etc.

The puzzle can start only on the presupposition that undetached proper parts of substances exist. For example, that "all of Dion except his left foot", or "all of Dion except his pinky-tip", etc. are objects that can be meaningfully talked about. Inwagen simply denies that there are such objects.[193] Also, some would rather say that it is Dion who perishes with the amputation and not Theon. This is the position of those who take it that substances cannot either lose or gain parts without ceasing to exist. This position is backed by *mereological essentialism:* i.e. the doctrine that each part of each object is essential to the object's identity.[194] Chisholm espouses this view, while Simons, Inwagen, Geach, etc. reject it.

However, if mereological essentialism is rejected *and* sortal essentialism is not accepted either, then, clearly, both Dion and Theon can be taken to survive the operation.[195] But in this case we have to face the option that Dion and Theon make two *coincident* objects.[196] This suggestion needs some qualification. It seems disputable to postulate

---

[193] See van Inwagen (1990), also, Inwagen (2001) ch. 5.: 'The doctrine of arbitrary undetached parts'. Here Inwagen points out that this doctrine entails mereological essentialism. Inwagen recasts the argument about undetached proper parts with "Descartes-minus" in the role of the torso and he expresses his position by saying that "there was never any such thing as D-minus". (2001., 82.)

[194] See Chisholm, R. (1973)

[195] Dion's survival would be ruled out by mereological essentialism along the lines just indicated and Theon's survival would be ruled out by sortal essentialism, much in the spirit of Burke's argument recapitulated in this chapter. However, if neither of these essentialisms hold, then both can survive.

[196] Doepke, F. (1982)

coincident objects of the *same sort,* since the occupancy of a spatio-temporal position uniquely singles out one individual substance and it would be absurd to superimpose many individuals for the same spatio-temporal position. Objects of *different sorts*, however, can occupy the same spatio-temporal region and they can share all the same proper parts and properties, except for their sortal and modal properties. For example, this is typically the relation of a substance and its constitutor. A statue and the piece of clay constituting it in the appropriate shape are coincident objects of different sorts. This restriction on coincidence, i.e. that it is applicable only to objects of different sorts, is accepted by Wiggins and Simons.[197]

Coincidence applies for Theon and Dion only at the times *after* the amputation. Just as coincidence is relative to time, so is identity, as some people claim. For example, Heller takes it that certain temporal parts of Dion and Theon are identical, notable those that exist after the amputation, while they have different temporal parts before the dismal event.[198] This solution relativizes identity to time. However, the relativization of identity to time goes with the acceptance of the doctrine of temporal parts that has been repudiated here. A further possibility would be to relativize identity to sortal concepts, in the fashion of Geach.[199] Then the claim would be that the object after amputation is Dion relative to the sortal "man", and the very same object is Theon relative to "the complement of the sortal 'man'". In this case the object is classified once as an instance of a sortal, and once as an instance of the complement of the same sortal. But it is clearly problematic, how one and the same thing could be classified both under a sortal *and* its complement. So it seems that identity relativized to sortal properties fails

---

[197] Simons (1987), Wiggins, D. (1980)

[198] Heller, M. (1984)

[199] Geach, P. (1967)

in such cases as the one under discussion where sortals and their complements are involved.

However, relative identity is not problematic if a thing is classified under different independent sortals: for example, a clay statue counts both as a work of art and a piece of clay. Still some would dispute this position by saying that relative identity under sortals violates Leibniz Law, since the identical thing is discernible from itself modally, with various sortal classifications. In a nutshell, these are the ramifications of the puzzle, and these are the trade-offs among the different positions.

Turning back to our original concern with substances, we can come to the insight that substances and their proper parts are vulnerable even to mere Cambridge changes provided that sortal essentialism holds. Obviously, this insight does not specifically apply to the trope-theoretical construal of substances; it applies for identification under some qualitative aspect. In the previous chapters we have already seen that substances qualitatively identified prove vulnerable under *set-theoretical essentialism* when it comes to change and identity through time. (Cleve says the same applies under *mereological essentialism*.) And the moral of the present chapter is that the proper parts of substances qualitatively identified prove vulnerable under *sortal essentialism*.

The question arises whether we should rather repudiate all sorts of essentialist commitments in view of these difficulties. I think it would be too hasty to embrace that option: we need the sortal essentialist principle for the identification of individual substances *qua* tokens of kinds. We cannot dispense with sortal essentialist commitments. What sortal essentialism gives us is keeping track of things qua tokens of kinds through time.[200] Estimating the trade-offs with the alternative views, the

---

[200] The interconnection of time and modality holds not only in case of substances. Obviously, it holds in the form of a parallel between the truth-conditions of temporal and modal propositions. See Ujvári, M. (2002)

best is to buy into sortal essentialism, despite complications with of Cambridge changes.

Sortal essentialism secures identity through time for *arbitrary* tokens of kinds. However, in some cases we need to go beyond the arbitrariness of tokens since we need to latch onto particular individuals. Therefore in the last chapter I defend the positing of individual essences.

VII. Individual Essences

Two arguments are offered in this chapter for postulating individual essences of concrete individuals on top of their sortal essences. One is the explanatory gap argument, the other draws on the analogy with the individual essences of events presupposed in single causal explanations. These arguments support qualitative individual essences with explanatory goals as opposed to hybrid impure relational essences accounting for origin and numerical identity. It will be highlighted also why origin properties as parts of impure relational essences do not yield genuine *de re* constructions. The distinction between the two types of individual essences will be traced back to the ambiguity of the very notion of individuation.

While sortal essences are mostly seen as impeccable, claims about individual essences are typically found dubious. Sortal or kind essences provide for the persistence conditions of individuals *qua* tokens of certain kinds. Sortal essentialism is explored also in disputes over colocation. These themes motivate largely the current revival of Aristotelian essentialism specifying sortal identity conditions.[201] Without questioning the importance of sortal essentialism, I argue here for a better reputation of individual essentialism.[202]

According to the standard existence-conditioned modal characterization of sortal essentialism, if P is a sortal essential property

---

[201] See: Burke (1994), Burke (2004), Matthews (1990), Ujvári (2004a) (2004b), Haslanger Kurtz eds. (2006), Brody (1980).

[202] The earlier version of the paper has been presented in the form of an invited lecture at Zagreb University, Dept. of Philosophy, in May, 2012. I am grateful to colleagues for their comments, especially, to T. Janovic and P. Gregorits.

of an object o, the latter cannot exist, *qua* the token of the given sortal, without having P, that is, o has P necessarily if it exists. Sortal essences are typically approached via sortal essential properties but the connection between essences and essential properties is not at all obvious. The natural intuition would be to say that car-hood, for example, is not a feature over and above all those mechanical, electrical, chemical, etc. properties every car necessarily has, but also, it seems that being a car is not equivalent to the mere conjunction of the properties necessarily had by every car. So, even if sortal essences can be explicated by sortal essential properties, the former is not fully reducible to the latter.

The modal characterization of sortal essences is inadequate, as Fine has pointed out, because a property's being 'essential' in the metaphysical sense does not always amount to its being had 'necessarily'.[203] Say, properties like 'being such that 2 is a prime number', or, for any object o, the property of 'being the sole member of a unit set containing o', or, 'being self-identical', etc. while necessary, cannot be rightly claimed to be 'essential'. For these reasons I adopt Fine's way of separating 'essential' from 'necessary'.

As an alternative, Fine's Aristotelian-new approach connects up essences and/or essential properties with the *nature* of things, or, in other words, *what it involves to be a given thing*. In this approach, an essential property P of an object o contributes to answering the question *what o is*. It is only by illuminating the real nature of object o that P can qualify as one of its essential properties. Notice that the 'what' in '*what it involves to be a given thing*' is ambiguous: it can mean 'what type' (kind, sortal) but also, it can mean 'what individual thing'. The latter question is not about an arbitrary token of a type but is about an *individual entity*. The ambiguity is resolved, both by Aristotle and Fine, by intending to capture *sortal* essence under the 'what' question. But one can also take this question as a departure to individual essences.

---

[203] Fine (1994)

Despite their intuitive appeal, Quine's familiar objection to *de re* essences may still intimidate many metaphysicians. Quine invites us to consider the obstacle: how *de re* modal properties can be claimed to hold independently of language? Recently, L. A. Paul has given a partial reply to this worry by drawing on the analogy between *de re* attributions and the standard treatments of vagueness.[204] The analogy consists in that both constructions require precisifications that vary with the contexts. The analogy is meant to explain the diversity of epistemic perspectives via the 'same' objects without telling against the admission that modal properties can be had independently of contexts. If Paul's point is sound, *de re* essentialism is in a better position than it has seemed to be with Quine.

The recognition of individual essences gets support from that they are explored to various metaphysical topics. Losonsky has summarized, quite long ago, the motivations for their admission: "they have been used in modal semantics to account for 'transworld identity' as well as the possibility that there are objects that in fact do not exist, without resorting to the hypothesis that there are merely possible individuals. They have been used to defend the Identity of Indiscernibles and the view that individuals are mere bundles of properties. They have been used to account for the knowledge we have of ourselves and other persons. Historically, philosophers have used individual essences to individuate objects in space and time (for example, Duns Scotus), and recently they have been used as principles of individuation for events. Finally, individual essences have been used in theories of sense and reference for singular terms." [205]

Losonsky's list is ambitious, covering practically the whole of metaphysics. Here I am not going to discuss the relevance of the bundle view and the knowledge of persons for individual essences; also, I do not

---

[204] Paul, L.A. (2004)

[205] Losonsky, M. (1987), 253.

want to tailor individual essences to actualism in an *ad hoc* manner; and, for the same reason, I ignore Plantinga's Boethian semantics as a motivation for the disputed entities. But I find particularly persuasive the reliance on individual essences in the modal individuation of individuals, that is, their identity through worlds. Also, the individuation of events and the role of their essences in the explanation of singular event causation suggest a powerful analogy for continuants; I will explore this analogy.

I suggest that we need qualitative individual essences, with many but not all individuals, on top of sortal essences and back my position with two arguments: one might be labelled as the argument with *explanatory gap*; the other will be an *analogical reasoning* exploring the analogy between continuants and individual events.[206]

According to the *explanatory gap argument* the explanation of the modal traits of the individuals would be gappy if sortal essences plus accidental features were the only conceptual resources for the explanans. Indeed, the typical position is that these two together do all the required jobs and consequently no room is left for the putative individual essences. Socrates is human, Greek, philosopher, etc. as to his sortals *plus* accidentally snub-nosed, married to Xanthippe, etc. A long enough list of both kinds of features exhausts what it is for being Socrates. Moreover, the objection continues, it is not worth postulating a haecceistic feature like 'being Socrates', on top of the elements of the list, for the feature of 'being Socrates' remains vacuous and explanatorily inert. Thus, while sortal essences (supplemented with accidental features) have their proper explanatory role, and, consequently, sortal essentialism seems unobjectionable, individual essences do not seem to play any explanatory role. Hence there does not seem to be any reason for postulating such dubious entities.

---

[206] See Ujvári (2012)

The explanatory gap argument I offer is ready with the retort: we need individual essences, on top of sortal ones, because many of the genuine metaphysical possibilities of individuals would remain unexplained and unexplainable if sortal essences *plus* accidental features were the only candidates for the role of explanans. In other words, metaphysical explanation about genuine possibilities of individuals would remain gappy without postulating also individual essences. For example, to answer the modal question whether it is possible *for me* to be a credit card it is enough to point to my general human essence which precludes such possibility. But the possibility, say, of me becoming a basket ball champion is not ruled out by my sortal essence; it is ruled out only by my idiosyncratic features, like being clumsy in ball games, having slow reflex, lacking the ability to cooperate in sports with team members, etc. Similarly, it is not possible for me, *not* as an instance of 'human' but as the individual who I am, to become an astronaut, a deep sea diver, etc. None of the precluding features are part of my sortal or kind essence, still, they determine a lot about me as an individual. To use a minimum modal jargon, it is not only *actually not possible* for me, for some accidental reasons that happen to obtain, to become a basket ball champion, (astronaut, deep sea diver, etc.) but it is *not possibly possible* either, since I would be another person, in some strong sense of 'another', if I had the missing skills.[207] In this sense the options *not possibly possible* for individuals are those that are precluded by their individual essences while not precluded by their sortal essences. Or, to take another example, Socrates and his persecutors are all humans, Greeks, etc. as to their sortals, but have different individual essences determining their possibilities. It would be a seriously defective explanatory reasoning to say that it is 'possible' for Socrates to behave in a morally inferior way because his sortals of being 'human', 'Greek', 'philosopher', etc. admit that. No, it would be only *possibly possible* for

---

[207] By 'strong sense of "another"' I mean difference in terms of at least one essential property and *not* mere property-discernibility in terms of any qualitative feature.

him to be morally inferior, since he would have to have another personality with that despicable moral character. What is 'possible' from the perspective of the sortal(s) may not, in each particular case, be 'possibly possible' from the perspective of the individual essence. With iterated modalities we can flesh out the distinguished modal contribution of the individual essences within the overall constraint of the sortal essences.

The job performed by individual essences does not compete with the job performed by general essences: individual essences have to be conceived within the constraints imposed by the sortal(s) of the individual in question. Here I confine myself to genuine sortals and I am not going to discuss gerrymandered objects although their case is also instructive, as is shown by Forbes.[208]

Forbes makes a point which proves to be particularly helpful with individual essences. In his polemic about the possible world semantic approach to *de re* modalities, he shows that while worlds are complete circumstances, possibilities are not complete in this sense.[209] Possibilities can be loose compared to worlds. The significance of his point, for our present concern, is this: his notion allows *local de re* possibilities of individuals such that their possibilities need not be arranged in a whole network of interrelated possibilities specified by the laws and the law-like features of the broad contexts called 'worlds'. That is, his local notion of possibility does not require the dovetailing of the possibilities of each and every individual with the possibilities of the rest of the individuals. In short, we do not fall a prey to the Leibnizian requirement of pre-established harmony. This is not to say, of course, that the

---

[208] Forbes shows that gerrymandered objects like Shoemaker's "klable" cannot be ruled out by *de dicto* impossibilities: "the transworld heirline of an object for which all is possible but a *de dicto* impossibility is no more the heirline of a real thing than the spatio-temporal path of a klable is the path of a real thing". *op.cit.*, 236.

[209] See Forbes (1985), 19.

individual possibilities flowing from the individual natures of things can ignore the laws and law like features of the broad context. The individual possibilities are confined by the sortal possibilities. Simply, it means that the former are not completely determined by the latter. This margin of tolerance makes room for individual possibilities.

The explanatory gap argument suggested here for postulating individual essences presupposes the *explanatory role* of essential properties and essences. The explanatory *role* is not independent of the *explanatory characterization* of essential properties. Such characterization is yielded by Gorman. According to him the essential properties of a thing are those that are not explained by any of its other characteristics. The essential properties so conceived are not simply unexplained explanans; the main point is that their explanation, if they have any, does not rely on any of the other characteristics of the given thing. Gorman has put forth his view as an alternative to the prevailing modal view found by him inadequate. He says that the modal view "falls short by treating both explained and unexplained necessary characteristics as equally central". He claims that his view "does the intuition far more justice. By picking out, from among a thing's necessary characteristics, those that are unexplained, it identifies what is truly at the core of what the thing is".[210]

The explanatory characterization of essential properties goes back to Aristotle's *Posterior Analytics* 74b5ff. Not surprisingly, the other two current characterizations also trace back to him: the existence-conditioned modal characterization has its roots in *Topics* 102b5ff; the roots of the definitional characterization favoured by Fine can be found in *Metaphysics* 1031a12.[211]

---

[210] Gorman, M. (2005), 286.

[211] Robertson, T. (2008), 6.

Explanations typically appeal to some general connection but they need not always take that form. For example, in the accounts of causal explanation, beside general causal connections *singular event causations* are widely recognized from Davidson, through Kim to Bennett. Here individual essences are appealed to as "principles of individuation for events" as has been noticed by Losonsky.[212] However, I put emphasis on the explanatory role: individual event-essences play a role in the explanation of singular event causation and the analogy with explanations about continuants is suggestive.

The classical major argument of Davidson for singular event causation consists in pointing out that events as causal relata are particulars, moreover, unique particulars since they are unrepeatable dated happenings.[213] In the 2nd chapter I have discussed Davidson's particularist view of events. It should be noted now that his event-particularism is motivated mainly by the recognition of singular event causation. This view presupposes, albeit tacitly, that the event-particulars have their individual essences, on top of their particularized sortal essences. The reason being that the whole point about event-particularism is the conviction that there is more to the causal explanation, and hence to the explanatory role, of particular events than instantiating general features and relations. Particular events as causal relata are not just the tokens of kinds but there is something special and unique about them in virtue of which they can play an explanatory role in a unique single case. Some essentialists, e.g. Lombard, claims that times and the subjects involved are essential to event-individuals.[214]

---

[212] Losonsky, M. (1987), 253.

[213] See Davidson, D. (1980), (1993).

[214] Lombard says that the theory of events he supports "is a theory which construes events as particulars, that is, as concrete, datable, non-repeatable occurrences". (Lombard, L. B. 1979. 361). Now if events are non-repeatable occurrences, as he claims, their identity should be sought not only in their kind-essence, by being arbitrary tokens of a kind, but also, in their individual essence.

Here I can not decide what specifically the essences of individual events consist in. It suffices to realize that they *have* individual essences. Particularism about events and singular event causation widely accepted would not make sense without the postulation, whether tacitly or explicitly, of individual event-essences. Moreover, since events can be analyzed by triples with continuants, properties and times, the individual essences of events fit well with the putative individual essences of continuants. This completes my second argument for the individual essences of continuants: the analogy with the individual essences of events holds. So, the way to the individual essences of continuants is paved by the particularist notion of singular event causation presupposing the individual essences of particular events.

One might object that the argument with events is circular, since events are not *per se* entities but entities dependent on the subject whose property-changes they are. So, if they have individual essences they have them only in virtue of their respective continuant-subject's having an individual essence; but this is what the argument is supposed to establish rather than simply presuppose. My reply is this: the ontological dependence of events does not preclude their being recognized as individuals and they are treated so in the contemporary analyses. Further, the way of explanation does not have to follow the ontological way. I am here after the explanation of individuals *qua* individuals; and concrete events are perfectly good candidates for the role of individuals strongly defended by the particularists. Therefore, the analogy with individual events supplies a further argument, beside the explanatory gap argument, for postulating the individual essences of continuants.

Obviously, when I urge this postulation I do not wish to render individual essences to tokens of each sortal; e.g. to tokens of car-sortal, rabbit-sortal, etc. I am not going to overpopulate the forest of the metaphysical Midsummer Night with individual spirits of each bush, tree, etc. All I am claiming is that it is reasonable to postulate, in certain cases, individual essences on top of sortal ones since they are implicitly appealed to whenever we try to give an account of these special individuals *qua* individuals. This applies to persons in the first instance; and derivatively for works of arts, including unique engineering works and natural places unique in certain projected respects. We treat them as unique individuals in the explanations and not just as arbitrary tokens of their respective kinds.

The recognition of individual essences can be found in the literature. Emphasizing the qualitative aspect, Graeme Forbes characterizes the individual essence of an individual as follows. 'An individual essence of an object x is a set of properties **I** which satisfies the following two conditions: **I**(i) every property **P** in **I** is an essential property of x; **I**(ii) it is not possible that some object y distinct from x has every member of **I**.'[215] He means non-trivial essential properties and, as a consequence, non-trivial individual essences. The non-triviality constraint is stressed also later by Della Rocca.[216] The set of non-trivial essential properties of an individual x excludes existence, self-identity and their cognates; properties had as a consequence of some *de dicto* truths; and properties x has in virtue of some necessary truth about items of another category.

While being sympathetic to the non-triviality constraint, I think that most of the trivial cases can be ruled out quite easily by making a distinction, in Armstrong's fashion, between genuine properties and predicates. Further, it is seen that the definition applies the Leibniz principle of the Identity of Indiscernibles (**PII**). However, the most important point, for our present concern, is that Forbes evaluates the significance of individual essences from the perspective of *counterfactual identity*: 'an individual essence of an object x, in virtue of its non-triviality, would give necessary and sufficient conditions for

---

[215] Forbes, G. (1985), 99.

[216] see Della Rocca (1996a)

crossworld identification of x without employing the property of being identical to x or any of its cognates'.²¹⁷

Actualism in possible world semantics also supplies, as I have already said, strong motivations for the haecceitistic version of individual essences. For example, Plantinga's position requires individual essences as surrogate inhabitants at those worlds where the respective individuals fail to exist. By actualist insights only actual individuals exist; and instead of talking about non-actual but possible individuals, the possibilities are captured by abstract proxies for individuals. But these abstract proxies are more haecceitistic rather than being the rich complete concepts of individuals in a Leibnizian manner. Now the actualist position towards merely possible individuals as a motivation for haecceitistic individual essences will not be explored here. First, because I am sceptical with individual essences taken haecceistically; the quidditative version seems to have more virtues. Second, while possibilia are a burden for actualism, the account of individual essences need not be tailored to the specific needs of actualism. I find strong enough those motivations for individual essences that concern only the modal traits of this-worldly individuals.

A dominant trend in the last decades is to accept 'hybrid individual essences' with origin properties or properties of material constitution as yielding a principle of individuation. Recently, Roca-Royes has spelled out this position, relying on the arguments of Adams and P. Mackie against purely qualitative individual essences.²¹⁸ Obviously, Kripkean claims about the necessity of origin strongly support this approach.

Losonsky also defended 'impure individual essences' arguing that "every individual has at least one relational essence, and that this essence is an individuating component of this individual's *haecceity*".²¹⁹

---

²¹⁷ Forbes, *ibid.*, 100.

²¹⁸ Roca-Royes (2011), Adams, R. (1979), Mackie, P. (2006)

²¹⁹ Losonsky, M. (1987), 258.

His individual essences are captured by definite descriptions containing predicates of origin and also making essential reference to some other individual (hence the impurity of the specification). For example, "*being the human being that grows from Alpha in suitable environments*" where Alpha is the particular zygote, contains Alpha as the "individuating component". Singularity is achieved thus, in a Russellian way, with an individual as the individuating component warding off the threat of generality. And the descriptive part of the specification of the individual essence saves it from collapsing into a mere non-qualitative haecceitas. The significance of this hybrid account is that the main challenges to individual essences, apart from their impurity, have come from associating them to haecceitas.[220]

An explanation-motivated argument for individual essences is put forth by the Leibniz scholar Brandon C. Look: "the specific essential properties of an individual are few; the individuating essential properties are many; and the specific essential properties are in fact so few that they do little work".[221] Although the point is not further elaborated, one may guess that individual essences are required in the *explanatory work* about individuals.

The brief survey shows that suggestions for individual essences fall roughly into three types: A) qualitative individual essences, B) non-qualitative haecceitistic essences, C) hybrid impure individual essences. This raises a host of closely related questions: provided that individual essences are useful posits, shall we take them partly/wholly qualitative (or, quidditative, in the scholastic terminology) or, shall we take them non-quidditative haecceitistic entities (either in the style of Duns Scotus or that of Kaplan); a further question is, whether origin properties, and relational essences in general, are proper candidates for the role of

---

[220] Individual essences are taken as *haecceitates* by Armstrong, Chisholm and Loux. See reference to, and critical discussion of, this position by Losonsky in Losonsky (1987)

[221] Brandon C. Look, *ibid.*, 11.

making up individual essences, or, alternatively, should we insist with Leibniz and his scholastic predecessors that an individual's individual essence must be wholly its intrinsic feature as opposed to some relational feature?[222]

Individual Essences and Individuation

The choice among the haecceitistic account, the hybrid theories with origin properties/material constitution *and* the qualitative approach in Forbes's style depends, I claim, on *what prior notion of individuation* is adopted. The problem is that the very notion of individuation is ambiguous, striving for two different, albeit related, desiderata: one desideratum is to divide the species over the range of individuals falling under it so as to arrive at a particular individual; the other is to ensure the diachronic and/or counterfactual identity of a particular individual by making recourse to its individual nature. Both desiderata are legitimate and widely appealed to; but there lies behind this duality of desiderata the very ambiguity of the notion of individuation. On one reading successful reference to a unique individual is all what is required to individuation; on the alternative reading, individuation is tied to the uncovering of the qualitative individual nature of the thing.

In more familiar terms, individuation as a means for keeping track of an individual may be directed either at securing unique reference or, alternatively, achieving the richest possible content. When the former desideratum prevails, it is superfluous to burden the task with the requirement of rich content: one can single out a unique individual successfully with relational means without being omniscient about it. However, with the explanatory task in mind, the singling out of an individual from among other individuals of the same species will not be sufficient for the explanation *why* that particular individual is the way it is; *why* it behaves as it does; *why* prediction concerning its behaviour is

---

[222] About the intrinsic/extrinsic dilemma concerning sortal properties, see: Ujvári (2011a)

reliable on the supposition of its determinate individual nature within the species, while a prediction calculating with another individual nature would fail, etc.? By contrast, qualitative individuation suffices for explanatory purposes and it also has an intimate bond with *qualitative* individual essences here argued for. Part of the goal of the paper is to point out this ambiguity of the notion of individuation and explore its consequences for coping with individual essences in different ways.

Typically, the two desiderata of individuation are not duly separated. Urging to recognize individual essential properties apart from specific essential properties, Brandon C. Look writes: "there may also be *individuating essential* properties, those which single x out from the other members of the same species and which are nevertheless such that, lacking them, x would no longer be x".[223] The indiscriminate use of the two goals is not new. For example, even 'Leibniz has never distinguished the questions "what accounts for the numerical distinctness of a thing" from "what accounts for its being the very individual that it is"', as has been pointed out by Cover and Hawthorne.[224]

But the gap has widened since Leibniz's times: today it is realized that numerical distinctness is achievable by indexical or other direct referential devices or by relational predicates, i.e. by means wholly accidental from the perspective of the individual nature of the individual. But neither Leibniz nor most of his scholastic predecessors would have accepted individuation by accidental features, albeit for slightly different reasons. Individuation by relational accidents, like the having of a spatio-temporal position, was ruled out by Leibniz relational view of space and time. Individuation by material constitution, in Aquinas's terms, by the 'designated matter' constituting a given individual, was criticised by Duns Scotus who argued that accidents cannot

---

[223] Brandon C. Look (2008), 10.

[224] Cover-Hawthorne (1999) reprinted in (2008), 41.

individuate.[225] The role of causal ancestry recognized today was not explored either. If one wants to find conceptual continuity, it is current haecceitism that claims to have a link to the medieval role of proper names as vehicles of individual essences.[226]

It is extremely difficult to assess the relevance of medieval and early modern positions to current discussions of individuation since the conceptual framework of metaphysics has drastically changed. For example, when the scholastic authors protest that accidents cannot individuate, depriving thus themselves from the ubiquity of relational (location, origin, stuff, etc.) individuation applied in current 'hybrid theories', the reason for their doing so is the adoption of the *substance/accident framework*. In this framework substances ground the existence of entities of other kinds, like accidents (proper and contingent ones), events, etc. all inhering in, and depending on, the substance. From this perspective, Leibniz also claims, repeated at various places, that 'there is no denomination so extrinsic that it does not have an intrinsic denomination as its basis'.[227] Due to this ontological dependence, substances cannot be individuated by items that depend on them, except on pain of circularity.

Now the substance/accident framework does not match with the current metaphysical framework of property-functions and individuals typically occupying the argument position. The current metaphysical framework yields a perspective for the problem of individuation and individual essences different from the perspective of its medieval predecessor. For example, for Duns Scotus haecceitas is a kind of *entity* falling 'within the category of substance'. As Woosuk Park explains, not being an accident, the only possible option for interpreting haecceitas within that conceptual scheme is to treat it as a *substance-like* entity.

---

[225] See Woosuk Park (1990), 386-7.

[226] See Plantinga, A. (1978)

[227] See Leibniz (1969), 267-70.

However, for Kaplan, equipped with set-theoretical resources, haecceitas is a non-qualitative *property* having, as its extension, a singleton with an individual. Such differences are often overlooked and friends of haecceitas move too hastily from Scotus to Kaplan in their efforts of legitimation.

Having disambiguated individuation into two different readings, the question arises whether we have an open choice between them. Not quite so. While not denying the relevance of referential individuation with relational impure essences, the qualitative version seems to be more basic: it is the *pendant*, on the individual level, of general essences on the species level. Further, there is a compelling argument, to be exposed in the next section, why origin properties cannot be taken as part and parcel of individual essences, supporting their relational impure reading. To anticipate briefly, the point I have elaborated elsewhere is that origin properties in modal contexts do not admit *de re* reading.[228] They can be parsed only as contributing to general possibilities. For these reasons I find Forbes's notion of qualitative individual essence more promising than the rival views.

Various problems may arise though disturbing the seemingly impeccable claim for qualitative individual essences; I try to cover some of these. Lastly, I shall spell out my dissatisfaction with the alternative views.

As to the former set of problems, for example, it is tempting to replace the need for individual essences by the need for the particularization of common natures. In Fine's definitional approach to essences the 'natures' talked about are general natures. According to Fine the essential properties of things are those that are part of their 'definitions' but one may wonder how things as first order individuals can have 'definitions'. Therefore, it is the *kinds* of things that have definitions and not directly the things falling under them. Consequently,

---

[228] Ujvári, M. 2011b

individual essentialism cannot benefit from the definitional approach; since individuals have no definitions, only kinds have.

Individual essences are not simply the instantiations of common natures; though they exist in cohabitation with the instantiated common natures. Sortal essential properties and sortal essences are shared and sharable; they can be instantiated and can fail to be instantiated. But it would be misleading to say that an individual essence is instantiated or fails to be instantiated since the relation between the individual essence and the individual is *not* that of instantiation but some closer and more intimate bond.

Therefore, when the individual essences of ordinary individuals are talked about, the proper starting point is *not* the relation of *property instantiation*. The perspective of the individuals with their genuine possibilities should be adopted, i.e., what makes them the particular entities they are, preserving their identity through times and worlds, etc., rather than adopting the perspective of properties, i.e., how properties contribute, through being instantiatied, to various truths about individuals. Viewed from the perspective of ordinary (non-abstract) individuals, instantiation explains only that something is a particular token of a kind. It only particularizes the kind without telling what makes a particular token what *it is*, different from every other token. In short, instantiation captures only particularization without capturing individuation. Instantiation is not applicable as a relation between a particular individual concept *and* the bearer individual: it will not be proper to say that I 'instantiate' my individual concept and a duplicate of me instantiates the *same* concept. A duplicate of me is a replica of me but not another *instance* of the same individual concept.[229] Perhaps, it is

---

[229] According to Plantinga, at those possible worlds where a particular individual does not exist, its individual concept exists, which, being abstract, exists necessarily. I am not quite sure whether Plantinga thinks that at those worlds where the individual in fact exists, the relation between the individual's existence and its individual concept is that of *instantiation*.

the relation of *constitution* that captures the connection between individuals and their individual essences.

For the reasons just clarified I find misleading Sonia Roca-Royes discussion of individual essences in terms of *instantiation*. Moreover, she connects essential properties of a thing with its 'sufficient-for-existence-properties'. These latter are the properties and circumstances of the material constitution of the thing. ` Roca-Royes claims that since 'an individual essence [has] to be both essential and sufficient', the essential properties and the sufficiency properties have to be conceived to 'interact' in a special way. But her requirement of tying individual essence to the sufficiency properties of material constitution leads to troubles: just as a given individual might have '*another* sufficient-for-existence-property', (recall Salmon's 'principle of modal tolerance' for material constitution), equally, different individuals, presumably with haecceistic differences, can be the 'possible instantiations' of a given sufficient-for-existence-property either in different worlds, or, what is worse, in the same world. [230] Roca-Royes acknowledges these difficulties, but the moral she draws from these cases is that one needs to accept '*flexible* individual essence', where 'flexibility is directly inherited' from the flexibility of material constitution.

Now assuming the non-rigidity of individual essences, I think their flexibility is *not* to be conceived in terms of the flexibility of material constitution.[231] Instead, the desired flexibility obtains in virtue of some

---

[230] These difficulties concerning the poor discriminating capacity of material constitution has been remarked earlier by Forbes; see his (1992). As to the principle of modal tolerance, see Salmon, N. (2002).

[231] Duns Scotus has already argued against Aquinas' incorporating matter into the definitional essence of things. For Aquinas the definition contains only the 'non-designated' matter. Say, human essence contains *some* flesh and bone, but it does not contain a piece of determinate, 'designated' matter. According to Scotus even such concession to the material component would be in conflict with the *principium individuationis*: the individuality of substances cannot be explained by differences in accidental features, such as the material component. See: Borbély, G. (2008), 234-5. The synoptic interpretations offered by medievalists suggest to me that

other kind of tolerance: it obtains as tolerance in the determinates of essential determinables that might play a role during the career of an individual. For example, Socrates is sarcastic, essentially, but he exhibits this essential determinable with various determinates as he develops from youth to maturity.

So the determinable/determinate distinction that I have already explored earlier when discussing the content of the nucleus, has an application to flesh out the putative flexibility of individual essences. These determinate qualities associated to qualitative individual essences sound pretty much as *trope*-like features. The virtue of taking these qualities as tropes rather than universal properties is obvious: the latter are shared and sharable, therefore they can never specify the individual essence of a unique individual.

Recall, I have already addressed the worry of circularity in connection with trope **BT**. Briefly, again, if tropes are property-particulars ontologically dependent on the bearer substance they cannot individuate, except on pain of circularity, the bearer substance. My reply is this: the objection trades on the ambiguity of dependence in the ontological sense and dependence in the explanatory sense. Even though ontological dependence holds, the individuation of *abstract* tropes and the individuation of *concrete* individuals have separate resources due to abstractness in one case and concreteness in the other. Thus the charge of circularity is evaded.

Failure of Origin Properties in de re Constructions

Scotus presumably took the principle of individuation in some stronger sense than accounting for the mere numerical difference of things. The point is that pieces of matter are capable of providing for mere numerical difference, and, consequently, he would not have had reason to object to material constitution if he had taken individuation in the sense of numerical identity. Therefore, his notion of individuation must be more pertinent to individual natures than to numerical identity.

It has been left to show why origin properties fail to yield genuine *de re* constructions. According to the familiar thesis about the essentiality of origin, it is essential for a given table to have been originated from a certain hunk of matter, or, for a person to have been originated from a given sperm and egg, etc. Is this thesis plausible enough to support the incorporation of the sufficient-for-existence properties into individual essences?

Well, once a given individual is already an existing thing, presumably no different origin could be rendered to it for that would yield another individual. Still, the property of origin is not a suitable candidate for an essential property, at least not in the usual sense of being a *de re* essential property required to individual essences. In order to see this more clearly we have to consider the challenge that radical-coming–into-being poses with respect to *de re* possibilities of individuals.

The fact that radical coming-into-being is metaphysically different from piecemeal change has been perceived by many philosophers. Aristotle is one of the first and later Kant used two different terms, Wechsel and Veränderung respectively, to indicate the difference. In recent times, Arthur Prior elaborated his polemic on whether radical coming-into-being is a *genuine de re possibility* of the individual substances.[232] To anticipate, he argues to the conclusion that there is no such possibility concerning radical coming-into-being as opposed to piecemeal change.

Prior considers the thought experiment of swapping the properties of two individuals through worlds. Say, we have in the actual world the person Julius Caesar with the usual Caesar-like properties ascribed to him by contemporaries and late descendants as well; we have also Mark Antony as inhabitant of the actual world with his properties agreed on by contemporaries and late descendants. Suppose now that through chains of accessible worlds we reach a world, being such that Caesar has all and

---

[232] Prior, A. (1968), chapter VIII on 'Identifiable Individuals'

only the properties of Mark Antony and vice versa. Surely, this world is qualitatively indistinguishable from the original world. The thought experiment is typically explored for highlighting our intuitions whether the world resulting in complete property swap is different in any sense from the original world. Those who say that the two worlds are actually one, for what matters only is what properties are instantiated and co-instantiated in a world and the instantiating entities are nothing over and above the properties they instantiate, are Leibnizian metaphysicians who subscribe to **BT** and, with it, **PII**, i.e. the principle of the identity of indiscernibles. Others, who feel that there is a genuine difference between the two worlds support they claim by maintaining that Caesar and Antony still differ by their haecceistic properties of *being Caesar* and *being Antony* respectively whatever other properties are swapped. As a retort, it is typically pointed out by people of the other camp that haecceistic properties are not genuine properties since they are fully parasitic on individuals.

Prior finds his way out from this dilemma as follows. He does not endorse the Leibnizian horn but equally does not rely on haecceistic properties, admitting them though. Instead, Prior finds that the property which is necessarily exempt from property-swap is the property of origin (in this case: the property of being originated from certain definite parents). This property, i.e. the property of having the actual ancestors one has is *the* property which is resistant, for reasons clarified soon, to property-exchange.

After having considered several possible property-swaps, Prior asks: 'can we not go further and suppose Caesar to have had the whole of Antony's life, including being born to Antony's parents?' (*op.cit.,* p. 85.) This question would obviously be merely rhetorical if it referred to a logical possibility since the proposition asserting Caesar's having born to Antony's parents contains no internal inconsistency. There is nothing in the individual concept of Caesar, if there is such concept at all, which rules out being born to Antony's parents.

As a question about a *temporal* possibility, however, the question is more substantial. For now we ask: '*when* was it possible?' And it is easy to see that '*after* his birth ... it was clearly *too late* for him to have had different parents.' (*ibid.*) This insight is fairly obvious. Why not ascribe, then, the *de re* possibility of having different parents '*before* Caesar existed'? Intuitively speaking, the remoter the present, viewed from a distant future, is, the more possibilities are still open concerning that present (taken indexically). Alas, the crucial point, highlighted by Prior, is that whatever broad the general possibility is in this case, 'there would seem to have been no individual identifiable as Caesar, i.e. the Caesar who we are now discussing, who could have been the subject of this possibility'.(*ibid.*)

It is clear from Prior's account that there is an overkill in this argument: for, if Caesar (or any other actual individual) could not have been the subject, before his birth, of the (later) unrealized possibility, equally, *he* could not have been the subject of the *later realized* possibility either. Which means, that none of us who was going to be born could have been the subject of a *de re* possibility of being (going to be) born – *i.e.*, at least not before our conception. What amounts to saying that what is once actual is always preceded by what is non-possible, contradicting thus the logic of propositional modalities.

The parallel reasoning above has an undeniable merit: it helps to repudiate the doctrine of the *necessity of origin*. For Prior is not only saying that the unrealized (logical) possibilities concerning origins are ruled out; he also perceives that the realized courses of originating by birth are not possible either, at least *not* in the *de re* sense. For there is no identifiable individual to ascribe the *de re* possibility to. Hence, there is no identifiable individual to ascribe the putative *de re* necessity of origin either. The realized and the unrealized *de re* possibilities/necessities are in a symmetric situation relative to each other: both require the semantic precondition of the successful referring of the term in the referential position which is not fulfilled in either case. Note that these cases of origin as temporal *de re* modalities show a close similarity to the familiar cases of empty names in extensional contexts.

Prior is quite right in claiming that any genuine *de re* possibility/necessity presupposes that the subject of the modal ascription, even if just a 'thin' individual, be fixed referentially. Since this is not satisfied in case of the putative *de re* possibility of origin, the latter must be denied of being a case of *genuine de re* possibility. Further, I suspect that Prior finds not only demonstrative reference missing in this case when there is not yet anybody before birth to refer to. I take Prior missing a *descriptive* device of referring to an individual in order to consider the possibilities ascribable to that specific individual. This claim can be supported by the fact that possibilities obtain always relative to a certain background. As Prior himself notes 'as new distinguishable individuals come into being, there is ... a multiplication of distinguishable logical possibilities'.[233] Now it is fairly obvious that the basis of distinction among individuals and their possibilities are of a qualitative nature. For example, there must be people identifiable qualitatively as different applicants to a job for opening the logical possibility of competition for that job. So I take Prior implying some descriptive notion of individuals even if not fully endorsing **BT** in the Leibnizian sense. It is a further question how 'thin' or 'thick' his implied notion of individuals is, but it seems to me evident that he must adhere to some qualitative, as opposed to merely haecceistic, identity condition of individuals.

Once the semantic precondition of reference is not satisfied with the *de re* possibility of origin, it is hard to see how one can satisfy the natural intuition that it is still meaningful, in some sense, to talk about the possibility of someone's having had a different origin.

The air of paradox is easily dissolved for there is no subject, strictly speaking, of such possibilities. Just as the promise of giving someone a horse, in Burleigh's example, may be disambiguated *not* as the promise of a specific horse but as the promise that can be fulfilled by giving someone *any* horse, so is the case with the possibility of origin. As Prior

---

[233] Prior, A. (1957), 91.

puts it, 'the possibility that *an* individual should begin to exist ... is like promise of the second kind'.[234] In other words, this possibility is 'general', rather than specific. Which is tantamount to saying that the possibility of origin is not a *de re* but a *de dicto* possibility. It is possible *that* someone be born to such and such parents, but it is not possible *of someone* that *he* should be born to these or other parents.

So, Prior's solution to the problem of *de re* possibility with radical coming-into-being consists in denying that there is such *de re* possibility and satisfying, instead, our modal intuition with the *de dicto* form of possibility. *De re* possibility with respect to radical coming-into-being is, at best, a *post factum* possibility: as Thomas Aquinas put it, quoted also by Prior, it is an 'accident' which 'is subsequent to the thing' that has already come into existence.

The temporal possibility just discussed is obviously different from possibility in the logical sense. Caesar could have been born to persons who actually turned to be the parents of Mark Antony in the logical sense of 'could' for there is no inconsistency in the proposition stating this course of events. (Leibnizians would, perhaps, object that there is, for the 'complete concept' of Caesar excludes the relational property of being born to those other people.) Logical possibility seems then to be permissive about a case explicitly ruled out by temporal possibility.

The gap between the two kinds of possibilities is smaller though: for, both possibilities *as de re* possibilities have an existential precondition such that 'before [Caesar] existed it was not logically or in any other way possible that he should *come to have* those people, or any other people, as his parents'.[235] As possibilities dependent on an (empirical) existential precondition the logical and the temporal readings of possibility behave much the same way.

---

[234] Prior (1957), 86.

[235] Prior (1957), 92.

It is clear from all above that radical coming-into-being is not change in the piecemeal sense of a thing's acquiring/dropping properties over time. Coming-into-being should not be taken, as Prior points out, to mean that 'once X's non-being was the case and now its being is'. It should be taken to mean, instead, that 'it is *not* the case that X *was*, but it *is* the case that X *is*', and this does not express a change but two contrasting present facts'.[236]

Paradoxical as it may sound, radical coming-into-being does not have the features of a genuine change. Radical coming-into-being is not unique, however, in this respect: Cambridge changes are typically not taken to be genuine changes either, even though they can threaten the identity through time of individual substances as I have shown in the previous chapter. So, this property should be exempt from the range of properties that afford opportunity for *de re* locutions: in contrast to the *factuality* of radical having-come-into-being, the *de re* possibility of radical coming-into-being is simply a non-possibility. And, as Prior indicates, this holds not only for temporal possibility, but for logical possibility as well (the latter covering, presumably, Lewis S5).

Undeniably, the property of origin is not suspect of being a haecceistic property like 'being identical to Caesar'. It is similar though to the latter in being an impure relational property. Further, it can ensure that there is a difference between two worlds even after all admissible property-swaps; that is, it can be used to distinguish worlds from each other. However, this property does not yield genuine *de re* possibilities of identifiable individuals with individual natures.

This insight about the special metaphysical status of radical coming-into-being is in complete consonance with Prior's aim at showing that the property of origin does not admit swap, unlike other properties of individuals, for its lacking the existential precondition. *After* this precondition being fulfilled, the property of origin is an accident

---

[236] Prior (1957), 88.

subsequent to the individual; in fact, a peculiar accident that can be had only *post factum* and it is resistant to property-swap. As a consequence, the property swaps between individuals through worlds must stop at the impure relational property of origin.[237]

To sum up, the need for qualitative individual essences has become clear by now. It is only by presupposing individual natures that the metaphysical explanation does not become gappy and certain possibilities can be spelled out which, while not being precluded by one's sortal essence, are still precluded by something else, i.e. one's individual essence. Hence sortal essences are relevant to individual ones: the features the individual essences comprise are compatible with the sortal-definitional essence, just like any determinate is compatible with its determinable(s) and vice versa. Also, the several relevant sortals of a given individual are compatible with each other so that they are capable of yielding, separately or collectively, the intelligibility constraints for the individual essence. E.g. Socrates falls under the sortals of being human, philosophers, Greek, etc. so that each of these sortals are capable of admitting him to be 'sarcastic', while each ruling out for him to be a 'prime', or a 'credit card', etc.

Apart from suggesting the *explanatory gap* argument, I have also drawn on the parallel with the explanation of singular event causation. Just as the latter tacitly presupposes the individual essences of events, similarly, the accounts of continuant-individuals presuppose their individual essences as parts of the explanans. This is not to claim that individual essences are always lurking behind the sortal essences with each token of every kind. The more modest claim is that they are not to be dismissed on board since there are certain explanations requiring them as parts of the explanans. In this role individual essences demonstrate the insufficiency of the twofold modal scheme of accounting for individuals only with definitional sortal essences and purely accidental features.

---

[237] See: Ujvári (2011b)

References

Abela, P. (2002) *Kant's Empirical Realism* (Oxford:Clarendon)

Adams, R. (1979) 'Primitive Thisness and Primitive Identity', *Journal of Philosophy* 76: 5- 26.

Armstrong, D.M. (1978) *Universals and Scientific Realism.* I. *Nominalism and Realism* (Cambridge: Cambridge University Press)

Armstrong, D.M. (1989b) *Universals: An Opiniated Introduction.*(Boulder:Westview)

Aristotle, *Categories*, in McKeon (1941)

Aristotle, *Metaphysics Z*, in McKeon (1941)

Bacon, J. (1995) *Universals and Property Instances: The Alphabet of Being* (Oxford: Blackwell)

Bacon, J. (2011) "Tropes", **The Stanford Encyclopedia of Philosophy (Winter 2011 Edition)**, Edward N. Zalta (ed.), URL = <http://plato.stanford.edu/archives/win2011/entries/tropes/>

Bennett, J. (1987) 'Event Causation: the Counterfactual Analysis' in: *Philosophical Perspectives. Metaphysics.* ed. J.E. Tomberlin, California, Ridgeview, 367-386.

Bennett, J. (1988) *Events and Their Names* (Oxford: Clarendon)

Bennett, J. (1999) 'Introduction to Events. Events Are Tropes' in: *Metaphysics. Contemporary Readings* ed. S. D. Hales, Belmont, CA, Wadsworth, 319-324.

Black, M. (1952) 'The Identity of Indiscernibles' *Mind* v. 61. 152-64.

Borbély, G. (2008). *Civakodó angyalok. Bevezetés a középkori filozófiába* (in Hungarian) [*Eristic disputes of angels: introduction to medieval philosophy*] (Budapest: Akadémiai Kiadó)

Brand, M. (1975) 'Particulars, Events and Actions' in: *Action Theory* eds. Brand, M, Walton, D. (Dordrecht: Reidel) 133-57.

Brody, B. (1980). *Identity and Essence* (Princeton: Princeton University Press)

Burke, M. (1994) 'Dion and Theon: an essentialist solution to an ancient puzzle', *Journal of Philosophy* v. 90. 129-39.

Burke, M. (2004) 'Dion, Theon, and the many-thinkers problem', *Analysis* v.64. n.3. 242-250.

Campbell, K. (1990) *Abstract Particulars* (Oxford: Blackwell)

Castaneda, H. N. (1977) 'Perception, Belief and the Structure of Physical Objects and Consciousness' *Synthese* v.35. 285-351.

Casullo, A. (1988) 'A Fourth Version of the Bundle-Theory' *Philosophical Studies* v.54. 125-39. repr. in *Metaphysics. Contemporary Readings*, ed. M. J. Loux, Routledge, 2001.

Cleve, J. (1985) 'Three Versions of the Bundle Theory', *Philosophical Studies* v.47. 95-107. repr. in: *Metaphysics. Contemporary Readings*. ed. S.D. Hales, Belmont, Ca: Wadsworth, 1999.

Cleve, J.(2000) 'John Bacon: Universals and Property Instances: The Alphabet of Being' (review) *The Philosophical Review* v.109. 107-9.

Chisholm, R. (1970) 'Events and Propositions' *Nous* v.4. 15-24.

Chisholm, R. (1971) 'States of Affairs Again' *Nous* v.5. 179-89.

Chisholm, R. (1973) 'Parts as Essential to their Wholes' *Review of Metaphysics* v. 26. 581-603.

Chisholm, R. (1981) 'First Person. An Essay on Reference and Intentionality' (Minneapolis: University of Minnesota Press)

Cover, J. A., Hawthorne, J. O'Leary (1999). *Substance and Individuation in Leibniz* (Cambridge: Cambridge University Press) reprinted in 2008.

Davidson, D. (1980) 'The Individuation of Events' in: Davidson, *Essays on Actions and Events* (Oxford: Oxford University Press) repr. in Hales, 1999, 325-335.

_____ (1993). 'Causal Relations', in: Ernest Sosa, Michael Tooley eds. *Causation* (Oxford: Oxford University Press)

Della Rocca, M. (1996a) "Essentialism: Part 1", *Philosophical Books*, 37: 1-13.

Denkel, A. (1997) 'On the Compresence of Tropes' *Philosophy and Phenomenological Research* v.57. n.3. 599-606.

Denkel, A. (2000) 'The Refutation of Substrata' *Philosophy and Phenomenological Research* v.61. 431-497.

Descartes, R. (1985) *The Philosophical Writings of Descartes* trans. J. Cottingham *et al.* (Cambridge: Cambridge University Press)

Doepke, F. (1982) 'Spatially Coinciding Objects' *Ratio* v. 24. n. 1., 45-60.

Geach, P. (1967) 'Identity' *Review of Metaphysics* v. 21. 3-12.

Geach, P. T. (1972) *Logic Matters* (Oxford: Blackwell)

Ehring, D. (1999) 'Tropeless in Seattle: the cure for insomnia' *Analysis* v.59. 19-24.

Ehring, D. (2001) 'Temporal Parts and Bundle Theory' *Philosophical Studies* v. 104. 163-168.

Fine, Kit (1994) 'Essence and Modality' *Philosophical Perspectives* 8: 1- 16.

Forbes, G. (1985) *The Metaphysics of Modality* (Oxford: Clarendon Press)

_____ (1992) 'Worlds and states of affairs: how similar they can be?' in: *Language, Truth and Ontology* ed. Mulligan, K. Dordrecht: Kluwer, 118-32.

Gorman, M. (2005) 'The Essential and the Accidental', *Ratio* XVIII. 276-289.

Haslanger, S., Kurtz, R.M. eds. (2006) *Persistence: Contemporary Readings* (Cambridge: MIT Press)

Heller, M. (1984) 'Temporal Parts of Four-Dimensional Objects', *Philosophical Studies* v. 46. 323-334.

Husserl, E. (2002) *Logical Investigations* vol. II. trans. J. N. Findlay, (London: Routledge) first published in 1970.

Inwagen, P. (1990) *Material Beings* (Ithaca: Cornell University Press)

Inwagen, P. (2001) *Ontology, Identity and Modality* (Oxford: Oxford University Press)

Kim, J. (1976) 'Events as Property Exemplifications' in: *Action Theory* ed. M. Brand, Dordrecht: Reidel, 159-177. repr. in: Hales, 1999.

Leibniz, G. W. (1969) *Philosophical Papers and Letters* ed. and trans. Leroy E. Loemker, (Dordrecht: D. Reidel) repr. in 1976.

Leibniz, G.W. (1981) *New Essays on Human Understanding*, ed. P.Remnant, J. Bennett, Cambridge: University Press

Lewis, D. (1983) *Philosophical Papers* vol.1. (New York: Oxford University Press)

Lewis, D. (1986) *On the Plurality of Worlds* (Oxford: Blackwell)

Locke, J. (1975) *An Essay Concerning Human Understanding* ed. P. H. Nidditch, Oxford: Clarendon

Lombard, L. B. (1979) 'Events', *Canadian Journal of Philosophy*, 9. repr. in Steven D. Hales ed. *Metaphysics. Contemporary Readings* (Wadworth, Belmont, CA, 1999, 348-369.)

Look, Brandon, C. (2008) *Stanford Encyclopaedia of Philosophy*, entry: 'Leibniz's Modal Metaphysics'

Losonsky, M. (1987a) 'Individuation and the Bundle Theory' *Philosophical Studies* v. 52. 191-198.

Losonsky, M. (1987b) 'Individual Essences' *American Philosophical Quarterly*, v. 24. 253-260.

Loux, M.J. (1978) *Substance and Attribute. A Study in Ontology* (Dordrecht: D. Reidel)

Loux, M. J. (1998) *Metaphysics. A Contemporary Introduction* (London: Routledge)

Lowe, E.J. (1998) *The Possibility of Metaphysics. Substance, Identity and Time.* (Oxford: Clarendon)

Lowe, E. J. (2002) *A Survey of Metaphysics* (Oxford: Oxford University Press)

O'Leary-Hawthorne, J. (1995) 'The bundle theory of substance and the identity of indiscernibles' *Analysis* v 55. n.3. 191-196.

Mackie, P. (2006) *How Things Might Have Been: Individuals, Kinds and Essential Properties* (Oxford: Clarendon)

Martin, C. B. (1980) 'Substance Substantiated' *Australasian Journal of Philosophy* v. 58. 3-10.

Martin, R. M. (1975) 'Events and Actions: Comments on Brand and Kim' in: *Action Theory*, eds. M. Brand, D. Walton, Dordrecht, D. Reidel, 179-192.

Matthews, G. (1990) 'Aristotelian essentialism', *Philosophy and Phenomenological Research* 1: 251- 62.

McDaniel, K. (2001) 'Tropes and Ordinary Physical Objects' *Philosophical Studies* v. 104. 269-290.

Mertz, D. W. (1966) *Moderate Realism and its Logic* (New Haven: Yale)

Mulligan, K. *et.al.* (1984) 'Truth-Makers' *Philosophy and Phenomenological Research* v. 44. 287-322.

Park, Woosuk (1990) '*Haecceitas* and the Bare Particular', *The Review of Metaphysics* 44. 375-397.

Paul, L. A. (2004) 'The context of essence', *Australasian Journal of Philosophy* 82: 170-84.

Plantinga, A. (1987) 'The Boethian Compromise', *American Philosophical Quarterly*, 15. reprinted in: Plantinga, *Essays in the Metaphysics of Modality*, OUP, 2003. 122-138.

Quine, W.V. (1960) *Word and Object* (Cambridge, Mass.: MIT)

Robertson, T. (2008) 'Essential vs. Accidental Properties', **The Stanford Encyclopaedia of Philosophy (Fall 2008 Edition)**, Edward N. Zalta (ed.), URL = <http://plato.stanford.edu/archives/fall2008/entries/essential-accidental/>.

Roya-Royes, S. (2011) 'Essential Properties and Individual Essences', *Philosophy Compass* 6: 65 -77.

Robinson, H. (2004) '*Substance*', entry in *Stanford Encyclopedia of Philosophy*, pp. 27.

Rodriguez-Pereyra, G. (1999) 'Resemblance Nominalism and the Imperfect Community' *Philosophy and Phenomenological Research* v. 59. 965-983.

Rosenkrantz, G. S. (1993) 'Haecceity. An Ontological Essay' (Kluwer: Dordrecht/Boston), reprinted in 2009.

Russell, B. (1940) *Inquiry into Meaning and Truth* (London: Allen and Unwin)

Russell, B. (1948) *Human Knowledge, its Scope and Limits* (London: Allen and Unwin)

Salmon, N. (2002) 'This Side of the Paradox', *Philosophical Topics*, 30:187-197. repr. in Salmon *Metaphysics, Mathematics and Meaning.*(Oxford, Oxford University Press, 2005).

Sellars, W. (1963a) *Science, Perception and Reality* (London: Routledge)

Simons, P. (1987) *Parts. A Study in Ontology*. Oxford: Clarendon. (repr. in 2000.)

Simons, P. (1994) 'Particulars in Particular Clothing: Three Trope Theories of Substance' *Philosophy and Phenomenological Research* v.54. 553-575. repr. in Hales, 1999.

Simons, P. (2000) 'Identity Through Time and Trope Bundles' *Topoi* v.19. 147-155.

Schneider, B (2002) 'A Note on Particularised Qualities and Bearer Uniqueness' 4th Conference of *ESAP*, Lund, 2002 June

Stone, J. (2002) 'Why sortal essentialism cannot solve Chrysippus' puzzle' *Analysis* v.62. n.3. 216-223.

Stout, G.F. (1971a) 'The nature of universals and propositions' repr. in: *The Problem of Universals*, ed. C. Landesman, New York, Basic Books, 154-166.

Stout, G. F. (1971b) 'Are the characteristic of particular things universal or particular?' in: *The Problem of Universals*, ed. C. Landesman, New York, Basic Books, 178-83.

Ujvári, M. (1989) 'Why Kantian Transcendental Philosophy cannot be a Metaphysical Foundation to Analysis of Language?' *Kant Studien*, 186-198.

_____(2000a) 'Events as Tropes and Tropes of Substances' staff lecture, University of Liverpool, Department of Philosophy, March

_____ (2000b) 'The Trope Theory of Events' *8th International Conference of Philosophy*, Bled, June

_____(2002) 'Time, Modality and the Limits of Indexical Analysis' *Abstracts of Contributed Papers*, 4th Congress of the European Society of Analytic Philosophy, Lund, Sweden, June

_____ (2004a) 'Cambridge Change and Sortal Essentialism' staff lecture, University of Nottingham, Department of Philosophy, February

_____(2004b) 'Cambridge Change and Sortal Essentialism' *Metaphysica* v.5. n.2. 25-34.

_____(2005) 'The Trope-Bundle Theory of Substance and Identity through Time', Abstracts of Contributed Papers, *ECAP 5*, Lisbon, p.185.

_____ (2011a) 'Intrinsic, hence Real; Extrinsic, hence Unreal? The Modal and the Sortal Properties of Continuants', *Prolegomena* 10: 53-67.

_____ (2011b) 'Prior's Fable and the limits of *de re* possibility' *Synthese,* special issue: *From a logical angle. Some studies in A.N. Prior's ideas on time, discourse, and metaphysics*. Peter Øhrstrøm, Per Hasle & Ulrik Sandborg-Petersen eds., *Synthese*: Volume 188, Issue 3 (2012), Page 459-467

_____(2012) 'Individual Essence: gibt es solche?' *Metaphysica,* online first: http://www.springerlink.com/openurl.asp?genre=article&id=doi:10.1007/s12133-012-0107-9

Vallicella, W.F. (1997) 'Bundles and Indiscernibility: a Reply to O'Leary-Hawthorne' *Analysis* v.57. 91-94.

Vallicella, W.F. (2002) 'Relations, Monism and the Vindication of Bradley's Regress' *Dialectica* v.56. n.1. 3-37.

Weberman, D. (1999) 'Cambridge Changes Revisited: Why Certain Relational Changes Are Indispensible' *Dialectica* v.63. n.2. 139-149.

Wiggins, D. (1980) *Sameness and Substance* (Oxford: Blackwell)

Wiggins, D. (2001) *Sameness and Substance Renewed* (Cambridge: Cambridge University Press)

Williams, D.C. (1953) 'On the Elements of Being' *The Review of Metaphysics* v.7. 3-18. repr. in: *Metaphysics. Contemporary Readings*, ed. M.J. Loux, Routledge, 2001.